THE ORTHODOX CHURCH

THE
ORTHODOX
CHURCH

*Its Past and Its Role in the
World Today*

BY

JOHN MEYENDORFF

Translated from the French by John Chapin

PANTHEON BOOKS

First published in French under the title
L'Église orthodoxe: hier et aujourd'hui
© 1960 by Éditions du Seuil
English translation © 1962 by Pantheon Books,
a Division of Random House, Inc.
Library of Congress Catalog Card Number: 62-14260

FOREWORD

ONE OF THE most typical and hopeful signs in contemporary Christianity is the determined search of
Christians for unity.

"As thou, Father, art in me, and I in thee; so that
the world may come to believe that it is thou who
hast sent me" (John xvii.21). This prayer of the Head
of the Church establishes a definite causal relation-
ship between the unity of Christians and their witness
in the world. That is, in order that the world may
believe in Him, the Christian faithful must manifest
their unity in God and summon all their nonbelieving
brethren to share it with them. There is a real danger,
however, that the hard facts of history may cause the
world to believe the very opposite, namely, that the
Father has not heard the prayer of his Son, that the
work of Christ's redemption has brought not peace
but dissension into the world, and that the Gospel,
after all, is only one creed among many, no one of
which has ever been able to conquer the whole world
so far.

This is the scandalous state of affairs which con-
fronts missionaries above all. In response to this challenge they have done their best to stimulate an interest in the "ecumenical" approach and to make people realize the true seriousness of the problem of
Christian unity. Experience has taught them that this
problem is not one of interest to specialists alone,
but that it has to do with the very nature of the
Church, with the efficacy of its mission in the modern

world, and ultimately with the answer that shall be
given to the will of God.

It is our desire to offer this book on the Orthodox
Church as a contribution to the ecumenical movement, in harmony with the spirit animating those who
are so actively promoting the ideal of Christian unity.

We shall have more to say later on with regard to
the historical factors which gradually led to a break
in the unity of the Greco-Roman world, after the latter
had witnessed the preaching of the Gospel in the first
century, and which contributed ultimately to the
ecclesiastical division between the Eastern and Western halves of Christendom. It is obvious that these
factors no longer play the same role today as they
once did, and have in fact been superseded by other
events of momentous importance which have occurred
and are still occurring in the world. The political and
economic centers of the world have shifted away from
the Mediterranean basin, and even the traditional concepts of East and West have now lost much of their
meaning except in a purely historical sense. Orthodox
communities are today found widely scattered over
the "Western world," and by the same token, the
Roman Catholic Church, as well as the various Protestant denominations, is to be found in the Near East,
in the Balkans, and in Russia. It has become a com-
monplace to say that the world is small and that we
must be prepared to abandon our isolated ways of
living and thinking. The new countries of Asia and
Africa are eager to receive the Gospel in its original
purity and to know the Church as its divine Founder
intended it to be, but they are not eager to become
involved in the interminable medieval quarrels which
have resulted in the disunity of Christendom.

All this points to the fact that we are without doubt
on the threshold of a new age in which the ecumenical
problem will be viewed in its true light, that is, as a

debate concerning *the faith.* History itself is helping
to rid us of secondary issues by breaking down the
old confessional barriers, by causing all Christians to
come to grips with the *same* problems, and by compelling them to adopt identical solutions. The fact
that we are as yet not all members of the one Church
of Jesus Christ is something which—ultimately—must
receive an adequate explanation, for our contemporaries and our descendants will find it increasingly
difficult to justify schisms except on the basis of real
credal differences. Without doubt, one of the most
hopeful signs of our times is the desire to have done
with purely secondary issues and to take up the real
issues at long last. What a magnificent opportunity
is now open to all Christians, if this is indeed true!
They can now debate the real issues underlying the
problem of reunion and deal with them, fairly and
constructively, with a view to furthering the great
cause of reunion.

Now the Orthodox Church has a very special role
to fulfill in this debate. As a matter of fact, it has
remained very much on the sidelines during the great
controversy of modern Christianity, the perpetual
quarrel between the churches which have emerged
from the Protestant Reformation and the Roman
Catholic Church. It can fairly claim, in this respect,
to be the church of continuity and tradition. This is
actually the meaning of the term "orthodox" which it
applies to itself so frequently.

During the course of the doctrinal disputes following the Peace of Constantine, the Greek adjectives
katholikos and *orthodoxos* were used interchangeably
by the followers of the true faith. About A.D. 100, St.
Ignatius of Antioch was the first to employ the term
"catholic" with reference to the Christian Church—
the Catholic Church—intending thereby to stress the
fullness, the universality, and also the corporate na-

ture of the Christian message. That is to say, as opposed to the opinions of "individuals," the Church
claimed to teach a doctrine which is a whole and is
destined for all mankind. The term was widely used
in the baptismal creeds and finally found its way into
the Nicaean-Constantinopolitan Creed: "the Church
one, holy, catholic, and apostolic." Use of the term
was quite widespread in the West, where it was the
custom to speak of "Catholic" Christians and the
"Catholic" faith. In the East, on the other hand,
"Catholic" was used more frequently with reference
to the Church itself, whereas the Church's members
were more commonly called the "orthodox"—"those
having the right opinion"—in contrast to heretics.
Finally, during the Middle Ages the custom developed
of referring more and more frequently to the "Orthodox
Church" in opposition to Western Roman "Catholicism."

The Orthodox Church, therefore, takes part in the
ecumenical debate as the guardian of the true faith,
the faith of the Apostles and Fathers of the early
Church. It maintains that all Christians must return
to the one true faith, the faith of the first ecumenical
councils, as the condition for true reunion.

In many respects this claim and this hope may
appear to be purely utopian in nature. Would not a
return of this kind to the sources, declared to be
essential if unity is to be restored, amount to a mere
artificial return to the past which can never be resur-
rected? And there is another serious objection: Are
the notorious historical weaknesses of the Orthodox
Church, which claims to have preserved the heritage
of the past, such as to make this claim plausible?
How then can we possibly pretend that such a course
of action would be justified?

We shall try to show in this book that it is unfair to
pose the question in this manner. When Orthodoxy

speaks of a "return to the sources" it does not mean
a return to the dead past, but has in mind a continuity with and fidelity to divine Revelation. This
Revelation is judge of the past, as well as the present
and future, of East and of West. One of the basic
problems confronting theologians today is to be able
to distinguish clearly between the holy Traditions of
the Church—the faithful voice of Revelation—and
mere human traditions which only express the former
imperfectly or, as is often the case, are contrary to it
or obscure it. How many traditions of the latter kind
the Orthodox must abandon before they can persuade
other Christians to accept their claim to possess the
one true Tradition! It is to their credit, however—
and the Christian East can justly pride itself on this
—to have left the door wide open for an eventual
examination of conscience.

Thus our book will be concerned with two aims:
we shall attempt to describe the Orthodox Church—
both in its past and its present state—for the benefit
of Western readers, who for the most part must have
recourse to very inadequate or all too brief accounts
of the subject; and, for the benefit of the Orthodox
themselves, we shall begin that examination of conscience which they need to make.

Our plan will be first to outline the historical development of the Orthodox Church from ¹apostolic
times down to the present. By explaining the various
stages in this historical process we hope to enable
the reader to understand better the basic dogmatic
positions of Orthodoxy. The fundamental dogmas
relative to Scripture and Tradition, the Church, and
the teaching authority (magisterium) of the Church,
will thus all be examined in the very first chapters.
Then in conclusion we shall take up certain other
doctrinal questions and discuss them from a contemporary point of view.

It is not our purpose here to give a systematic account of all the details of the Orthodox faith, but to provide the reader with a general introduction to the Orthodox way of life by describing its past history, present status, and future prospects.

CONTENTS

THE ORTHODOX CHURCH

CHAPTER I

THE APOSTLES. HOLY SCRIPTURE.
THE APOSTOLIC FATHERS.
THE EARLY CHURCH

"IT WAS IN the fifteenth year of the emperor Tiberius' reign, when Pontius Pilate was governor of Judaea, when Herod was prince in Galilee, his brother Philip in the Ituraean and Trachonitid region, and Lysanias in Abilina, in the high priesthood of Annas and Caiphas, that the Word of God came upon John, the son of Zachary, in the desert" (Luke iii.1-2). It is in this exact, historically accurate way that the Evangelist St. Luke begins his account of the messianic work of Jesus. Christianity, as a matter of fact, is based on a historically attested intervention of God in the concrete affairs of mankind, namely, the incarnation of his Son. We find the same concern for historical accuracy in the Creed, which tells us that Christ suffered "under Pontius Pilate." Why should this relatively obscure provincial official be mentioned in a short, solemn statement of the Christian faith, except in order to impress upon us the fact that Jesus was indeed a real historical person, a man like all of us, a Jew who suffered under the Roman yoke like all his compatriots, and to emphasize the fact that living men had heard him, had seen him with their own eyes, and had touched him with their hands (cf. 1 John i.1)?

This historical nature of the messianic work is also attested by the way in which the Gospel was transmitted to the Greco-Roman world and later generations. When he was about to leave his disciples and ascend to heaven, the Master solemnly declared to them: "The Holy Spirit will come upon you, and you will receive strength from him. You are to be my witnesses in Jerusalem and throughout Judaea, in Samaria, yes, and to the ends of the earth" (Acts i.8).

Like all other historical facts, the acts performed by Jesus—and especially the most extraordinary act which God ever performed in him: his resurrection on the third day—must be attested by witnesses: "There were Peter and John, James and Andrew, Philip and Thomas, Bartholomew and Matthew, James the son of Alphaeus and Simon the Zealot, and Judas the brother of James. All these, with one mind, gave themselves up to prayer, together with the women, and Mary the Mother of Jesus, and his brethren" (Acts i.13-14). They were rather dull-witted witnesses, at best, those twelve fishermen from Galilee—who were only eleven after the betrayal of Judas—and the few close relatives of Jesus. After the tragedy of Golgotha, after the Resurrection, after all that the Master had told them regarding his kingdom, they still persisted in asking him when he intended to restore the monarchy of David (Acts i.6). However, they had followed him from the beginning of his ministry: this was the necessary condition for being a member of the apostolic college, as is clear from the account of the election of Matthias to succeed Judas: "There are men who have walked in our company all through the time when the Lord Jesus came and went among us, from the time when John used to baptize to the day when he, Jesus, was taken from us. One of these ought to be added to our number as a witness of his resurrection" (Acts i.21-22).

Eager as they were to serve as witnesses of the risen Master, they were not fully capable as yet of grasping the overwhelming universality of the ministry with which they had been invested. It was only after a promise which Jesus had repeatedly made had been fulfilled that they were able to exchange their Galilean dialect for the universal language of the Gospel: the Holy Spirit alighted on each one of them and they "began to speak in strange languages, as the Spirit gave utterance to each" (Acts ii.4). Only then did Peter feel himself authorized to announce to Israel the beginning of the true messianic reign, the fulfillment of the prophecies: "Let it be known, then, beyond all doubt, to all the house of Israel, that God has made him Master and Christ, this Jesus whom you crucified" (Acts ii.36).

In order to establish the community of the New Covenant, it was necessary both to have eyewitnesses of the risen Christ and for the Holy Spirit to descend on the infant Church in order to make this witness plausible and its fruits immediately evident to all: "And about three thousand souls were won for the Lord that day" (Acts ii.41).

To this day the Church lives only by the witness of the Apostles and thanks to the Holy Spirit, who dwells in it from the day of Pentecost: it is thus both "holy" and "apostolic." The Spirit, actually, has *added* nothing to the work performed by Christ, for "it was God's good pleasure to let all completeness dwell in him" (Col. i.19). The Spirit "bears witness, because he is the truth" (1 John v.6): "And he will bring honor to me," said Jesus, "because it is from me that he will derive what he makes plain to you" (John xvi.14). The coming of the Spirit therefore does not make the human witness of the Apostles with respect to the historical resurrection of the Lord superfluous: it places a seal upon it and authenticates it.

This last point is particularly important when we consider the significance of the *books* of the New Testament and the formation of the canon of Holy Scripture. The four Gospels, the book of Acts, the epistles of Paul, and the Apocalypse are primarily concerned with furnishing information concerning the person of Jesus Christ, the nature of his sacrifice, and the fact of the Resurrection: they constitute, in other words, a written account of the message of the Apostles. Their authority comes both from their apostolic origin and from their inspiration. Tradition insists, as a matter of fact, on the apostolic origin of the Gospels of Mark and Luke, although their authors were not members of the college of the Twelve and probably did not know Jesus; in order to establish the authenticity of these Gospels it appeals to the authority of Peter and Paul, whose preaching was taken down by Mark and Luke. This rather elastic conception of authenticity has allowed the inclusion in the canon of such works as the Epistle to the Hebrews or the Apocalypse, with regard to which there have been doubts since the earliest times of the Church: hence we may say that apostolic authenticity does not necessarily mean material authenticity, but that it is a guarantee, vouched for by the Holy Spirit, of the apostolic origin of the contents of the Holy Books.

As a matter of fact, the witness of the Apostles would have been valueless without the miracle of Pentecost, unless the Spirit had come not merely to the Twelve but to the entire Church. The Church is thus founded not only *by* the Apostles but *on* them, as well as in the Holy Spirit. It occurred to no one to add to the Scriptural canon a work that was not of apostolic origin, because the Spirit does not reveal anything except Christ, to whom the Apostles witnessed. But it is the Spirit who defines the canon of Scripture in the Church and preserves the Church

through the centuries in truth and in faithfulness to
its Head.

These are the basic elements of the Orthodox conception of Scripture and Tradition. Scripture includes
the *totality* of the apostolic witness and nothing can
be added by way of completing our knowledge of
the person of Jesus, his work, and the salvation which
he brought us; but this written witness regarding
Christ was not launched in a void—after the manner
of the Koran, which, according to Islamic tradition,
fell from heaven and is read by men in a form fixed
once and for all—but was given to a community which
had been founded by these Apostles and which had
received the same Spirit. This community is the
Church, which has received the Scripture and acknowledges in it the Truth, fixed in its limits for all
time, and interprets this corpus of writings with the
help of the Spirit. This interpretation and this ac-
knowledgment are what is known as Tradition.

The early history of the Church is described in the
book of Acts, written by St. Luke, the author of the
third Gospel. The book is divided, somewhat sche-
matically, into two rather unequal parts: the first part
(chapters i to xi) is concerned with the primitive
Church at Jerusalem, its foundation at Pentecost, its
internal organization, and the activities of its leaders;
the second part comprises the rest of the book and
has to do no longer with the Church at Jerusalem but
with the person of the Apostle of the Gentiles, whom
Luke here calls Paul (Acts xiii.9), whereas in the
previous chapters he was known as Saul.

The community of Jerusalem is governed by the
college of the Twelve, but in this college the Apostle
Peter clearly occupies the first place: he speaks in the
name of all and acts as head. It is probable that the
famous words of Jesus on the road to Caesarea re-

ported by the Jerusalemite Gospel of Matthew relate
to this predominant role of Peter at Jerusalem: "Thou
art Peter, and upon this rock I will build my Church"
(Matt. xvi. 18).[1] The Church of Jerusalem, of course,
was not one church among many; it was actually *the*
Church, the only Church, the "remnant" of Israel,
foretold by the prophets, which had received the Messiah. The Church of the Gentiles, for which Paul would
be the special Apostle, could only be a "wild olive"
grafted on the authentic olive tree (Rom. xi.17). Governed by the twelve Apostles, the original Judaeo-
Christian community was an anticipation of the heavenly Jerusalem, the holy city that will descend from
heaven and concerning which the seer of the Apocalypse says: "The city wall, too, had twelve foundation stones: and these too bore names, those of the
Lamb's twelve Apostles" (Apoc. xxi.14). History and
eschatology are so intimately bound up with each
other in the first chapters of the book of Acts that it
is difficult to isolate the distinguishing features of
each. In Peter's speech, the day of Pentecost, the
coming of the Spirit, is interpreted as the fulfillment
of the eschatological prophecy of Joel, and the life
of the infant community is portrayed as a constant
miracle: "They used to gather together with one accord in Solomon's Porch. No one else dared join them,
although the people held them in high honor" (Acts
v.12-13).

Chapter xii brings this exceptional period in the
history of the Church to a definite close. The college
of the Twelve ceased to exist: Herod caused "James,
the brother of John, to be beheaded" (Acts xii.2),

---

[1] See my article "Sacrements et hiérarchie dans l'Église.
Contribution orthodoxe à un dialogue oecuménique sur la
Primauté romaine," in *Dieu vivant*, No. 26 (1954), pp. 81-91;
also V. Kesich, "The Problem of Peter's Primacy in the New
Testament and the Early Christian Exegesis," in *St. Vladimir's
Seminary Quarterly*, Vol. IV, Nos. 2-3 (1960), pp. 2-25.

and no one thought of replacing him by electing a successor in order to keep up the symbolical number of Twelve, as they had in the case of Judas. Peter, after his arrest and miraculous escape, "left them and went elsewhere" (Acts xii.17). He will retain his personal authority as "First Apostle," but this authority will not be regarded as absolute, since he will be directly contradicted by Paul (Gal. ii). Moreover, at Jerusalem the first place will henceforth be assumed by James, the brother of the Lord (Acts xv), who was not a member of the college of the Twelve. The part played by Peter in the foundation of the Church will be perpetuated—as we shall see later on —by the episcopal office, but he will henceforth be confined to being the "Apostle of the Circumcised" (Gal. ii.7-8), a ministry which, unfortunately, was not destined to have a brilliant future inasmuch as Israel would definitely reject its Messiah, the miserable "remnant" which actually did receive him being finally swallowed up by the disaster of A.D. 70 which swept over Palestine.

From then on the future will belong historically to the Apostle of the Gentiles, Paul, to whom chapters xiii to xxviii of the book of Acts are devoted. As a result of his missionary journeys throughout the Mediterranean basin Christian communities will spring up everywhere. All "churches of God," like that of Jerusalem before them, will receive the Gospel and the Holy Spirit. However, the community in Palestine was always regarded by Paul as enjoying a peculiar authority and a special primacy because of its early foundation, even after the college of the Twelve had left Jerusalem. He tried in particular to get its approval—after a great deal of trouble—for the basic principle underlying his mission to the Gentiles, and he never forgot the collection "for the brothers of Judaea," a symbol and expression of the unity of the Church. However, for

him, every church was the "Church of God," in
which "there was neither Greek nor Jew." He insisted
that all Christians who lived in one place should belong to one church, a point that was a source of friction with the parallel missions to the Jews which did
not share this view. He was indignant with them at
Corinth where they wished to form two distinct communities: "Each of you has a cry of his own: I am
for Paul, I am for Apollo, I am for Cephas, I am for
Christ. What, has Christ been divided up?" (1 Cor.
i.12-13). Christians, as a whole, "form" Christ; they
are one indivisible body which ought to be evident
in its entirety and its fullness in each church.

These frictions with Jewish Christians do not seem
to have affected Paul's relations with Peter, the Apostle of the Circumcised. According to Tradition, both
Apostles came to Rome and bore witness by their
blood, perhaps only a few months apart, to the universality of salvation in Jesus Christ. This communion of the two "first Apostles" [2] in death in the
capital of the Empire—the first of the Twelve who
presided over the Church at Jerusalem, and the first
Apostle of the Gentiles—contributed greatly to the
prestige of the Roman Church, where the memory
of their teaching and presence remained alive and
where their relics would soon be venerated.

Among the earliest witnesses to the Resurrection we
also find the mysterious figure of the "beloved disciple," John, the son of Zebedee. He too, like Peter
and Paul, is regarded as the author of certain books
of the New Testament and is associated with a particular locality, namely Ephesus. John was one of the
outstanding members of the apostolic college, personally very close to Peter, and because of this he
played a very important role in the life of the primi-

[2] The Byzantine liturgy regularly refers to Peter *and* Paul
as *koryphaioi* (leaders).

tive Church at Jerusalem. His intimacy with the Master seems to have conferred on him a kind of spiritual primacy among the Apostles, a primacy which some have opposed or compared to the more institutional primacy of Peter, and which is reflected in the pages of his Gospel.[3] Nevertheless, his name is mentioned only once in the epistles of Paul: John is referred to along with James and Peter as one of the "columns" of the Church of Jerusalem (Gal. ii.9). We do not know whether he later assisted Peter with the Jewish mission of this church. According to Tradition he resided during the latter years of his life at Ephesus—a church founded by Paul (Acts xix.8-9)—but he does not appear to have been connected with any kind of opposition to Pauline doctrine. His works, the last to be included in the New Testament canon, are strongly marked by the author's own personal, visionary conception of the Christian message, and the Byzantine Church has therefore accorded him the title of "the Theologian." John emphasizes particularly the sacramental side of this message, and it is not unreasonable to conclude, as some have done, that the monarchic episcopate derives from the Johannine tradition.[4]

In our time, Protestant exegesis is coming to admit more and more the importance of the sacramental element in the life of the early Church.[5] Now it is beyond dispute that baptism and the Eucharist, the essential elements in the earliest Christian preaching, are acts of a ritual and corporate nature and presuppose a certain organization of the community which

[3] See Mgr. Cassien, "Saint Pierre et l'Église dans le Nouveau Testament," in *Istina*, No. 3 (1955), pp. 261-304.

[4] See J. Colson, *L'Évêque dans les communautés primitives: tradition paulinienne et tradition johannique de l'épiscopat des origines à saint Irénée* (Paris, 1951).

[5] See for example O. Cullmann, *Early Christian Worship* (London, SCM Press, 1953).

celebrates them. Our present knowledge of the primitive eucharistic prayer points to a close parallel between Jewish worship in the time of Christ, especially the prayers—preserved in the Talmud—that were recited by certain Jewish brotherhoods when common meals were celebrated, and its Christian counterpart. Christ and his disciples formed one of these brotherhoods and celebrated such a ritual meal immediately before the Master's death, a meal described for us briefly by the Evangelists, in the course of which Jesus blessed bread and wine, declaring them to be his Body and his Blood, and directed his disciples to "do this" in remembrance of him.

The fact that we find liturgical elements of contemporary Judaism in the earliest Christian anaphoras is a clear indication of the apostolic origin of the Christian rite of the Eucharist: that is to say, the earliest communities celebrated the Supper in the same way that it was celebrated by Jesus in the Upper Room. But this still leaves us with the problem of determining who presided over these Christian gatherings and therefore took the place of the Jewish head of the family or president of the fraternity. This problem has a particular relevancy for us, because the Last Supper, as the prototype and origin of the Christian Eucharist, was presided over by the Master in person, and consequently the president of the Christian assembly would be the logical person to pronounce the words which He pronounced and to perform the acts which He performed.

The problem can be solved almost certainly, it would seem, for the primitive community at Jerusalem. The first twelve chapters of the Acts show clearly that the Apostle Peter was the head of the apostolic college and the head of that church. This role of Peter at Jerusalem appears to follow naturally from the words of the Lord: "Thou art Peter, and upon this rock I

will build my Church" (Matt. xvi.18); "When, after
a while, thou hast come back to me, it is for thee to
be the support of thy brethren" (Luke xxii.32); "Feed
my sheep" (John xxi.15-17). Jesus was himself the
Rock and the Shepherd, but he gave to one of his
disciples the power to perform this ministry: the Apostle Simon Peter was the disciple who performed this
function in the primitive Jewish-Christian community
at Jerusalem, which came to be regarded as the unique
model for all future Christian churches.

But Peter left Jerusalem "for another place" (Acts
xii.17) and was replaced by James as the head of
the Church at Jerusalem. From then on, the Apostles
—the Eleven (James, brother of John, being dead:
Acts xii.2), Paul, and certain others—were the itinerant witnesses of the risen Christ: everywhere they
went they founded Christian churches, leaving to
others the responsibility of presiding over them and
performing the sacramental rites. The Apostle Paul,
for example, celebrated the rite of baptism only on
extraordinary occasions, for, he said, "Christ did not
send me to baptize; he sent me to preach the Gospel"
(1 Cor. 1.14-17). For the postapostolic period, the
Didache specifically states: "Let each Apostle, when
he comes to you, be received like the Lord; but let
him remain only one day, or two days in case of need;
if he remains three days, he is a false prophet" (xi.4-5).
After Peter and the other members of the apostolic
college had ceased to preside over the Church of Jerusalem, the apostolic ministry became itinerant, and
no ancient document has survived indicating that the
Apostles personally presided over any particular
church. St. Irenaeus of Lyons in the second century,
for example, describes the role of the Apostles as
being that of "founders" or "builders": "After having
founded and built the Church, the blessed Apostles
entrusted to Linus the charge of the episcopate . . .

Anacletus succeeded him. After him, in the third place from the Apostles, it is to Clement that the episcopate fell. . . ." (*Against the Heresies,* iii.3).

A sharp distinction thus came to exist between the apostolate—an itinerant and universal witness—and the episcopal office, or a sacramental, administrative, and *local* function.

The book of Acts and the epistles of Paul seem to assume that there was a certain collegiality in the government of the earliest churches: we hear of *episkopoi* (overseers), *presbyteroi* (elders), *proistamenoi* (presidents), in the plural. By the end of the first century, however, all the churches were presided over by one person, the *episkopos,* or bishop. Did a revolution take place in the organization of the Church? No, for there is no evidence of any protest being made by Christians of the earliest period against the establishment of a "monarchic" episcopate. As a likely explanation we must remember that the sacramental orientation of the primitive Christian community naturally called for and presupposed the existence of a single head.

The whole life of the community, as a matter of fact, was centered around the celebration of the Eucharist. Now the Supper has to be presided over by one person, the image of the Lord. This function of president was performed by Peter at Jerusalem. Since all the local churches founded by the Apostles were essentially identical in organization with the Church of Jerusalem and were reproductions, as it were, of the same communal and eschatological prototype, this primitive community, as described in the first twelve chapters of the book of Acts, served as a model for all the rest, and Peter himself, when reporting at Jerusalem on the baptism of Cornelius and other pagans, declared that "the Holy Spirit fell upon them, just as it was with us in the beginning" (Acts xi.15; cf. x.44, 47; xi.17). St. Ignatius of Antioch, the earliest and principal witness to the monarchic episcopate (about A.D. 100) describes the Christian church at Magnesia or Smyrna as having a single bishop—the image of God—who was assisted by the "presbyterium," which corresponded to the college of Apostles at Jerusalem: "I conjure you, have a heart to do all things in the divine concord, under the presidency of the bishop who holds the place of God, the presbyters, who hold the place of the senate of Apostles, and the deacons who are so dear to me, to whom has been entrusted the service of Jesus Christ" (*Magn.* vi.1); "Let us all revere the deacons like Jesus Christ, as well as the bishop who is the image of the Father, and the presbyters as the senate of God and as the assembly of the Apostles" (*Trall.* iii.1).

The essential point about the ecclesiology of St. Ignatius is that the local church is not regarded as a *part* of the body of the Church, but as the whole, having at its head the Lord himself and *all* the Apostles. If St. Ignatius is aware of an apostolic succession in the Church, it is to be found in the collegial ministry of the presbyters. The bishop's function is to represent the Father, to be the source and unique center of church unity, as the Father is the source of the Divinity.

Moreover, the episcopal office, by definition the function of a single individual, was thought of in the primitive Church as a continuation in each church of the ministry which Peter performed at Jerusalem. It is in this sense that we must interpret the words which Christ addressed to Simon Peter on the road to Caesarea. The great exponent of this idea in the third century was St. Cyprian, the bishop of Carthage. For St. Cyprian the episcopate is "one" by virtue of the identity of faith—the faith of Peter—of all the churches and all the bishops sit on the one chair (*cathedra una*), namely, that of Peter, by confessing this true faith.[6] Representing the "image of the Lord" in the Christian community, the bishop thus appeared not only as the consecrator of the Eucharist but as the teacher of true doctrine.

The definite hierarchic structure of the early Christian communities is thus determined by their sacramental nature.

The Sunday eucharistic gathering, the meal in common which serves to proclaim and anticipate the joyous feast of the Kingdom to come, is the moment when the Church fully became the Church, for it was then that all communicated in the Lord, then also that baptism was conferred, instruction in the faith was given, and bishops and presbyters were elected; it was then too that bishops came from neighboring communities to consecrate new bishops; it was then that discussions were held regarding the common problems facing the community. Nothing, not even the persecutions, was allowed to interfere with Christian participation in the Sunday Supper of the Lord. Because these Christian gatherings were rather sizable, they were inevitably known to the Roman police, and the corporate worship of the *religio illicita* thus had the effect of making Christians vulnerable to attack by their enemies. Yet they insisted upon meeting together for worship, and refused to substitute any kind of personal or private prayer for the corporate gatherings. The reason for this was simply that they regarded these liturgical gatherings as belonging to the very essence of their faith. Like the Church at Jerusalem, "they occupied themselves continually with the Apos-

[6] There is a consensus today regarding the interpretation of St. Cyprian's famous treatise *De catholicae ecclesiae unitate* in this sense; cf. in particular the translated text in *Ancient Christian Writers*, No. 25, with notes by M. Bévenot (Westminster, Md., 1957); also P. T. Camelot, "Saint Cyprien et la primauté," in *Istina*, No. 4 (1957).

tles' teaching, their fellowship in the breaking of bread, and the fixed times of prayer" (Acts ii.42). They could not give up this custom without violating the commandment of the New Covenant.

The cautious historian of course must be wary about painting too bright a picture of the early Christians and portraying them as perfect in all respects. Yet, as long as the fledgling status of the new Church lasted, as long as being a member of the New Covenant entailed a certain risk or at least a conscious effort to profess the faith, it was natural that the faithful should be more aware than later generations of the true nature of the Christian community. In this sense and in this only, the Church of the first three centuries can be said to be the golden age of Christianity—and also, to a certain extent, a criterion by which to judge the rest of Christian history.

Unfortunately we cannot linger over this interesting formative period but must content ourselves with having pointed out some of its salient features, of particular importance because of their influence on later church history.

CHAPTER II

THE CHRISTIAN CHURCH AND
THE ROMAN EMPIRE.
THE CHURCH OF
THE ECUMENICAL COUNCILS

FOR MORE THAN three centuries the Roman Empire adopted a hostile attitude toward Christianity, varying from indifference or scornful toleration to outright violent persecution. Nevertheless the earliest Christian apologists were on the whole well disposed toward the Empire and even viewed it optimistically on the grounds that it performed a useful function as an educator of the nations on the purely natural level, in so far as the Kingdom of God was not yet fully realized on earth: "Every soul must be submissive to its lawful superiors; authority comes from God only, and all authorities that hold sway are of his ordinance. . . . A good conscience has no need to go in fear of the magistrate, as a bad conscience does. If thou wouldst be free from the fear of authority, do right, and thou shalt win its approval; the magistrate is God's minister, working for thy good" (Rom. xiii.1-4).

Unfortunately these hopes were not justified. "God's minister, working for thy good" required the disciples of Christ to deny their Master and thus merited the anathemas hurled at him by later Biblical writers (Apoc. xiv.8; xvi.19-20; xviii.9-24). The politico-religious outlook of the Roman state was both totalitarian and syncretistic and could not brook the absolute claims of a gospel which stripped the imperial power of its sacral nature and showed an absolute hostility to the other cults of the Pantheon. The fact that Christians thus refused to acknowledge any religious basis whatever for the Empire caused them to be regarded not only as religious but as political criminals, and the law declared: *Non licet esse christianos* (It is not lawful to be a Christian).

The radical transformation which was brought about in the fourth century in the relations between the Christian Church and the Roman state has long been a subject of study, and scholars have endeavored to determine exactly what effect it had on the state and on the Church. When the state ceased to persecute the Christians, did it somehow undergo a fundamental change in character and in outlook? Or was the change in the Church? The traditional view, since the Middle Ages, has been that the emperors were suddenly transformed from persecutors into the "equals of the Apostles" and henceforth everything they did was in accordance with the mind of the Gospel. Liberal theologians, on the other hand, especially Protestant historians of the nineteenth century, maintained that Christianity was so enslaved by the state and so contaminated by the introduction of pagan elements in the fourth century that it amounted to a betrayal of the evangelical message. As a matter of fact, however, the historical truth lies somewhere in between these two extremes.

While the Emperor Constantine granted all kinds of favors and privileges to the Church, he did not become a full-fledged Christian himself until he was on his deathbed. Throughout his reign he remained largely faithful to the syncretistic principles inherited from his father, while at the same time professing Christian beliefs. Christian monotheism had for him simply taken the place of solar monotheism as the ultimate rallying point for all cults and religions. In many respects this was an acceptable attitude from the Christian point of view, all the more so in that the personal convictions of Constantine himself and those of his successors were continually developing in the direction of greater devotion to the doctrines of the Church. This development gradually brought about the emergence of that phenomenon known as the "Christian Empire," an empire whose ruler bore the official title of "faithful king in Christ-God" and whose governmental system came to be permeated more and more by the Christian outlook and Christian doctrine. From the fourth to the sixth century the various emperors, especially Constantine himself, Theodosius I, and Justinian I, granted the Church very extensive privileges of all kinds, allowed it to share the state's judicial authority, and turned over to it the control of public welfare. Magnificent churches were raised over the holy places of Christianity and the tombs of the martyrs, and their new capital, Constantinople or the New Rome, was adorned no longer with temples to Victory or Justice, as in the pagan past, but with churches dedicated to Christ-Wisdom (Hagia Sophia) or Divine Peace (Hagia Eirene).

In adopting the new religion and employing it more and more as the basis for their policies, the emperors were clearly trying to inject new life into the state, and above all, to assure the unity of the Empire. Secure at last in the enjoyment of imperial protection, the Church opened its gates wide to the masses who sought admittance, and when Justinian closed the last pagan university at Athens in 529, he could justly pride himself on being the head of a completely Christian state, for the boundaries of his political power coincided with those of the Church. The people of God, taken as a whole, were thought of as united under the scepter of a single monarch; Church and state were no longer two separate entities, concerned about defining their mutual relations, but one single society governed by two hierarchies: the ecclesiastical and the political, the latter headed by the emperor.[1] The status of Christianity in the East during the medieval period was thus practically identical with its status in the West, except for the fact that in the East no one succeeded in gathering into his hands the supreme power over both temporal and spiritual affairs as the popes did in the West.

The Byzantine emperors, it is true, made certain efforts along these lines, particularly from the time of Justinian. The politico-religious unity which they dreamed of bringing about was being constantly threatened by dogmatic controversies, for the universal Church which they regarded as a prop for the Empire was distressingly divided, first by the Arian controversies, and then by the endless later Christological disputes. In order to restore church unity the emperors had recourse to the method of holding ecumenical councils, but this proved to be time-consuming and the outcome was sometimes uncertain. From the time of Justinian they began to embark on the dangerous path of issuing dogmatic decrees on their own, but they at once came up against a stubborn fact: the Church was not disposed to recognize their claim to infallibility.

Besides, Justinian and his immediate successors had much too good a grasp of theological principles to take seriously the formal claims of caesaropapism. Their attitude is indicated by Justinian's Sixth Novella, dated March 16, 535: "The greatest gifts which God has granted to men are the priesthood and the em-

---

[1] For the theocratic ideas of Justinian, see A. Schmemann, "Byzantine Theocracy and the Orthodox Church," in *St. Vladimir's Seminary Quarterly*, Vol. I, No. 2 (1953).

pire, the priesthood concerns things divine, the empire presides over mortals." The goal to be achieved
was an agreement or "symphony" between these two
institutions, and not the subjection of one to the
other. As far as Byzantium was concerned, this harmony was never worked out in precise juridical terms:
we have to do rather with a state of mind than a system of government, which allowed certain emperors
to act arbitrarily but did not formally subject the
Church to the state. The Byzantine Church was always capable, especially after the ninth century,
of producing patriarchs willing to stand up to arbitrary emperors. Abuses of power for which the latter
were responsible, although accepted by weak-willed
prelates, were almost always condemned later on by
the church authorities.

In fact, there is no basis in Christian teaching for
the religious power claimed by the emperors, even
indirectly. The sacral character of the imperial office
under the old pagan empire could not survive in a
Christian empire, except in popular fancy or as a mere
survival. Nevertheless it is a fact that, because the
emperor reigned over an empire at least theoretically
Christian, because of the universal nature of his power,
and because the Church, equally universal, had accepted his support and his protection, the Byzantine
emperor was regarded as the Chosen of God, as the
earthly reflection of the celestial power of Christ, and
the Biblical titles applied to the Jewish kings in the
Old Testament were applied to him in court ceremo-
nies.

This whole field of relations between the emperor
and the ecclesiastical hierarchy, between state and
Church, remained rather vaguely defined. This vagueness and pragmatism reveal a positive fact: the awareness of the fundamental instability of the relations
between the Church and the world, between the King-

dom of God and that of the fallen world, had not been wholly lost. That unsteady balance, established during the early centuries of the Christian Empire, was really only upset for the first time by the iconoclastic emperors Leo III (717-741) and Constantine V (741-775). Of all the Eastern emperors they were the only ones who formally claimed the plenitude of both powers, spiritual and temporal. Their campaign against the cult of images amounted to an attempt to establish imperial control over all the manifestations of religious life and to inaugurate in Byzantium a theocratic type of totalitarianism. Doubtless they were influenced in this respect, either consciously or unconsciously, by the example of the Moslem khalifs, for it is well known that in Islam, the people of God, there is no distinction between temporal and spiritual, between Church and state. Constantine V wished to be both "priest and king" (*basileus kai hiereus*) and to realize the fond ambition, already guardedly entertained by Justinian, of making the terrestial Empire an exact replica of the Kingdom of Heaven.

After a crisis lasting for more than a century (725-843), the iconoclastic party in Byzantium was finally defeated. A balance was once more achieved between Church and state on an even firmer basis, later expressed by Patriarch Photius in a document called the *Epanagoge,* which clearly distinguishes between the rights of the emperor and those of the patriarch.[2] In spite of many extravagant ideas about Byzantine caesaropapism which are current, it is a fact that from the ninth century on the emperors of New Rome were no longer in a position to impose their doctrinal will on the Byzantine Church. The brief efforts in this

[2] An English translation of this text is to be found in W. K. Medlin, *Moscow and East Rome* (Geneva, 1952), pp. 232-33.

direction by the Comneni and even more so by the Palaeologi were all brought to nought and cannot possibly be compared with the doctrinal decrees of a Zeno, a Justinian, or a Heraclius in the fifth, sixth, and seventh centuries.

The true legacy of the Christian Empire founded when Constantine was converted, therefore, was not caesaropapism but the ideal of a single "Christian state." Empire and Church no longer constituted two societies but a single society, the "Christian society" (*christeponymon politeuma*), the orthodox *oikoumene* (world), in which the political and the religious powers would henceforth be regarded only as two complementary aspects of the same organized society. Confronted by the evident danger inherent in this state of affairs, namely the risk of forgetting that the Kingdom of God present in the Church still remains an entity that will be fully realized only in the future, proclaimed and anticipated by the sacraments but not identifiable with the earthly Empire, the Church, responding to the voice of conscience, reacted in various ways, particularly by placing a special emphasis on the liturgy and by the promotion of monasticism.

Before the fourth century Christian worship had been the worship of a persecuted minority. This had helped to emphasize the corporate nature of the liturgy. Only true Christians, those who were prepared to accept the Gospel in all its fullness and in the full awareness of its meaning, were members of the Church. Christian worship was the mystery of the community meeting together. From the fourth century onward, however, it gradually became a worship dominated by the sanctuary. Was a development of this kind not inevitable once the liturgy came to be celebrated in the great basilicas which Constantine had erected throughout the Empire—in the "Great

Justinian 558

"Church" of Hagia Sophia, for example, which held thousands of worshippers? Moreover, the faithful themselves felt that they now belonged to a privileged religion, to an imperial Christianity, and they were no longer a group hated by the "world."

But, basically speaking, the Church did not modify either its stand toward the world or its consciousness of being "outside the world." In the new circumstances in which it found itself it could not help devising new methods for protecting the Christian mystery. Formerly the nonbaptized had been forbidden to enter the *ecclesia* (church); henceforth the laity were forbidden to enter the sanctuary since many of them were only superficially baptized at best. . . . The liturgy was gradually transformed into an "office" chanted by the clergy in the "presence" of the people. In sermons, theological works, and the symbolism of church art, from now on there would be much more emphasis on the terrifying mystery of the divine presence in the Church, on the dangers of an unworthy reception of the "communion" in this mystery, and on the role of the clergy as mediators between the people and the Mystery.

This increased emphasis upon ecclesiastical formality, which obscured but did not deny the essential traits of Christian worship, was necessary in order to maintain the sense of the Sacred in the Church over the centuries. This was particularly true at a time when confusion between the sacred and the profane was quite general. Taken over, protected, used by the Kingdom of this world, the Church had to continue to assert that its true Master was the King who was to come again one day and who wished to manifest himself now only under the sacramental veils.

Certain Christians, however, went even further. They refused outright to have anything to do with the new "Christian society": they abandoned it altogether and retired to the desert to witness there to the super-natural and eschatological nature of the Church.

It is rather odd but nevertheless a fact that the Church of the first three centuries was not acquainted with the institution of monasticism, as the word is generally understood. This is strange, because we know what close bonds there were between the early Christian community, its liturgy, organization, and out-look, and contemporary Judaism, for the Apostles were all Jews. Now Judaism had a long tradition of ascet-icism which was experiencing a revival precisely in the time of Christ. St. John the Baptist was the most outstanding example of this tendency, and Christian monks later adopted him as their chosen model. Had the Lord himself not withdrawn into the desert to fast for forty days before beginning his ministry? The New Covenant was first preached in the desert, as if to show that history was being given a new beginning and that the New City should owe nothing to the old. But Christians did not follow this precedent, because it was all too apparent to them that wherever their communities were established they were surrounded by a hostile desert. The stark contrast between the Church and the world was all too apparent for them to wish to emphasize this factor by following a particu-lar way of life: their very existence was a prophetic announcement of the Kingdom to come.

Only after peace had been concluded between the Empire and the Church do we find thousands of Chris-tians fleeing into the desert.[3] A few of them preferred to live completely isolated lives there, others estab-lished communities and sought to reconstruct the ideal of the first community in Jerusalem: "All the

[3] See on this whole subject the penetrating study of L. Bouyer, La Vie de saint Antoine (Éditions de Fontenelle, Abbaye de Saint-Wandrille, 1950), pp. 7-11.

faithful held together, and shared all they had, selling their possessions and their means of livelihood, so as to distribute to all, as each had need" (Acts ii.44-45). Aware of having a prophetic mission to fulfill in the Christian world, these individuals, soon to be called "monks," practiced chastity, for was it not their role to announce the *supernatural* nature of the Kingdom of God? Now in this kingdom, "there is no marrying and giving in marriage; they are as the angels in heaven are" (Matt. xxii.30). They were constantly given up to prayer, either the chanting of the psalms in monastic communities or the "pure" or "monologic prayer" of the hermits. Soon monks began to take up residence in the towns, where they could make the full impact of their eschatological calling apparent to one and all in the very midst of the new society.

The monastic world was certainly not immune to temptations and deviations of all kinds, but by and large it can be said that the monks remained faithful to the doctrinal, hierarchic, and sacramental structure of the Church and in time became a permanent institution. Throughout the medieval period, both in the East and the West, the monastic ideal continued to attract the best elements in Christian society. In the East, from the sixth century, the episcopate was reserved exclusively to monks, while in the West the ideal of monastic celibacy was later extended to the clergy in general. The moral prestige of the monks, moreover, served as a kind of brake on the process of absorption and control by the state to which the Church was continually subject. Among them also the great traditions of mysticism and holiness flourished, which have nourished Orthodox spirituality throughout the ages.

The founding of a "Christian state" in the Greco-Roman world in the fourth century did not put an end to the doctrinal controversies of the early Christians. Constantine and his immediate successors had to cope with the Arian crisis and this was then followed by the Christological controversies of the fifth, sixth, and seventh centuries. Finally, in the eighth century, the Byzantine Empire was shaken to its very foundations by the iconoclastic controversy.

Before Constantine's time the Church had had to deal with schisms and heresies by relying entirely upon itself. Each bishop was doctrinally supreme in his own diocese and sat "on the chair of Peter." It was up to him to solve the various disputes that arose concerning the faith and to condemn heretics. Sometimes, however, disagreements between bishops or the spread of heresy made necessary a more solemn witnessing to the Christian truth. In that case synods or councils would be held. We employ the term "witness" here purposely to mark the true significance of these gatherings. The bishops were all depositaries of the same grace and all equal in office: they gathered not to add anything to the grace that each possessed in its entirety—*in solidum,* as St. Cyprian of Carthage used to say—but to witness to their unanimity in the true doctrine. That is why councils never adopted the procedure of modern parliamentary assemblies in their deliberations: it was not a question of causing the opinion of the majority to triumph, but of assisting the adoption by all of the true revealed doctrine. Heretical majorities—Arian, Monophysite, iconoclastic —sometimes succeeded in imposing themselves on "false councils." The mere fact of there being a majority therefore could not be regarded as a criterion of infallibility. The Church ultimately upheld a St. Athanasius or a St. Maximus, who, at one time, were almost alone in fighting for the truth. Nor have these "false councils" ever succeeded in bringing the institution

and authority of councils into disrepute, any more
than heretical bishops have succeeded in undermining
the authority of the episcopate. Without ever being
considered infallible individually, the bishops—
separately or gathered in council—were the normal
witnesses to the true teaching and it was they perforce who bore witness to the final triumph of orthodoxy over heresy. After heresy had triumphed temporarily, later councils in which an orthodox unanimity was apparent would always succeed in reaffirming
the revealed Truth.

These ecclesiastical norms continued to be observed
in the fourth century as in the past. However, a new
factor was introduced when imperial support made
possible the holding of councils more frequently and
with a larger attendance. Hence, when Constantine
became worried about the spread of the Arian controversy, he decided on the summoning of an "ecumenical" council which would include all the bishops
of the whole "inhabited" (ecumenical) world.

Ecumenical councils are distinguished from those
which preceded Constantine by two features: they
were convoked by the emperor and their decisions
were held to be laws of the Empire. While the Church
had entered into an agreement with the Empire, the
Empire, for its part, had assumed the responsibility
for protecting the orthodox faith. It was natural, under the circumstances, that the emperor should be
eager to have an exact definition of the faith so that
he could appeal to it in his use of the political and
judicial machinery of the state. This was the real
purpose of ecumenical councils from the imperial
point of view.

In fact, however, the Church and its Tradition
never bowed completely to the imperial will. The
ecumenical councils never became organs of infal-

libility whose decisions were accepted automatically.
They rarely won the acceptance of the whole Empire
at once. The first council, that of Nicaea (325), was
rejected for more than half a century before it obtained general recognition and came to be regarded as
the symbol of an ecumenical council par excellence.
Again at Ephesus, in 449, a council formally declared
to be ecumenical was repudiated and has gone down in
history as the *Latrocinium* or "Robber Council."
The Council of Chalcedon (451), held under exceptional circumstances with regard to freedom of attendance and discussion and with representatives of different theological schools present, should have been able,
it would seem, to work out an acceptable synthesis of
various views, but its decisions were never received by
the majority of the non-Greek elements in the Eastern
Empire.

The Western Christian today may find himself
somewhat perplexed by this absence of a precise and
definite theological criterion. If he is a Roman Catholic he is accustomed to think of Tradition as something that is recognized or can be defined by the
doctrinal authority of the Roman see, or, if he is a Protestant, as something which is determined ultimately by
Scripture alone. He has difficulty in seeing how the
Church can continue to express itself *organically* in
the maze of dogmatic controversies without a permanent criterion of truth. He will prefer the apparent
security offered the West by the medieval papacy, or
he will take refuge in the principle of *sola scriptura.*
The Roman Catholic will maintain that a certain "dogmatic development" was necessary to bring some
measure of order out of the initial chaos of conflicting
doctrines during the early centuries and to make apparent the concept of the doctrinal authority of the
Roman see which the Fathers had only recognized im-

plicitly. The Protestant will generally reject the very basis for these dogmatic controversies, since in his view those who took part in them had already departed from written Revelation. The Orthodox historian, however, sees in the ecumenical councils an obvious sign of the continual fidelity of Christ to his Church, a miraculous fidelity that no definite juridical institution can express fully. Of course our theological handbooks speak of the infallibility of ecumenical councils, but the fact remains and cannot be denied that several councils, regarded as ecumenical today, were not so recognized at the time, while others, declared to be ecumenical, were later repudiated. Russian theologians of the nineteenth century, particularly A. S. Khomiakov, made much of this "reception" of conciliar decisions by the entire Church, though they were not the first to do so. In fact, it would be wrong to see an opposition between this idea of "reception" and that of the infallibility of the councils, as is sometimes done. An ecumenical council truly representative of the Church and gathered together in the name of Christ will certainly be inspired by the Holy Spirit and will therefore be infallible. However, it belongs to the Spirit and to the Church guided by him to judge whether a gathering which declares itself or is declared to be ecumenical is actually so or not. The council is not an organ external to the body of the Church. The Church's infallibility is ultimately always the infallibility of the Spirit of Truth alone, who resides in the whole organism of the Church. This organism is subject to its own special law, the law of the Spirit, and has its own peculiar form or structure, the hierarchic organization of the Church, both being dependent upon a deliberate personal profession of the true faith, by all and at all times.

The Orthodox regard the period of the ecumenical

councils as a *normative* period. It was then, by and
large, that the dogmatic and canonical norms of the
Orthodox faith were laid down, as we know them today, rather than in later ages as was the case with
Western Christianity.

The Orthodox Church acknowledges seven ecumenical councils:[4]

1. *The First Council of Nicaea* (325), which condemned Arius and defined the incarnate Son of God as
"consubstantial" with the Father.

2. *The First Council of Constantinople* (381),
which finally settled the Arian controversy. Later on,
this council was credited with having adopted the
present Creed known as the Nicaean-Constantinopolitan Creed.

3. *The Council of Ephesus* (431), which condemned Nestorianism and declared that there were
not two persons existing side by side in Christ—God
and a man called Jesus—but that the divinity and
humanity were united in one person (the "hypostatic
union"), the Person of the Word, the Son of God incarnate. Consequently, Mary, the Mother of Jesus, is
the Mother of God (*Theotokos*).

4. *The Council of Chalcedon* (451), which, while
confirming the existence in Christ of a single Person,
condemned the Monophysites, because the latter refused to distinguish between the concepts of Person
(*hypostasis*) and Nature (*physis*). If Christ were one
Person, they claimed, he could not have two natures
but only one (*mono-*, "one," *physis*, "nature"). The
council affirmed that the Son of God must be confessed
in two natures "unconfusedly, immutably, indivisibly,
inseparably, united . . . in one Person or 'hypostasis.'"
Many of the non-Greek elements in the Empire

---

[4] An English translation of the canons and dogmatic decrees
of the seven councils may be found in *The Nicene and Post-
Nicene Fathers*, Second Series, Vol. XIV (Grand Rapids, 1956).

(Copts, Ethiopians, Syro-Jacobites, Armenians) left the Orthodox Church at this time and formed schismatic Monophysite churches.

5. *The Second Council of Constantinople* (553). The Emperor Justinian was anxious to win back the Monophysites and wished to prove to them that the Council of Chalcedon had not fallen into Nestorianism and was not contrary to the doctrine proclaimed at Ephesus. Summoning a new council, he had three theologians of the fifth century (the "Three Chapters") suspected of entertaining Nestorian views condemned.

6. *The Third Council of Constantinople* (680), which condemned a bastard form of Monophysitism known as Monothelitism. According to the Monothelites (*thelesis*, "will"), while Christ has two natures he has only one will, his divine will or "energy." The council maintained that the humanity is not an abstract entity in Christ but is manifested by its own will, subject freely and in all things to the divine will. Christ therefore has two wills.

7. *The Second Council of Nicaea* (787), which defined the Orthodox doctrine concerning the images (icons) which represent Christ or the saints. The Word of God was truly incarnate and became true man. He may therefore be pictorially represented, and the same is true of the saints. While sacred images ought to be venerated, the one whom they represent is the true object of the veneration. However, it is not lawful to pay to them the highest form of worship (*latreia*), which is due to God alone (the distinction between "veneration" [*proskynesis*] and "true worship" [*latreia*] has become classical in theology). The veneration of images was opposed by several Byzantine emperors, who were responsible for the iconoclastic controversy.

The work of the ecumenical councils was not limited to deciding these purely dogmatic questions, but was also concerned with the Church's constitutional and administrative organization.

During the pre-Constantinian period there were no precise juridical norms governing the relations of local churches with each other. These relations were determined ultimately by the awareness all Christians had of belonging to the one Lord and to the one Catholic Church. Church unity was manifested in a practical way: for example, when the bishops from neighboring districts convened in a city which had lost its chief pastor for the consecration of a new bishop. Occasions of this kind soon came to be used for the holding of synods, which became a regular feature in the life of the Church. In this way local churches came to be grouped into provinces, which generally coincided with the administrative divisions of the Empire. Moreover, it was inevitable that the bishops of the larger sees, the heads of sizable and wealthy communities, should preside over these synods, or councils, and although they exercised no jurisdictional power over their colleagues, the latter were nevertheless prepared to acknowledge their *de facto* authority. Their votes were often the determining factor in reaching common decisions.

The councils of the Constantinian period simply codified and gave juridical form to this state of affairs in their *canons*.

The canons of the Council of Nicaea (325) are almost all concerned with the adjustment of the government of the Church to that of the Empire, which was now of course well-disposed toward the Church: the local churches were grouped together in ecclesiastical provinces which had the same boundaries as the civil provinces, and the provincial synod, which was to meet regularly, was to be presided over by the bishop of the capital of the province, or "metropolitan." Canon 6 allows for an exception to this rule in the case of the three greater sees of Rome, Alexandria, and Antioch, whose jurisdiction in any case by this time extended far beyond the limits of a single province. The Council of Nicaea officially granted them the right to approve the episcopal elections in several civil provinces. The overwhelming importance of these cities—by far the largest in the Empire—was certainly the determining factor in this decision. Later an attempt would be made to explain Canon 6 on the basis of the *apostolic* origin of the three churches, but the objective historian cannot be unduly impressed by this argument (to which the council never refers!) for it could be alleged more convincingly on behalf of certain other churches, especially Jerusalem. In spite of the honor conferred on him by Canon 7, Nicaea still decreed that the bishop of Jerusalem should be subject to the metropolitan of Caesarea in Palestine.

The second ecumenical council at Constantinople (381) decreed a similar exception in the case of the Church of Constantinople, because of its status as the New Rome, the capital of the Empire, but it remained subject to the over-all primacy of the Elder Rome (Canon 3).

Still later, especially at Chalcedon (451), the Roman world was divided into five "patriarchates"—Rome, Constantinople, Alexandria, Antioch, and Jerusalem—which had the privilege of presiding over the metropolitan elections in groups of provinces, while the metropolitans themselves continued to consecrate the bishops under their immediate jurisdiction.[5] The

[5] Within each patriarchate, as a matter of fact, a different procedure was followed: the bishop of Alexandria, for example, had abolished the privileges of metropolitans as early as the fourth century and himself consecrated all the bishops of the civil "dioceses" of Egypt, Libya, and the Pentapolis.

Novellae of Justinian refer to the five patriarchates as the five senses of the Empire.

This gradual evolution of the Church's governmental structure did not take place without certain clashes. Beginning in the fifth century, for example, we can discern the seeds of future conflict over the exact role which the Church of Rome was destined to play. Whereas for the Orientals—who were always in a majority at the ecumenical councils—the privileges of Rome, universally recognized, were based on the numerical importance of the Roman see and also on the fact that it was located in the capital of the Empire, in Rome itself there was an awareness that this interpretation could lead to the complete disappearance of the Roman primacy, for was Constantinople not the new capital and thus capable of eclipsing the glory of the old capital? On the other hand, Rome was the *only* "apostolic" Church in the West; the relics of the holy Apostles Peter and Paul had long been venerated there and there was no question at all that, for the Western Christian, Rome was the center of Christianity. By appealing to these considerations the popes, particularly St. Leo the Great (440-461), attempted to oppose the rise of the see of Constantinople, but they could not succeed in their purpose, except temporarily, for its rise was logical and in the nature of things. From the time of the Patriarch John the Faster (528-595), the bishops of New Rome adopted the title of "ecumenical patriarch," which was partly of honorary significance, but which in any case was not intended to infringe upon the Roman primacy.

However this may be, it is undeniable that as a result of these differences two opposing ecclesiologies began to take shape, each with its own view of what the primacy meant which all the world acknowledged belonged to Rome. For one side this primacy was of direct apostolic and hence "divine" origin, while for the other it was only a primacy of "ecclesiastical law" and origin, the exact significance of which it was up to the councils to define and which in any case could only function with the consent of and subject to control by the other churches. The canons of the councils definitely favor this latter interpretation.[6]

It is impossible to dwell any longer on the history of the councils. We must be content with having pointed out their importance for the Orthodox Church. Later ecclesiastical writers have sometimes compared them with the Seven Pillars of Wisdom or with the Seven Gifts of the Holy Spirit. But such symbolical explanations stressing the number seven have only a relative importance. They indicate that the councils have indeed been venerated by tradition, but they have no real theological meaning. When the Orthodox Church says that it recognizes only these seven councils as ecumenical, it is not claiming, of course, that its authority is confined to one historical period, or that other councils or witnesses to tradition—the Church Fathers or liturgical formulas—may not also witness to the Truth. We shall see further on that certain local councils, recognized later as having universal validity, defined the Orthodox position on grace in the fourteenth century, and a similar function was performed by still other councils which met between the seventeenth and nineteenth centuries.

The seven ecumenical councils recognized as such by the Orthodox Church were held under certain definite historical circumstances, those prevailing at the time of the Christian Roman (or Byzantine) Empire. Now while it is perfectly true that the Church remains

---

[6] For a more detailed study of the question, see our article "La Primauté romaine dans la tradition canonique jusqu'au concile de Chalcédoine," in *Istina*, No. 4 (1957), pp. 463-82; see now also the remarkable study of Prof. F. Dvornik, *The Idea of Apostolicity in Byzantium and the Legend of the Apostle Andrew* (Cambridge, Mass., 1958).

essentially the same at all times, historical circumstances vary from time to time. Consequently it would
be foolish to think that we can simply reproduce the
forms and procedures that governed the ancient councils. New forms and procedures will be called for in
keeping with the new conditions that will prevail, and
we must not suppose that this natural evolutionary
process detracts in any way from the permanence of
Truth in the Church. Moreover, the Roman Catholic
Church commonly recognizes twenty councils as ecumenical today, but it does not pretend to claim that the
later ones were held in accordance with the same forms
and procedures governing the earlier ones. . . . In fact,
the word "ecumenical" is used today in such a variety
of senses that it has become rather vague. What
matters is not the number of councils recognized as
"ecumenical," but the awareness which the Church
has of itself and of the Truth. The Orthodox Church
claims that it remains faithful to the ancient councils—
the common heritage of Eastern and Western Christendom—and it believes itself to be the One Church
to which the ancient councils bore witness.

CHAPTER III

SCHISM AND
ATTEMPTS AT REUNION

THE SCHISM between Byzantium and Rome was without doubt the most tragic event in the history of the Church. Christendom became divided in two halves, and this separation still endures today and has determined the destiny of both East and West to a very great extent. While the Eastern Church claimed—and still claims today—to be the only true Church of Christ, it saw its cultural and its geographical field of vision restricted: historically, it became identified with the Byzantine world. The Church of the West, as viewed by the Orthodox Church, lost the doctrinal and ecclesiological balance of primitive Christianity and this lack of balance was ultimately responsible for provoking the reaction of the sixteenth century, the Protestant Reformation.

If we wish to assess the true meaning and extent of this catastrophe, we must avoid the romantic fallacy of thinking that there was ever an "undivided Church" which lasted for some nine centuries. As a matter of fact, the Church has experienced a succession of heresies and schisms from the very earliest times. A particularly important and long-lived separation began in the fifth and sixth centuries over Christological issues,

when whole nations—Egypt, Ethiopia, Armenia, and
large segments of the Syrian population—abandoned
the communion of the orthodox "Great Church,"
which they referred to scornfully as the "Melkite" or
"imperial" Church. The latter was thereby deprived of
communion with various venerable non-Greek traditions of Christianity, those of the Semites and Copts,
and found itself reduced, practically speaking, to the
Greek and Latin parts of the Empire. In the ninth
and tenth centuries this Greco-Roman world was in
turn divided into two great branches, along the linguistic and political frontiers which then demarcated
the two zones of the ancient Roman Empire.

However, these various schisms cannot be regarded
merely as evidence of an inescapable tendency toward
fragmentation on the part of the churches. The Greek
and Latin Churches both continued to exhibit the
signs of true Catholicity. Neither allowed itself to be
transformed into a purely national church. Both continued to direct their energies outward toward the
spreading of the Gospel. While Rome was preoc-
cupied with the conversion of the new nations of the
West, the "barbarians" of the North, Byzantium could
claim credit for the conversion of the Slavs and was
continually active throughout its history in the attempt
to win back the Monophysites to union with the
Church. We have to admit, therefore, that in addition
to the various linguistic, cultural, and political reasons
for the separation, theological differences of a profound nature were also at work toward this end.
In attempting to explain the nature of the schism
we are forced to admit that both theological and non-
theological factors were hopelessly mixed up together.
It would be pointless to deny either the one or the
other. We shall find later on, however, that theological
causes are at the root of the matter because all attempts at conciliation and reunion have been frus-

trated by the failure to overcome these hurdles. Moreover, they still constitute today the major obstacle to the ultimate goal of ecumenism.

We have seen that from the fourth to the eighth century tension already existed in the Church between East and West over the true significance of the Roman primacy. This tension, however, was not always readily apparent, because of the flowery rhetoric and studied vagueness used by Eastern prelates when writing to the popes. The latter, for their part, avoided pressing their claim to universal jurisdiction over the whole Church, in all its implications, for the claim was contrary to the traditions and customs of the Church. The latent tension only came to the surface in the ninth century, when it developed into open hostility.

The political event which occasioned this conflict was the founding of the Carolingian Empire in the West.

History textbooks are fond of portraying Charlemagne as the great restorer, for his own benefit, of the Roman Empire in the West which had disappeared in the fifth century. It is asserted that when Charlemagne was crowned in 800 by the pope in Rome, he was occupying a throne that had long been vacant. But, as a matter of fact, many contemporaries regarded him as a usurper, for the legitimate Roman Empire with its capital at Constantinople had not ceased to exist, and its claim to rule the entire Christian Roman world had never been given up. One of the primary objectives of the reign of the Frankish king was to get Byzantium's approval for the step that had been taken in the West. When a project for the marriage of Charles and the reigning Byzantine empress fell through, the Frankish king decided to ruin Constantinople's claim to universal jurisdiction. One of the means used to achieve this end was to bring the charge of heresy against the East. The Eastern emperor could not claim to be the successor of earlier Christian *basileis* because he worshipped images and because he confessed that the Holy Spirit proceeds "from the Father by the Son" insted of "from the Father and the Son." These allegations by Charlemagne in his famous *Libri Carolini,* sent to the pope in 792, formed part of the Frankish refutation of the decrees of the second ecumenical council of Nicaea (787) and prepared the way for the interminable quarrel between East and West over the question of the *Filioque.*[1] Several Western bishops and theologians—Paulinus of Aquileia, Theodulphus of Orleans, and Smaragdus, abbot of St. Mihiel—took up the cudgels against the Greeks at the invitation of the Frankish court at Aix-la-Chapelle. Alcuin was thus able to write to Charlemagne in 799:[2]

> Three persons have been at the head of the hierarchy of the world: firstly, the representative of the apostolic sublimity, the vicar of blessed Peter . . . secondly, the occupant of the imperial dignity which exercises secular sway in the second Rome . . . thirdly, the royal dignity which our Lord Jesus Christ has reserved to you in order to rule the Christian peoples. . . . It is now on you alone that the Churches of Christ must rely, from you alone that they expect salvation. . . .

[1] During the sixth century certain anti-Arian councils in Spain had inserted in the Nicaean-Constantinopolitan Creed the word *Filioque* which was not in the original (*Credo . . . in Spiritum Sanctum . . . qui ex Patre Filioque procedit*). This new version of the Creed spread to Gaul and the Frankish lands in the eighth century. It was not accepted by the Church of Rome, which opposed the interpolation until the eleventh century. The most complete account of the question of the origins of the *Filioque* remains that of H. B. Swete, *On the History of the Doctrine of the Procession of the Holy Spirit (From the Apostolic Age to the Death of Charlemagne),* (Cambridge, 1876).

[2] *Letters of Alcuin,* No. 174, Monumenta Germaniae historica Epistolae, IV, Epistolae aevi Carolini, II (Berlin, 1895), p. 288.

These words are very revealing with regard to the true nature of the new empire in the West: it was dominated by the ideals of caesaropapism—it seems that the Frankish court was influenced by the example of the iconoclastic emperors of Byzantium, whose theology was taken over by Charlemagne, at least in part—and it was intended to supplant both the traditional empire (in the East) and the papacy.

Fortunately for the cause of church unity, while the Roman Church approved Charlemagne's political aims, it was decidedly opposed to his theological attack on Byzantium. Popes Hadrian I (772-795) and Leo III (795-816) defended the Council of Nicaea and formally rejected the interpolation in the Creed. We must acknowledge frankly that the Christian world is indebted to them for having preserved its unity, if only for a relatively short time. When political interests finally caused the Byzantines to extend recognition to the Carolingian Empire—though with reservations—the Western attacks on the Greeks ceased, but they left behind a certain amount of ill feeling; and because of this and because of the existence of polemical tracts, it was not long before animosity flared up again.

The most serious consequence of the creation of Charlemagne's empire was the appearance of a new type of Christianity in the West, the work of men from the "barbarian" parts of Northern Europe, who were only very vaguely acquainted with the intellectual atmosphere of the Roman-Byzantine world in which the Fathers of the Church had lived and in which the ancient councils had been held. More serious still was the fact that the learned men at Aix-la-Chapelle felt free to define theological issues without reference and even in opposition to the East. The *Libri Carolini* and the whole literature connected with them have no other meaning. On the other hand it must be admitted that while the Byzantines were wise enough not to pay any attention to the doctrinal attacks of Charlemagne, they were unable to adopt toward the new Carolingian learning and culture a sympathetic and charitable attitude which might have helped to smooth off its rough edges. The Emperor Michael III was indiscreet enough in 864 to refer to the Latin language as a "barbarous" and "Scythian" tongue, incapable of expressing the finer shadings of theological thought. This self-satisfaction of the Byzantines with their own culture, which could boast a Photius or a Psellus while the medieval West was scarcely able to cope with the rudiments of learning, prevented them from taking the theological position of the Franks seriously.

The Church of Rome alone was capable of maintaining the bridges. It was the only religious authority which the Franks respected; it had preserved enough of the Greek traditions to be able to understand both East and West. We have seen how, when they were opposed by Charlemagne, the Roman popes had been able to perform their role as supreme judges worthily, and Photius publicly acknowledged the Church's indebtedness to Pope Leo III a century later.[3]

The open breaks between East and West in the ninth and eleventh centuries occurred when the political aims of the Frankish Empire became confused with the canonical pretensions of the popes and both found themselves united in a common opposition to the East.

From the eighth century the history of the papacy is dominated by its relations with the new Carolingian Empire. At first, in the eighth century and then again particularly in the tenth and eleventh centuries, the bishops of Rome were hardly more than mere tools

[3] In his *Mystagogia*, written against the *Filioque*, Photius mentions with approval the opposition of this pope to its insertion in the Creed.

in the hands of the Western emperors, whose outlook was thoroughly caesaropapist. However, a few great popes managed to assert themselves and react against this tendency, Nicholas I in the ninth century, and especially the great theoretician of the medieval papacy, Gregory VII (1073-1081), who was preceded by the vigorous but short-lived Leo IX (1049-1054) and Nicholas II (1059-1061). This papal reaction, which ultimately led to the triumph of the papacy over the Empire, was inspired by a new consciousness of the meaning of the Roman primacy. The see of Rome must become something more than a mere patriarchate of the West, something more than one apostolic see among others, if a Henry IV were to be forced to go to Canossa. Its traditional primacy of honor and authority must be transformed into a real power of jurisdiction, universal in scope and absolute in nature.

Antipapalist writers have often seen in this development a sign that the popes had succumbed to a wicked desire for domination. But this is to read the signs incorrectly and miss the essential point. The great reforming popes were sincerely attempting to restore the Church and free it from excessive lay control. They fought the evil of simony and raised the standard of clerical morality. The result of their efforts was the birth of a Christian Europe and a new civilization. However, these great pontiffs, almost all of whom were of Northern European origin and closely identified with the Cluniac reform movement, were the heirs of that Carolingian civilization which, as we have seen, had dared to reach definitions by itself in opposition to the East and had developed without being influenced to any extent by the Greek Fathers. Basically Latin and Western in outlook, this civilization was shared by both Roman popes and Western emperors. This is why, ultimately, the controversy be-

tween the *Sacerdotium* and the *Imperium* appeared to
be more of a political than a religious quarrel. The
popes turned the emperor's own arms against him,
they adopted his methods and identified themselves
with his ambition to destroy the prestige of the old
but legitimate Roman Empire at Constantinople. The
Orthodox historian therefore will not question the
sincerity of the reforming popes or their zeal for the
welfare of the Church. He will simply feel obliged to
question the theological and ecclesiological basis of a
theory of power which appears to him as alien to
the spirit of the Gospel. He will refuse to regard the
development of the medieval papacy as something
absolute and will attribute to this development, at
least in part, those secularizing, reformist, and anti-
clerical tendencies which will begin to appear in the
West later on.

When reforming the Western Church the popes
tried to extend their reforms to the East but failed.
This failure would serve more than anything else to
strengthen the unity of Western Christendom and
make it monolithic and self-contained.

Nicholas I (858-867) was without question the
greatest of the reforming popes of the early Middle
Ages. In the West he was confronted by the three
kingdoms into which the Carolingian Empire had become divided, and in the East by the Byzantine Empire which was experiencing a violent quarrel between two factions in the Church. Appeal from both
sides was made to his tribunal, in accordance with
tradition. But whereas his predecessors in the time of
Charlemagne were called upon to arbitrate *between*
the two Christendoms, he was obliged to deal with
quarrels within each side. This gave him the opportunity to press those reforms which he deemed necessary, on the one side as well as the other.

We cannot linger here over the crisis brought on by the divorce of Lothar II. Skillfully utilizing the rivalry between the latter and his uncles, Charles the Bald and Louis the German, Nicholas succeeded in annulling the sentences of several councils of the Frankish episcopate, in judging the archbishops of Cologne and Trier at Rome, and finally in compelling the royal power to yield. He attempted, also, in the course of a violent quarrel with Hincmar, the archbishop of Reims, to limit the authority of metropolitans in the West, which had been decreed, as we have seen, by the First Council of Nicaea, and to establish a system which would have subjected the entire Western episcopate directly to the Roman see. In support of its new policy the latter now began to appeal—in good faith, of course—to the celebrated False Decretals, which were compiled about this time and which aimed at substituting for the old conciliar legislation a new system exalting the prerogatives of the Roman see, that is, in effect, a papal monarchy.[4]

All this might have had little effect on relations with the East. Precedents could have been cited, particularly the example of Alexandria, showing that it was lawful for powerful patriarchs to gather the reins of power into their own hands. But Nicholas was clearly of the opinion that his reforms had to do with rights which the Roman see ought to claim as properly

[4] The compiler of the Decretals (whether of Roman or Frankish origin) was interested primarily in combatting the authority of strong metropolitans like Hincmar by an appeal to a great many alleged ancient papal decretals which he forged, rather than in exalting the authority of Rome, but this was the net effect of his work. The decretals were accepted as genuine and incorporated in later canonical collections. See P. Fournier and G. Le Bras, *Histoire des collections canoniques en Occident*, Vol. I, pp. 126-33; cf. E. Amann, *L'Époque carolingienne*, in Fliche-Martin, *Histoire de l'Église*, Vol. VI (Paris, 1947), pp. 352-66, 387.

belonging to it and therefore of universal validity. It was on this point that he clashed with the Eastern Church.

The Patriarch Ignatius of Constantinople had been compelled to resign his throne in 857 to Photius, the great scholar and student of antiquity, as well as theologian and politician. The imperial government was of course responsible for the change, but at Byzantium as elsewhere in the West at this time no one questioned the right of the emperor to decide who was to sit on the patriarchal throne. This right naturally entailed a certain influence by the patriarchs over political affairs. This dyarchy of emperor and patriarch was, as it were, the very foundation stone of the Byzantine theocracy. However, it would be highly inaccurate to think of this system as merely a form of caesaropapism, particularly after the defeat of the iconoclastic party. In the case of Ignatius, moreover, things took their accustomed course and due forms were observed: Photius was elected only after his predecessor had formally resigned.[5]

However, a group of Ignatian partisans decided to keep up the struggle and persuaded the ex-patriarch to revoke his abdication. In keeping with the canons of the ancient Council of Sardica, both parties then appealed to Rome. This move on their part was tantamount to an unprecedented act of deference by the Byzantine Church toward the see of Rome, for until then the popes had never intervened directly in the purely disciplinary affairs of the powerful ecumenical patriarchate. So the legates of Nicholas I presided over a council of bishops at Constantinople which confirmed the election of Photius (861). On the very eve

[5] The fundamental work on the Photian crisis is by F. Dvornik, *The Photian Schism, History and Legend* (Cambridge, 1948).

of the conflict, therefore, Byzantium was displaying a more deferential attitude toward Rome than it had ever done in the past.

Since Photius continued to be opposed by an Ignatian minority at Constantinople, Pope Nicholas determined to profit by the occasion and extend to the East the reforms which he was pressing in the West. If he could limit the authority of metropolitans in one half of Christendom, why could he not humble the much more important obstacle to Roman centralization in the other, namely the Byzantine patriarchate? He decided therefore to annul the Council of Constantinople and compel both Ignatius and Photius to appear before his tribunal, as he had attempted and partially achieved in the case of the archbishops of Cologne and Trier. It hardly needs to be observed that there was no precedent in the conciliar legislation then in force to justify such a procedure. The patriarchate of Byzantium remained silent and failed to reply to the papal letters.

The situation was further complicated by the activities of Byzantine and Western missionaries in Bulgaria. Most of the Slavic tribes were on the verge of adopting Christianity about this time and were hesitating between East and West in view of the political and religious pressure being exercised by the two rival empires, the Byzantine and the Frankish. The brothers St. Cyril and St. Methodius, the Apostles of the Slavs, encountered wherever they went, in Khazaria and later in Bohemia, the opposition of German missionaries eager to impose on their new converts the Latin language and ritual and the singing of the *Filioque* in the mass. Now the Bulgarians were actually baptized in 863 by missionaries from Byzantium, but when the Bulgarian Khan, Boris, failed to get Byzantine approval for the autonomous status of his church in 865, he decided to transfer his spiritual allegiance to the West and allow the Frankish clergy to organize his church.

Up until this time the popes had been fairly successful in acting as arbiters between the Franks and Byzantines. It was possible for them to appear to be neutral as long as the Roman see did not have direct control over the German missionaries in Slavic countries. But this is precisely what Nicholas sought to bring about by his curtailment of the autonomy of local churches and extension of Roman jurisdiction. He was bound therefore to take a stand on the minor quarrels which until then had not been regarded as within the sphere of the papacy. In the case of Bulgaria, he decided to support the Franks against the Byzantines. He even succeeded in obtaining that the new head of the Bulgarian Church should be appointed by himself and not by the Germanic emperor Louis II, though only after some difficulty. The pope was thus creating at the very gates of Constantinople a situation until then undreamed of, namely, a church of Frankish rite subject to Roman jurisdiction. This church would of course recite the *Filioque* in the Creed, although this was not done at Rome itself. Nicholas was thus not only supporting the political and cultural enemies of Byzantium, but implicitly giving his blessing to this controversial interpolation in the universal creed.

In 867 the Patriarch Photius accused Pope Nicholas of heresy in his famous Encyclical and broke off communion with him.

It is impossible to go into the details of the long conflict which ensued. Before long Photius was deprived of his patriarchal throne by a dynastic revolution in Byzantium. In order to strengthen their position, the restored Ignatius and his followers needed the support of Rome. In a new council at Constantinople (869-870), under the presidency of papal legates, Photius was condemned and the Roman primacy forcibly asserted. However, this was tantamount to a mere diplomatic maneuver on the part of the Ignatian party, for they could not be expected to go on appealing to principles that were so much at variance with the age-old conceptions of the Eastern Church. While the council was being held Ignatius received word that the Bulgarians had returned to their allegiance to Byzantium. Khan Boris drove out the Franks and requested the Byzantine Church to consecrate an archbishop for his church. Ignoring the protests of the papal legates Ignatius welcomed the Bulgarian move. Only his death (877) prevented him from being excommunicated by Pope Hadrian II. It is not accurate, therefore, to describe the Ignatian party at Byzantium as a "papal" party.

Meanwhile Photius had been reconciled with Ignatius and now found himself once again on the patriarchal throne (877). Since Providence willed that the successor of Popes Nicholas I and Hadrian II should break with the policy of these two popes, peace and harmony were once more restored to the Church.

All historical sources are in agreement that Pope John VIII (872-882) realized the danger to Christian unity inherent in the policy of his immediate predecessors. Like the popes of the time of Charlemagne he acknowledged the justice of the Greek point of view with regard to the use of the native languages in the liturgy and the exclusion of the *Filioque* from the Creed. He gave support to St. Methodius in the latter's trouble with Frankish missionaries in Moravia, and, most important of all, his legates at the Council of Constantinople in 879-880, which restored Photius, condemned the famous "addition" to the Creed, to-

gether with the rest of the Eastern Church.[6] For the
rest of his life Photius remained grateful to Pope John
for his restoration of the unity of the Church and cited
him as an example to those who wished to deny the
authority of the Roman popes at Byzantium. It cannot be denied, as a matter of fact, that the decisions
of the council of 879-880, which are included in every
Orthodox collection of canon law, must be regarded
as the very model of the way in which the Orthodox
Church conceives of Christian unity, that is, as a
unity in faith to which the Roman primacy may indeed bear witness, but of which it cannot itself be
the source.

The tenth century and the first half of the eleventh
were not marked by any outstanding clash between
East and West. During this time the papacy was passing through one of the most profound periods of deg-
radation in its long history, while for Byzantium, on
the contrary, this was an age of glory under the Macedonian emperors, whose conquests greatly extended
the boundaries of the Empire; an age of cultural progress, that of Michael Psellus, and Symeon the New
Theologian; the age also of important missions to the
Slavs and the Caucasus. The Byzantines could af-
ford to ignore the pope, the primacy, and its far-
reaching claims, because the pope was not in a position to enforce them.

Hence they paid very little attention to one event
of major importance—as things turned out, a portent
of things to come. In 1014 the German emperor Henry
II came to Rome to have himself crowned by Pope

[6] Until recently it was held that Pope John VIII later
repudiated his legates and excommunicated Photius anew. Modern Catholic historians (F. Dvornik, op. cit., cf. also V. Grumel,
"Y eût-il un second schisme de Photius?" in Revue des sci-
ences philosophiques et théologiques, No. 32 [1933], pp. 432-
57) have proved that the second Photian schism is merely a
"legend."

Benedict VIII, and he easily persuaded that pope,
who was completely under his influence, to allow the
use of a Germanic ritual in the coronation ceremony;
this meant that the *Filioque* would be sung in the
Credo of the mass in Rome.[7] Thus it came about that,
because of the laxness and indifference of the times,
the frankly caesaropapist outlook of the German mon-
archs became responsible for the adoption by Rome of
a doctrine which was rejected by the Christian East.[8]
In any case, from approximately the beginning of the
eleventh century there was no longer any *communio
in sacris* between Byzantium and Rome.

The controversy over the *Filioque* as well as other
points in dispute between Rome and Constantinople
could certainly have been settled, as had so many misunderstandings before this time. But the tragic thing
about developments in the eleventh century was that,
because they had mutually ignored each other for so
long, East and West had lost the *common ground*
which had formerly enabled them to come to an
understanding. Whenever they attempted to restore
communion—and this was done again and again in
the medieval period—they were always prevented

[7] We know this from Berno (*De officio missae*, in PL 142,
col. 1060-61), who does not explicitly mention the *Filioque*.
However, it is known that the popes of the ninth century had
forbidden the singing of the Creed in the mass (a Frankish
custom) in order to avoid the appearance of approving the
Frankish interpolation. Benedict VIII was no longer in a
position to keep up this opposition. It is worth noting that
Byzantine tradition regards Pope Sergius IV (1009-1012), the
predecessor of Benedict VIII, as the first pope to profess the
heresy of the *Filioque* and as having been excluded from the
diptychs at Constantinople on that account. The vagueness of
this information shows what little importance was attached to
the event by contemporaries.

[8] As G. Every aptly says in his book, the singing of the
Filioque in the Creed at Rome was interpreted as a sign of
allegiance to the Holy Roman Empire on the part of the pope
(*The Byzantine Patriarchate* [London, 1947], p. 170).

from agreeing upon a common language because of
their different understanding of the nature of the
Church. For one side, the see of Rome was the sole
criterion of Truth; for the other, the Spirit of Truth
resided in the whole Church and normally expressed
himself by means of the ecumenical councils.

One of these attempts occurred in 1053-1054, an occasion that has wrongly been considered as marking
the beginning of the schism.[9] It must be admitted that
the protagonists on both sides were reformers of their
respective churches and the spirit of their reforms
was hardly likely to be conducive to reconciliation.

The patriarch of Constantinople, Michael Caerularius, had determined on a reform of the Latin churches
in his own diocese and even in those throughout the
entire patriarchate. These churches fasted on Saturdays, sang the Alleluia during Eastertide, and otherwise followed Latin customs which were at variance
with Byzantine practice and which appeared to be
controversial. So the patriarch decided that they must
conform to Byzantine custom in the matters under dispute, and when they refused to do so, he ordered the
churches closed. It hardly need be said that the Latins
of Constantinople did not sing the *Filioque* in the
Creed and that is why there is little mention of
this subject in the controversial literature of the eleventh century.

In the West the Cluniac reform movement and its
sympathizers were pushing ahead with their projects
at this time. The most important of their measures
had already been widely accepted by the Germanic
world, but they were encountering a stiff resistance
on the part of the Italians. Pope Leo IX, former bishop
of Toul, and his entourage, particularly Cardinal Hum-

[9] On the events of 1054, see especially A. Michel, *Humbert
und Kerullarios* (Paderborn, 1924-1930); and G. Every, *op. cit.,*
pp. 153-69.

bert of Moyenmoutier, were strong advocates of the
new reform measures and were attempting to win
Italian acceptance of one of them in particular, the
celibacy of the clergy. The opponents of the celibacy
measure did not fail to point to the example of the
Greeks, whose secular priests were regularly married.
Endless controversy raged over questions that were
relatively unimportant in themselves, and was carried on by persons who were no doubt well-inten-
tioned, but who were not always so well acquainted
with the true traditions of the Church.

In spite of this mutual atmosphere of distrust, the
Patriarch Michael Caerularius dispatched to Pope Leo
IX, at the request of the emperor, a letter offering to
re-establish communion with Rome. In reply to this invitation and also in order to regulate the outstanding
disciplinary and liturgical differences between the two
churches, the pope sent legates to Constantinople in
1054, headed by Cardinal Humbert. They were received with honor by the emperor, but the patriarch
refused all contact with them. He charged that they
had come at the instance of Argyrus, the Byzantine
governor of Italy, a person of Lombard origin and a
follower of the Latin rite, whose pro-Germanic policies the patriarch disliked. Caerularius also questioned
the authenticity of the papal letters which the legates
had brought with them. His suspicions were perhaps
justified since Leo IX was at this time a prisoner of
the Normans in Italy and would thus not have been in
a position, it would seem, to sign official documents.

Thwarted by the non-cooperative and even hostile
attitude of the patriarch, the legates stalked into Hagia
Sophia during the celebration of the liturgy, deposited
their famous sentence of excommunication on the high
altar, and then stalked out again, shaking the dust
symbolically from their feet. The patriarch and his
clergy were excommunicated for the most unlikely

crimes: for having *omitted* (!) the *Filioque* from the
Creed and for allowing the marriage of the clergy,
among others. Caerularius replied by summoning a
synod and having the legates excommunicated, in
spite of attempts of the emperor to smooth things
over.

The events of 1054 which seemed to put a seal on
the break between Rome and Constantinople did not
in fact put an end to all contacts between East and
West. The other Eastern patriarchs remained in communion with the Latins for some time, and at Constantinople itself the Latin churches and monasteries
remained open.[10] The true and final rupture only took
place as a result of the Crusades.

Even today, it is rare for Western historians to pay
adequate attention to the really disastrous part played
by these great expeditions in worsening the relations
between East and West, from the viewpoint of church
unity. When they first reached the East, lands traditionally Christian but now occupied by the Moslems,
the Crusaders began by acknowledging the canonical
rights of the local bishops and entering into sacramental communion with them. There is much evidence,
in fact, which proves that the ecclesiastical rupture
was not yet regarded as finally consummated in the
eleventh or throughout the twelfth century. But the
Latin princes and clergy of Outremer gradually put
an end to this state of affairs by replacing the Oriental
clergy with Latin clergy. Most important of all, it
was the infamous Fourth Crusade which gave the
final blow to the last vestiges of church unity still
remaining. The Venetian fleet conveying the Crusaders
to the Holy Land purposely veered off its course toward Constantinople, with the approval of the Crusaders themselves, and the great city "guarded by
God" was captured and sacked in one of the most

[10] See particularly G. Every, *op. cit.*, pp. 153-69.

famous but also disgraceful events in history. The whole West was enriched by the precious relics and Byzantine treasure carried off, and a Venetian patri- arch, Thomas Morosini, was installed on the throne of Photius with the approval of Pope Innocent III. To the doctrinal differences separating the Greeks and Latins there was now added a new note, national hatred, which helped to make all future attempts at reunion more unrealistic than ever.

Yet these attempts were made, and rather frequently. Almost every one of the Palaeologi, particularly Mi- chael VIII, who won Constantinople back from the Latins and re-established the Byzantine Empire (1259- 1282), carried on discussions with the popes regard- ing reunion. Political motives were unquestionably uppermost in their minds: first the desire to protect their empire against Latin attempts to retake it; then the hope of being able, with Latin help, to ward off the Turkish peril, which finally reduced their empire to little more than a beleaguered city. Only a new Crusade (!) could save Byzantium. But before the popes would do anything effective in the way of mili- tary help, they insisted that there must first be re- union in ecclesiastical matters. Occasionally the By- zantine emperors would resort to force in order to break down the resistance of the Byzantine Church and impose a policy of reunion against the latter's will. Thus after taking part in the Council of Lyons (1274) through representatives and accepting the union personally, Michael VIII installed on the patri- archal throne a person sharing his own views, John Bekkos, but the reunion did not survive the emperor even by one day. Regarded as an apostate, he was even refused Christian burial. The Emperor John V (1341-1391) also embraced Catholicism on a personal basis (1369), but this too was without any effect in the ecclesiastical sphere. While remaining stubbornly opposed to any politically oriented reunion, the Byzantine Church was not opposed categorically to the idea of a negotiated peace in keeping with the ancient canons and ecclesiastical custom. In order to bring this about, the Church insisted that it was necessary to hold an ecumenical council which, it was certain, would result in the triumph of Orthodoxy. For a long time the popes refused to entertain the idea of holding a council in which both sides would be represented as equals, but the idea finally triumphed, nevertheless, during the first part of the fifteenth century, when the Great Schism of the West had shaken the papacy to its very foundations. The popes were afraid that the Greeks might reach an agreement with the schismatic council of Basel and decided to authorize at last a real reunion council.

The council met first at Ferrara, then at Florence (1438-1439), and the mere fact that it was held at all constituted a kind of moral victory for the East. An important Greek delegation headed by the emperor and the patriarch of Constantinople arrived in Italy and began theological discussions with the Western theologians and prelates. The course of these discussions showed how difficult it would be to reach an agreement on basic issues, for minds were not yet prepared to revise their thinking on certain points. The problem of the *Filioque*, for example, was complicated by the fact that the Roman Church held that it had already defined this matter dogmatically and was unwilling to go back on its previous decision. Regarding the problem of the Roman primacy, we can only say that it was hardly more than touched upon at Florence. After weeks and even months of wrangling, the Greeks finally had to face the unpalatable alternative of either yielding to the Roman point of view or breaking off the talks and attempting to cope with the Turkish threat alone. Moral and financial pressure finally conspired to force them to accept the first alternative. The majority at length yielded and signed the act of reunion. Only the metropolitan of Ephesus, Mark Eugenicos, held out and refused to follow suit. Another outstanding theologian, Scholarios, the future patriarch, left Florence before the end of the discussions.

As soon as they returned home the Greek delegates for the most part repudiated their signatures, when confronted by the general disapproval of the people. When the Metropolitan Isidore of Kiev reached Moscow to proclaim the reunion there, he was imprisoned and only succeeded in escaping to Rome with great difficulty. The Byzantine emperor John VIII and his successor, Constantine XI, remained faithful to the union, but they did not dare proclaim it officially in Hagia Sophia until 1452. The following year, in 1453, the Ottoman Turkish ruler Mohammed II entered New Rome as a conqueror and the Byzantine Empire had ceased to exist. The first task of the new patriarch, Gennadios Scholarios, was to repudiate the Union of Florence officially.

There can be no doubt, as we have said, that the really profound reasons for the schism between East and West are of a doctrinal and theological nature, the most important issues being those concerning the Holy Spirit and the nature of the Church. Different views about doctrine have also prevented agreement from being reached on a number of minor points of a political, canonical, or liturgical nature, for, in spite of all, both sides have made sincere efforts to come to some kind of understanding. If these efforts have failed, it can only be because the really basic issues of a doctrinal nature were never discussed seriously. From the thirteenth century on, all discussions between the popes and emperors regarding reunion took place in an atmosphere dominated more by political than by religious considerations, the Byzantine Church itself remaining largely outside the picture. Moreover, those discussions showed that the West harbored completely false ideas about the existence of Byzantine caesaropapism and thought that it was sufficient to win over the emperor to gain the allegiance of the whole Church. It was with this in mind that the popes encouraged the personal conversion of the Emperor John V in 1369. Even today the view is quite common that the Byzantine "schism" had its roots in caesaropapism; nevertheless it is a fact that from the eleventh century the emperors were almost consistently in favor of reunion with Rome because of the undoubted political advantages to be derived from it, and they tried to bring reunion about at all costs, even by the use of brute force. Equally consistently, since the time of Michael Caerularius, the patriarchs, or most of them at any rate, opposed their efforts in the name of the true faith. By relying so much on the emperors to bring about reunion, the popes were relying, actually, on a caesaropapism which did not in fact exist.

We must freely confess, however, that even if serious theological discussions were to take place, there can be no assurance that they would result in a speedy agreement on fundamentals. The discussions at Florence proved this, for they were serious from the doctrinal point of view regardless of the outcome. Agreement was possible only on the basis of a common tradition, but the overwhelming impact of scholastic theology, the doctrinal formulas and definitions connected with it (such as the approval of the *Filioque* by the Council of Lyons in 1274), and finally the far-reaching reforms affecting the very nature of the Church in the West brought about by the great popes of the Middle Ages made conversations extremely difficult.

CHAPTER IV

THE GOVERNMENT, LITURGY, AND
SPIRITUALITY OF THE
ORTHODOX CHURCH.
ORTHODOX MONASTICISM

WE HAVE SEEN how the Christological disputes in the
fifth century resulted in the loss to the Orthodox
Church of whole nations of non-Greek origin (Copts,
Armenians, Syrians, Ethiopians), some of whom refused to accept the decisions of the Council of Ephesus
(431) and adopted a Nestorian profession of faith,
while others accepted Ephesus but refused to acknowledge Chalcedon (451) and professed a faith that was
the very opposite of Nestorianism, namely, Monophysitism. Both the former and the latter looked upon
the Church of the Empire with undisguised suspicion,
regarding it as a tool of the emperors. That church
was now virtually coterminous with the Greek and
Latin portions of the Empire.

Nevertheless, despite the losses sustained in the
East, the Byzantine Church remained active in the
missionary field like its sister church in the West.
Most of the Slavic peoples were converted from Constantinople and received their Bible, liturgy, canon
law, and spirituality from there. The Byzantine method
of spreading the Gospel involved translating both the
Scriptures and the liturgy into the language spoken
by the people of the country and then establishing

new churches modeled in all respects on the "Great Church" at Constantinople. This method differed fundamentally from that pursued in the West, where missionaries were at pains to impose Latin as the common liturgical tongue; it sufficed, however, to preserve a unity of cult among the newly converted nations. This liturgical unity soon became uniform throughout the East in any case, for the peoples of non-Greek origin who had kept the ancient liturgies of Antioch and Alexandria abandoned the Orthodox Church for the most part, as we have seen. However, it is important to realize that this liturgical centralization was not a matter of principle with the Byzantines, for the Orthodox Church has always admitted the legitimacy of various rites, but the cultural and political prestige of Constantinople was so great, in the medieval period, that liturgical uniformity often came about of its own accord: the provinces naturally tended to imitate the magnificent and imposing ritual of the Queen City on the Bosporus. Thus it happened that the non-Greek Churches of Syria, Egypt, and Palestine, which remained Orthodox, sooner or later adopted the Melkite or imperial rite of the capital. The Byzantine liturgy was also adopted by the Georgian Church, a distant outpost of Chalcedonian Orthodoxy, founded in the fourth century and long subject to the influence of Antioch.

Thus, many if not all of the Slavs too came to adopt the Byzantine form of Christianity. The Bulgarians (863) and Russians (988), each in turn, were baptized en masse, following the example set by their ruling princes, Boris and Vladimir. The conversion of the Serbs, from the ninth century onwards, was more gradual, as was that of the Walachians, Latin colonists who had settled in the region of the lower Danube and would later be known as Rumanians. Byzantine missionaries also penetrated into Bohemia in the ninth century—where the archbishopric founded by St. Methodius was later taken over by the Germans and conformed to the Latin rite—and in the tenth century converted the Alans, a people residing north of the Caucasus. Thus the spiritual influence of Byzantium came to extend from the Mediterranean to the Arctic Ocean and from the Caspian Sea to the Alps. It was not seriously affected by the decline and fall of the Byzantine Empire, and this general area constituted what may be called the Orthodox world, until the modern Diaspora of Orthodoxy to other parts of the globe.

In accordance with the Twenty-eighth Canon of the Council of Chalcedon, the patriarch of Constantinople had the right to consecrate new bishops for the missionary churches. He also attempted to keep them as long as possible under his direct control, an aim that was sometimes difficult to realize. When the Slavs became Christians they were content to enter the ranks of "civilized peoples" and adopt Byzantine customs, but they were not happy about the continuance of Greek control. From Byzantium they took over the Byzantine theory of the state according to which there was only one Christian emperor on earth, that of Constantinople, the protector of the universal Church and the Chosen of God. The Bulgarians and Serbs, each in turn, attempted to conquer the imperial crown for their own rulers, but both failed before the stout walls of Constantinople. They consoled themselves for their inability to achieve this political goal by creating national churches for themselves. Constantinople was forced to recognize the situation and grant them the right to elect their own bishops, but as soon as conditions again became favorable the Byzantines would withdraw this right and re-establish

their direct control. This right of the national churches
to choose their own bishops will later be known as
"autocephaly."

Thus, in addition to the four traditional patriarchates
of the East, Constantinople, Alexandria, Antioch, Jerusalem—of which only the first had any real authority
—from the ninth to the fifteenth century, during
the Middle Ages, there was created a whole series of
Slavic autocephalous churches (Greek *auto-*, "self,"
kephale, "head"), whose heads were metropolitans
or archbishops but sometimes also received the title
of "patriarch." Byzantine canon law has always been
sufficiently flexible to allow for considerable fluctua-
tions in the course of its history: unity of faith rather
than unity of organization has been regarded as the
ultimate bond uniting the churches.

This system, the basic features of which are still in
effect, was tantamount to an organic development of
the principles of church government as laid down by
the first ecumenical councils. We may remember that
in the time of Justinian (527-565) the Church was
thought of as constituting a Pentarchy. The five patriarchs were invested with a kind of collective primacy
in the Church and consecrated the metropolitans in
their respective areas. Within the Pentarchy there was
an honorary order of precedence which accorded the
first place to the bishop of Rome, who was then followed by the bishops of Constantinople, Alexandria,
Antioch, and Jerusalem. Since the schism between
East and West has resulted in the breaking off of
communion with the first see, in the Orthodox Church
today the patriarch of New Rome is regarded as having inherited the Roman primacy. It hardly needs to
be stressed that this precedence of sees and transfer
of the primacy were not regarded as a matter of
"divine right," since all bishops are equal with respect
to the sacramental functions of their office. However,

the myth of an ideal theocracy and a single Christendom, as formulated in the time of Justinian, remained firmly rooted in the Byzantine consciousness. That is why the Byzantines continued to venerate the memory of the early popes and were always ready to restore the Roman primacy, provided Orthodoxy were restored in the West. This is the way Symeon, a fifteenth-century archbishop of Thessalonica, a theologian, a commentator on the liturgical rites, speaks of the possibility of reunion: "There is no point in quarreling with the Latins over the Roman primacy. Only let them show that he [the bishop of Rome] adheres to the faith of Peter and that of the successors of Peter, and he will then receive the privileges of Peter, he will be the first, the coryphaeus and head of all; he will be the supreme pontiff." [1] Canonical unity thus depends upon unity of faith, and the latter must be evident by itself and not determined by some external criterion.

The survival of the pentarchic conception did not prevent the Eastern patriarchs, with the exception of that of Constantinople, from being shorn, in the course of the Middle Ages, of most of their former splendor and power. The Moslem conquests reduced the size of their flocks and isolated them from the rest of Christendom. Henceforth the Church of Constantinople became the real center of the Orthodox world. The ancient canons conferring on her the right of appeal from the entire Church, the decline of the other patriarchates, the missionary conquests of the Byzantine Church, and the prestige of the "Great Church" of Hagia Sophia: all contributed to endow her with an authority without parallel. The political decline of the Byzantine Empire also helped to enhance the prestige of the ecumenical patriarchate, for the latter

[1] *Dialogus contra haereses*, PG 155, col. 120 B.

retained power in the spiritual sphere comparable to
that which was slipping from the hands of the emperor.[2] In the fourteenth century we find the patriarchs actively interfering in the religious as well as
the political affairs of Eastern Europe, settling domestic quarrels for the Russian feudal princes, negotiating
with the king of Poland over the status of his Orthodox
subjects, and frustrating all attempts at reunion with
Rome. But in exercising this authority they never
claimed to be infallible. History reveals moreover that
there were far too many heretical patriarchs for any
such claim to be taken seriously. As late as 1347, for
example, John Calecas was deposed for having supported the teaching of a condemned monk, Akindynos.

This centralized control over the Byzantine world
achieved by the ecumenical patriarchs from the ninth
century onwards has been effective in making the
Orthodox Church "Byzantine," somewhat in the same
way that the Catholic Church in the West was dominated by Rome and is today termed "Roman." This
process of Byzantinization may be observed in both
the liturgical and the devotional as well as in the
canonical spheres.

The Christian liturgy has been given various forms
and these in turn have gone through various transformations in the course of history, in both East and
West, in response to new conditions and in accordance with the peculiar genius of different peoples.
The Church of Constantinople, for example, did not
have any liturgical tradition of its own prior to the
fourth century, but it gradually created a new rite
which was greatly influenced by Antioch. This new
Byzantine rite already possessed all the essential fea-

[2] See on this subject, G. Ostrogorsky, *History of the Byzantine State* (New Brunswick, N.J., Rutgers University Press,
1957), pp. 577-78.

tures which it now has[3] by the ninth century, at the time when it was carried to the far corners of the Byzantine world and became *the* liturgy of numerous peoples. It is celebrated today in many different languages and is regarded as a powerful bond uniting divers nationalities who feel that it is an expression of their one Orthodox faith. The custom of translating it into a language understood by the people has helped to root the liturgy in the minds of the faithful, who look upon their participation in the common prayer of the Church as an important sign of belonging to the Body of Christ. This is not a question of mere ritualism, but an appreciation of the corporate significance of the Gospel message combined with the realization that the new life in Christ is indeed manifested by and communicated in the sacramental nature of Christian worship. This is why the Orthodox layman pays particular attention to the form and manner in which the liturgy is celebrated. He never regards it, as does his brother in the West who is accustomed to a liturgy celebrated in a language which he does not understand, as an act involving only the priest, but feels responsible himself for all that is done in the house of God. This awareness as to what is taking place, it can readily be appreciated, makes it difficult to carry out reforms, whether good or bad in nature. Actual schisms have resulted from attempts to change the liturgy in minor respects. This close control which the Church exercises over its own liturgy causes it to view as suspect rites with which it has not been closely in touch since the Middle Ages, especially Western variations—wrongly so, however. It is also true that this genuinely living liturgy, which

[3] Later changes, particularly by the Patriarch Philotheus in the fourteenth century, were concerned only with minor points and the rubrics.

is firmly rooted in the language of each country and
has often been instrumental in forming that language
itself, can often serve to keep the faith alive. Under
the Turkish and Mongol yokes the Christians of the
East were strengthened in their faith by the celebration of the liturgy, and so it is in Russia today, where
the liturgy remains the only means at the disposal of
the Church for communicating to the faithful the
truths of religion in the midst of a Marxist state. The
revival of Christianity in Russia shows once more that
the school of the liturgy can be a very potent influence.

It is not possible here to linger over the details of
the Byzantine liturgy.[4] Various liturgical cycles, daily,
weekly, annual, and paschal, correspond in large part
to similar cycles in other traditional liturgies, but in
contrast to the rather austere Latin liturgy these cycles
are much richer and much more elaborate. The Psalter
and other excerpts from the Bible which form the basis
for the daily office (vespers, compline, nocturn or mid-
night prayer, matins, prime, terce, sext, none) are sup-
plemented by a great many different kinds of hymns
which vary according to the season or feast day. These
hymns are collected in three books which are used at
different times of the year:

1. The *Triodion* and the *Pentekostarion* contain the
variable portions of the liturgy and office for Lent and
Eastertide. Many of the hymns are from the pen of
St. Theodore the Studite (beginning of the ninth century).

[4] The most comprehensive set of translations is to be found
in the *Book of the Divine Prayers and Services of the Catholic
Orthodox Church of Christ,* published by the Syrian Antiochene
Archdiocese of America. For a general introduction to the
Byzantine rite, see S. Salaville, *Eastern Liturgies* (London,
1938); and also Nicholas Cabasilas, *A Commentary on the
Divine Liturgy,* tr. by S. M. Hussey (London, 1960). This
fourteenth-century commentary on the Byzantine Eucharistic
service is very important for gaining an insight into the meaning and spirit of the Eastern liturgy.

2. The *Octoechus* (Greek *Oktoechos,* "book of eight tones") includes the cycle of eight weeks which begins with the first Sunday after Pentecost and is then repeated throughout the year until the following Lent. Each week has a different tone (*echoi*). The *Octoechus* establishes a link between each day in the year and Easter, the Feast of Feasts, since the main theme of the book is the Resurrection; it is traditionally ascribed to St. John of Damascus (eighth century).

3. The *Menaion* or *Menaia* (Greek *men,* "month"), finally, corresponds to the sanctoral of the Latin liturgy and contains the variable portions for the feasts of saints and other feasts throughout the year which are not connected with the paschal cycle.

Every day, therefore, has its own office composed of an invariable portion consisting generally of excerpts from the Bible, a variable series of hymns from the *Octoechus* or *Triodion* (sometimes during Lent the two are used together) or *Pentekostarion,* and finally portions of the *Menaion.* Only monasteries, of course, are in a position to celebrate the offices in their entirety, according to the rubrics in the *Typikon,* which goes back to the fourteenth and fifteenth centuries and describes the way in which the various cycles are to be combined. The Byzantine office is essentially a monastic office and parishes have to adapt it to their needs as best they can.[5] This is one sign of the strong influence which monasticism has traditionally had on the Orthodox Church.

The custom of celebrating the eucharistic liturgy on a daily basis was of relatively late origin, both in the East and the West. However, it has never become widespread in the East, hence the Orthodox Church

[5] The ecumenical patriarchate published an abridged *Typikon* about fifty years ago for the use of parish churches. This is used by Orthodox churches whose liturgical language is Greek. [The Latin office is also essentially a monastic office. —Translator]

is not familiar with any obligation for priests to celebrate daily—the liturgy is not regarded as their private
affair but as an act involving the whole Church—and
the liturgy has retained some of its meaning as a
"common work," a solemnity involving the whole community which normally takes place only on Sundays
and feast days. But while Orthodoxy does not at-
tach any particular importance to the frequency with
which mass is celebrated,[6] it has inherited from Byzantium a spirituality strongly oriented toward the sacramental life. Both as a memorial and as an anticipation of the world to come, the Eucharist is the place
where the Church identifies itself with the Kingdom of
God. This is the essential meaning of the celebration
held on "the eighth day" of the week, the Lord's Day.

The Byzantine rite has preserved a number of the
countless variations which once characterized the liturgy of the ancient Church: for example, it has two
eucharistic liturgies which are used on different occasions, that of St. John Chrysostom and that of St.
Basil. A third type of liturgy, celebrated at Jerusalem
and occasionally elsewhere, is traditionally attributed
to St. James, the brother of the Lord.[7] During Lent
it is customary not to celebrate the liturgy except on

[6] There is no rule either ordering or forbidding the daily
celebration of the liturgy. Only in monasteries and large parish
churches is it customary to have daily liturgies.

[7] We cannot go into the question of the authenticity of these
liturgies here; in any case whether they are to be attributed
to this or that person is a question of relatively minor importance because the liturgy has always been regarded as the
liturgy of the Church and not that of any particular person
as such. Liturgists seem to agree today that the hand of St.
Basil can be seen in the canon which bears his name. But St.
John Chrysostom certainly never compiled the liturgy which now
bears his name and which is of a later date. Both liturgies have
undergone modifications, even after the fourteenth century.
The Liturgy of St. James also appears to belong to the Byzantine type and therefore cannot have had any connection with
the brother of the Lord.

Saturdays and Sundays, in accordance with the canons of ancient councils; the fast is intended to impress on Christians the meaning of the fallen state in which they now are until the Parousia, despite the assurance of salvation which is even now within their grasp. Lent is therefore a period of expectation interrupted only by the dominical liturgies and terminating in the triumphal paschal liturgy, the anticipation of the Second Coming of Christ. On certain days during Lent, however, it is customary to celebrate a form of vespers when communion is distributed which has been reserved from the preceding Sunday. This is called the Liturgy of the Presanctified, a form of service traditionally ascribed to St. Gregory the Great, the pope of Rome.[8]

Like all traditional eucharistic prayers the Byzantine canon has the form of a solemn thanksgiving which the bishop or priest offers to God the Father. Because the Church is the Body of Christ, the Son of God, it is privileged to address itself directly to the Father in commemorating the redemptive work of the Son and in invoking the descent of the Holy Spirit "on us and on these Gifts here present" (Liturgy of St. John Chrysostom) so that they may be changed into the Body and Blood of the Lord. This trinitarian character of the canon, which reaches its culminating point in the solemn invocation of the Spirit (Epiclesis), is regarded as essential by the Orthodox Church, and the lack of this feature in the present Roman mass since the early Middle Ages is held to be a grave defect. It is the Spirit, actually, who reveals the grace of redemption in the Church after the ascension of Christ: "When the truth-giving Spirit, who proceeds from the Father, has come to befriend you,

---

[8] The Sixth Ecumenical Council (Quinisext, Canon 52) forbids the celebration of the liturgies during Lent, and prescribes the celebration of the "Presanctified."

he whom I will send to you from the Father's side, he will bear witness of what I was" (John xv.26).

Orthodox teaching always has emphasized the reality of the sacramental change (*metabole*) in the Eucharist by which the bread and wine are transformed into the Body and Blood of Christ. However, neither the liturgy nor the Fathers nor any authentic Orthodox text prior to the sixteenth century uses the term "transubstantiation" (Greek *metousiosis*) to describe this mystery. This term is employed in later Orthodox confessions of faith intended to define the teaching of the Church with respect to Protestant opinions on this matter, but there is always the reservation that the term is only one of several that could be employed and does not imply that the Church intends to adopt the Aristotelian philosophical theory of form and matter.[9]

Besides the Eucharist, the Church also acknowledges the existence of six other sacraments, without, however, holding that the number seven has the same absolute character assigned to it by Western post-Tridentine theology. No Orthodox council, as a matter of fact, has ever defined the exact *number* of the sacraments. The number seven was first mentioned in the East only in the thirteenth century, at the time of the "Latinizing" (*latinophronos*) emperor Michael Palaeologus VIII. Several Byzantine theologians such as Symeon of Thessalonica (fifteenth century) formally accept the number seven for the sacraments, but others in the fifteenth and sixteenth centuries held that certain other sacred rites ought to be regarded as sacraments, particularly the assumption of the monastic habit and the blessing of the waters at Epiphany. St. Gregory Palamas refers to Baptism and the Eu-

[9] See especially the *Confession of Dositheus* (1672), art. 17, in P. Schaff, *The Creeds of Christendom*, Vol. II (New York, 1889), p. 431.

charist as "recapitulating" (summing up) by themselves "all the works of the God-Man," [10] and thus
without denying the efficacy of other sacraments,
establishes a certain hierarchy among them. This apparent lack of a precise terminology is an indication
that Byzantine theologians regarded the Christian
Mystery as a unique mystery expressed in different
ways by the various sacramental acts. And there was
no doubt that among all these acts the Eucharist was
the Mystery of Mysteries, to use an expression of
Pseudo-Dionysius. The doctrine of Seven Sacraments
is frankly misleading if the impression is given that
Unction of the Sick is equally important as the Eucharist or Baptism, or that redemptive grace is not
imparted by sacramental acts such as the Blessing of
the Waters. It is a convenient tool, however, for
catechetical purposes and this is why it has been
adopted in textbooks and manuals. (We must now say
a word briefly about each of these sacraments.)

Baptism is conferred on infants in the form of a triple immersion in the water as the names of the three
Persons of the Trinity are invoked.

Confirmation is generally conferred along with Baptism in one rite. The Orthodox Church feels that the
process of Christian initiation, involving Baptism,
Confirmation, and Communion in the Holy Mysteries,
constitutes an inseparable whole, which ought to be
conferred on each new Christian as such, whether
child or adult. This belief that Baptism and Confirmation belong together is at the basis of the Orthodox custom of conferring them at one and the same time.[11] It
is customary for Orthodox priests to confer both sacraments, whereas in the West confirmation is normally

[10] See our *Introduction à l'étude de Grégoire Palamas* (Paris,
Éditions du Seuil, 1959), p. 395.
[11] Confirmation is only conferred apart from Baptism in
certain special cases when heterodox persons are reconciled
with the Church.

reserved to bishops.[12] Orthodox Confirmation consists of an anointing with the Holy Chrism, which has been specially blessed by the bishop;[13] hence the term Chrismation customarily applied to it in the East.

The sacrament of *Holy Orders* includes the three traditional orders: the episcopate, priesthood, and diaconate; and two minor orders: subdiaconate and lectorate. Ever since the sixth century (Justinian's law, later confirmed by the council *in Trullo*) it has been the rule to choose the episcopate exclusively from the celibate monastic clergy. Married men, on the contrary, may be ordained as deacons or priests.[14]

The *Marriage* rite is an impressive ceremony called "Crowning." The Lord's precept regarding the integrity and uniqueness of marriage is held to be of an absolute nature, and very strict regulations are in effect so far as the clergy are concerned; for example, it is impossible for anyone who has contracted a marriage with a widow to be ordained priest. Divorce, however, is allowed in certain cases where the grace of the sacrament has manifestly been deprived of its efficacy, whether by the fault of one of the spouses (adultery), or because of some material impediment to the fulfillment of the conjugal bond.

Penance has generally become an act of a private nature today, as in the West. It essentially involves the reconciliation of a sinner with the Church through a remission of his sins, and it is also a "healing of the soul" or confession. The various formulas for absolution in use are of the deprecative kind; that is, the

[12] The bishops were the normal ministers of both Baptism and Confirmation in the early Church.

[13] According to the present discipline only important episcopal sees have the right to prepare and bless the Holy Chrism (involving an elaborate ritual), which is then distributed to the various dioceses and parishes.

[14] Marriage after ordination and second marriages of widowed priests are strictly forbidden.

priest prays for the pardon of the sinner, the actual forgiveness coming from God, not from the priest. However, a seventeenth-century metropolitan of Kiev, Peter Moghila, did not hesitate to adopt a formula of Latin inspiration in the Slavic ritual which he published, in which it is the priest who absolves in the first person (*ego absolvo te*). This is the formula actually used by the Russian Church today.

Thus the liturgical life forms the very basis of Orthodox piety. It is the realization and expression of the mystery of the divine presence in the Church and proclaims the truths of the faith. It also governs to a large extent the moral behavior of the faithful, sometimes inviting them to do penance and fast, at other times summoning them to glorify the Creator and share in the messianic banquet. It governs their lives by associating each evening and morning, each day of the week, each season of the year, and also every important event in the life of man such as birth, marriage, sickness, and death with the great events of Revelation, and by communicating to him on such occasions the unique grace of Redemption.

Inasmuch as this liturgical life is essentially a corporate form of worship, the building where the gatherings of the faithful are regularly held acquires a special importance and significance. Here too, Byzantium has been remarkably successful in the course of its long history in creating a form of art admirably suited to express the dogmas of the faith pictorially and to give expression to religious feeling. This artistic expression assumed such an important place in the life of the Church that it brought on the iconoclastic controversy in the eighth and ninth centuries. Only an art intimately connected with dogma and religious feeling could either have aroused such fierce opposition or inspired so many valiant defenders. As a result of this controversy the Church came to define the dogmatic significance of the veneration which it paid to images. This is what the decisions of the seventh ecumenical council (the Second Council of Nicaea in 787) were about. "We define," proclaimed the Fathers of the council, "that the holy images, whether in color, mosaic, or some other material, should be exposed in the holy churches of God, on the sacred vessels and liturgical vestments, on the walls and furnishings, and in houses and along the roads, namely, the image of our Lord God and Savior Jesus Christ, that of our Lady, the immaculate and holy Mother of God, those of the venerable angels and those of all holy men. Whenever these representations are contemplated, they will cause those who look at them to commemorate and love their prototypes. We define also that they should be kissed and that they are an object of veneration and honor (*timetike proskynesis*), but not of real worship (*latreia*), which is reserved for Him who is the Subject of our faith and is proper for the Divine Nature alone. . . . The honor rendered to the image is in effect transmitted to the prototype; he who venerates the image, venerates in it the reality for which it stands."

The distinction established by the council between the "worship" or "adoration" (*latreia*) which is due to God alone, and the "veneration" (*proskynesis*) due to images of Christ and the saints, was intended to refute the charges of idolatry leveled against the Orthodox by the iconoclasts. It is also equally valid today in the dialogue with Protestants concerning the exact meaning of icons in the Orthodox Church. The words "worship" and "adoration" are frequently used for the veneration which the Orthodox Church pays to sacred images, whereas they ought only to be employed in circumstances which make it quite clear that they do not stand for the Greek *latreia*, in accordance with the rulings of the council. It needs to be stressed, however, that the Orthodox Church regards the veneration of icons as something dogmatically wholesome and sound. This is ultimately because of the reality of the Incarnation of the Word. The defenders of images from St. John of Damascus to the Patriarch Nicephorus never tire of repeating that the Son of God really became man: the Invisible, Unknowable, and Undescribable became visible, knowable, and describable in flesh which was really His own. However, this flesh is deified, that is, it has itself become the source of grace. The images which represent it therefore should reflect this divine character. That is why Byzantine art, with its strong emphasis upon the conventional and traditional, is peculiarly suited to be a Christian art. Like all the dogmatic controversies during the early centuries, the quarrel over iconoclasm was also connected with Christology. The iconoclasts refused, in effect, to admit the full reality of the Incarnation and upheld the notion of a wholly transcendent God. Their Orthodox opponents, while stressing the human nature of Christ, did not forget the fact that this nature was deified, that it belongs properly to the one hypostasis of the Word, and that the images of Christ, therefore, as well as those of the Virgin Mary and the saints, who have shared in Christ's deification, should be regarded as holy and as worthy of veneration.

Holy icons therefore form an essential part of Orthodox worship and piety. Some of them have been regarded as miraculous and this exceptional status has been recognized as such by the Church, which has instituted special feasts commemorating them. Just as the portraits of famous persons or those dear to us serve to remind us of these persons as individuals, sometimes in a very realistic and compelling way, so certain icons can cause a direct contact between the prototype and the faithful, stimulating the latter to

make acts of faith and ultimately helping to manifest
the whole divine power.

These various aspects of Orthodox piety and spirituality, which still characterize it, had their stoutest
defenders in the medieval period among the monks.
We have seen that Christian monasticism was a creation of the third and fourth centuries as an antidote to
the new situation of relative ease in which the Church
found itself under the Empire. A select group preferred to flee to the desert and show in this way that
the Kingdom of God is a future Kingdom that is to
come and that the Church cannot find any permanent
refuge here below. The continual attraction of the
monastic way of life throughout Byzantine history
proves that this eschatological awareness never slack-
ened. Byzantine monasticism even became the support of the Church when the latter was hard pressed
by willful emperors and helped to prevent it from
being transformed into an imperial (state) Church.
Byzantine society was grateful to the monks for the
important role which they performed, and that is why,
in essence, candidates for the episcopate were chosen
from the monasteries, why the Byzantine *lex orandi*
was modeled on that of the monks and was given its
final shape by them, and why it was the monks were
able to win such a brilliant moral victory over the
iconoclasts and thus restore Orthodoxy in Byzantium.

Orthodox monasticism has assumed various forms in
its long history, from the simple anchorites who first
appeared in the deserts of Egypt and Palestine to the
great monastic communities which lived under the
Rules of a St. Pachomius or a St. Basil.

The life of a *hermit* (also still called *Hesychast* in
the East, from *hesychia*, "quiet," "spiritual repose") is
a life of continual, "monologic" prayer: "Let the remembrance of Jesus be present with each breath,"

wrote St. John Climacus in the seventh century; "you will then know the value of solitude." [15] As a citizen of the heavenly Kingdom the monk is in constant communion with his Lord, by repeating continually and without any interruption, whether during his work or sleep, a short prayer in which the Name of Jesus is invoked. Sometimes it is the *Kyrie eleison,* at other times "Lord Jesus Christ, Son of God, have mercy on me." Sometimes he will also interpret the words of St. John Climacus literally and repeat the prayer rhythmically as he breathes. He will seek the Kingdom of God "within himself," for Baptism and the Eucharist confer on every Christian the privilege of being able to live in Christ and possess in their hearts the gifts of the Holy Spirit. The Hesychasts will give rise to great Orthodox mystics, such as St. Maximus the Confessor (seventh century), St. Symeon the New Theologian (eleventh century), and St. Gregory the Sinaite (fourteenth century). In the fourteenth century, led by the great theologian, St. Gregory Palamas, archbishop of Thessalonica, the Hesychasts will be the foremost defenders of Orthodoxy against the ravages of a philosophical school which denies the possibility of any real communion with God here below. This controversy offered Palamas the opportunity to obtain conciliar approval (1341, 1347, 1351) for theological formulas expressing the complete reality of communion with God, which is available to all Christians who are members of the Church, a communion which the Greek Fathers called "deification." [16]

Besides Hesychasm the Christian East was also

[15] *Ladder of Paradise, Twenty-seventh Step,* tr. by Lazarus Moore (London, 1959), p. 246.

[16] Cf. J. Meyendorff, *Saint Grégoire Palamas et la mystique orthodoxe, Coll.* "*Maîtres Spirituels*" (Paris, Éditions du Seuil, 1959); and *Introduction à l'étude de Grégoire Palamas, Coll.* "*Patristica Sorbonensia*" (Paris, Éditions du Seuil, 1959). Both of these books will soon appear in English translation.

familiar with another type of monastic life which came to be regarded as classical in the West, namely, that of the great disciplined, liturgically oriented community. St. Pachomius and especially St. Basil of Caesarea furnished the monks of all succeeding ages with a set of norms in their famous *Rules,* which have displayed such a remarkable vitality. St. Theodore, abbot of the great monastery in Constantinople called the Stoudios, and stout defender of Orthodoxy against the iconoclasts (ninth century), was the most important codifier of the monastic rule in the Byzantine tradition. The Studite monks were subject to an abbot and apportioned their time between the church, the refectory, and work. It was in communal monasteries of this type that the forms of the Byzantine liturgy and the style of Byzantine hymnography were perfected and achieved their final stage of development. The work of earlier hymnographers, such as the great poet of the sixth century, St. Romanus the Melode, was incorporated in the divine office. Byzantine hymnography has retained this inspiration and form to the present day, even now that it is no longer an exclusively monastic affair but has been adopted by the whole Church.

The Byzantine Church therefore was familiar with both the hesychastic and cenobitic (*koino-,* "common," *bios,* "life") forms of monasticism, and both continue to exist in the Orthodox Church today. While conflicts have sometimes marred their relations, both have been able to work harmoniously together. The great monasteries occasionally produced mystics capable of practicing the purest form of Hesychasm while continuing to conform to the ordinary rules of the community. St. John Climacus, for example, was the abbot of the great monastery of Mount Sinai; Hesychasm flourished even in the Stoudios, in the tenth and eleventh centuries, in the persons of St. Symeon the Pious and St.

Symeon the New Theologian. Monastic federations or republics, such as those of Mount Athos, Mount Olympus, or Mount St. Auxentius, allowed for the existence of imposing communities and the hermits' cells of Hesychasts side by side. Originally the monks of Mount Athos were all anchorites; then St. Athanasius founded the first great laura (tenth century), and later the whole territory was divided between federated monasteries under the authority of a central monastic government, the Protaton. However, the various charters in effect (which have been changed from time to time) have always allowed for the existence of the *skiti* and *kellia* in which Hesychasts may devote themselves to "pure prayer." The Rules of the monastic communities also provide for the practice of the Prayer of Jesus by the monks.

Thus, while displaying a remarkable unity of purpose and inspiration, Byzantine monasticism has been wise enough to allow for different ways in which individual temperaments could express themselves. Whether he lives apart or in a community, the monk is a witness and prophet of the Kingdom to come. His ministry is of the charismatic kind destined to serve the Church and the world. It is interesting to note in this respect that the Church has always refused to approve tendencies which would isolate the monks from the Church and imply that they had a mission that was *essentially* different from and superior to that of other Christians. Canonically speaking, the monasteries of the Orthodox Church are always subject to the local bishop and are therefore integrated in the life of the diocese. The Eastern Church has never recognized religious orders that were canonically "exempt" from diocesan control. It is therefore in the Church and for the Church that Byzantine monasticism is called upon to perform its special mission.

The Byzantine liturgy, the inexhaustible richness of Byzantine art, the spiritual influence of monasticism, the use of a language understood by the people in the liturgy, a married secular clergy and therefore one in close touch with the faithful, a conception of the Church which allows for a large amount of responsibility for all Christians in the life of the Church: all these factors, which were given their definitive form in the Byzantine period, have enabled the Orthodox Church to build up and to maintain a remarkably coherent corporate attitude toward the Church and the faith through the centuries. From Byzantium also it has inherited certain historical characteristics of a less important nature, particularly the concept of a sacral state which explains many of the excesses of modern nationalism. It is our task now to attempt to distinguish in this heritage between the Tradition of the Church, the expression of revealed Truth, on the one hand, and mere human traditions which have naturally tended to accumulate, on the other. This distinction will sometimes be painful to make, sometimes it can only be made gradually; but in any case the necessary adjustments can only be achieved with the help of the Spirit who teaches "all truth." For it is He who, without nullifying man's free will, guides the Church toward its final destination.

CHAPTER V

THE ORTHODOX CHURCH AND ISLAM.
THE CONFESSIONS OF FAITH.
THE SEVENTEENTH AND
EIGHTEENTH CENTURIES

ISLAM LAUNCHED its attack against the Eastern half of Christendom during the first part of the seventh century, toward the beginning of its historical drive to conquer the world. The Byzantine emperor Heraclius (610-641) had just succeeded in winning back from the Persians large tracts of the old *orbis Romanorum*, including the Holy Land, but this task had barely been completed before the Arabs, in a new wave, soon engulfed all of Syria, Palestine, Egypt, and North Africa.

The religious picture in these areas undoubtedly contributed to the rapid expansion of Islam. The Syriac- and Coptic-speaking churches were definitely anti-Greek in sentiment, and their hatred for Chalcedonian Orthodoxy, which the emperors had for so long endeavored to impose on them by force, made them welcome the new invaders with open arms. Occasionally even the Orthodox clergy, bowing before the inevitable and hopeful of being able to preserve the vital interests of the Church, adopted the same course. Thus St. Sophronius, the patriarch of Jerusalem and one of the leading opponents of Monothelitism, negotiated the surrender of the besieged

Holy City to the Khalif Omar in 638. By 678, however, the imperial armies and fleet had been able to stem the Moslem advance, and in 718 the Arab fleet was thwarted in its attempt to capture Constantinople, the "City protected by God." These Byzantine successes against the Arabs served much the same purpose in the East as the great victory of Charles Martel at Poitiers, in 732, at the other end of Christendom.

From the ecclesiastical point of view, the Arab conquest of the former Oriental provinces of the Empire meant that the ecumenical patriarch was now destined to play the leading role in the Eastern Orthodox Church. As we have seen, Photius, for example, was able to work out with Pope John VIII a kind of mutual agreement between Rome and Byzantium, dividing between them the government of the Christian world. Henceforth, the Eastern patriarchs of Alexandria, Antioch, and Jerusalem were almost wholly dependent upon their colleague in the imperial capital, in fact if not in theory, and would not dare to take up a position directly contrary to his in important matters.

Finally, in the eleventh century, the Empire was confronted by a new wave of invaders from Central Asia, the Turks, who soon gained control of the khalifate and renewed the threat of a militant Islam. Recent converts to Islam, and vigorous and warlike in habit, the newcomers proved to be formidable opponents and exerted a constant pressure on the Eastern frontiers, while the Crusaders from the West delivered their famous stab in the back in 1204. Nevertheless, in spite of reverses and threats, Byzantium managed to hold out against the Turks for another two and a half centuries.

This military struggle between the Cross and the Crescent, which lasted for so long, and which is still reflected in many Byzantine liturgical texts, was not the only contact between Islam and the Byzantine world during the Middle Ages. Orthodox theologians like St. John of Damascus (eighth century) and the Emperor John Cantacuzene (fourteenth century) were responsible for spreading at least a cursory knowledge of the Koran and its teachings by means of their refutations of Islam. The emperors of the eighth century, the very ones who won such decisive victories over the Moslems, were themselves much attracted by certain aspects of Islamic civilization. The result was the iconoclastic crisis, but also the establishment of cultural relations, direct or indirect, between Baghdad and Constantinople.[1] Important Byzantine prelates and scholars, such as Photius, Constantine the Philosopher, and Nicholas the Mystikos, were in touch with Arab scholars. Even in the realms of spirituality and mysticism it is likely that there was a certain amount of borrowing, for the Moslem concept of *dhikr,* the practice or technique of repeating the divine Name rhythmically as one breathes in and out, appears to have influenced the corresponding teaching of Orthodox Hesychasts in the thirteenth and fourteenth centuries.[2] It must be noted, however, that Arabic philosophy exercised virtually no influence on Byzantine thought, for the Byzantines were always able to have direct access to ancient Greek philosophy and never needed, like the Latins, to "discover" Aristotle by way of Arabic translation and commentaries.

All this exchange of knowledge undoubtedly helped to prepare the way for the survival of Christianity under the Turkish yoke. Many important Byzantine

[1] On the links between Islam and the iconoclastic movement, see the study of A. Grabar, *L'Iconoclasme byzantin.—Étude archéologique* (Paris, 1957).

[2] On this topic, see L. Gardet, "Un problème de mystique comparée: la mention du Nom divin (dhikr) dans la mystique musulmane," in the *Revue thomiste,* Vol. III (1952), pp. 642-79; Vol. I (1953), pp. 197-216. Cf. our *Introduction à l'étude de Grégoire Palamas,* pp. 201-3.

leaders foresaw the day when the Empire might fall. They knew that Christianity would be on the whole tolerated by the Ottoman rulers.[3] As later Byzantine emperors, in their desperate attempts to summon a Western Crusade to come to their assistance, were forced more and more to deny the Orthodox faith and to accept Roman "innovations," an important dignitary of the court, the Grand Duke Lucas Notaras, was led to assert publicly, on the very eve of the fall of Byzantium: "Better to see the turban of the Turks reigning in our city than the Latin miter."[4] His words certainly expressed the opinion of many.

The capture and sacking of Constantinople by the armies of Mohammed II in 1453 was nevertheless one of the greatest catastrophes in the history of Christianity. In 1456 Athens also fell and the Parthenon, which for a thousand years had been a church dedicated to the Virgin Mary, was transformed into a mosque, like Hagia Sophia in Constantinople. In 1460 the Turks conquered the Byzantine Morea and in 1461 Trebizond, the last remaining outposts of the Byzantine Empire. The two Serbian Orthodox states succumbed in turn, in 1459 and 1463. This meant that the Ottoman Empire now embraced the whole of the Christian East, with the sole exception of Muscovite Russia, which, just at this time, was liberating itself from the Mongol yoke and would become the principal bulwark of Orthodoxy in the East for several centuries to come.

Under Turkish rule, however, the Church preserved its canonical organization intact and was even able to strengthen itself as a result of certain privileges granted to the ecumenical patriarch by the conqueror.

[3] St. Gregory Palamas spent some time as a prisoner in Anatolia in 1354; he gives a favorable description of Christian life under the Turks there. (See our *Introduction à l'étude de Grégoire Palamas*, pp. 157-62.)

[4] Ducas, *Historia*, 38, Bonn ed., p. 264.

Mohammed II allowed the canonical election of a new patriarch, Gennadios Scholarios, who was both the leader of the anti-unionist party and a devoted admirer of Thomas Aquinas. The sultan personally handed the new patriarch the emblems of his office, saying: "Be patriarch, preserve our friendship, and enjoy all the privileges which the patriarchs your predecessors possessed." These privileges included the inviolability of the patriarch's person, and through him, of all the bishops, exemption from all taxes, and *civil jurisdiction over all Christians in the Ottoman Empire*. According to Moslem law all Christians were regarded as forming a single nation (*millet*) and no account was taken of confessional, linguistic, or national differences. The Christians had been conquered by Islam, the people of God, but they were allowed to retain the right to rule themselves so far as their domestic affairs were concerned, in accordance with the precepts of their religion and subject to the personal jurisdiction of the patriarch alone, who thus became a kind of Christian khalif, responsible to the sultan for all Christians. Thus the Greek hierarchy found itself invested with considerable power, both civil and religious, in some respects greater than the authority it had enjoyed before the Turkish conquest. The jurisdiction of the ecumenical patriarch was virtually limitless, for it embraced not only the faithful who belonged to his own patriarchate but also those in the other Eastern patriarchates—who were theoretically his equals according to canon law—and even heterodox Christians who happened to be living in the Ottoman Empire. The Orthodox bishops greeted the ecumenical patriarch as "their sovereign, their emperor, and their patriarch." [5] From now on the latter appropriated the special insignia of the Byzantine emperors; he wore a miter in the form of the im-

[5] *Historia patriarchica*, Bonn ed., p. 177.

perial crown, stood upon a rug which bore the emblem of a Roman eagle, and let his hair grow in the manner of the emperors and Byzantine officials.[6] In his role as *millet-bachi*, "head of the Christian nation," or "ethnarch" in Greek, the patriarch was now virtually the regent of an enslaved empire.

The ethnarchic system, as created by the Turks and as it has survived to this day on the island of Cyprus and in certain countries of the Levant, guaranteed the independence of the Christian Church under alien rule. It was based on an idea that Islam shared with Judaism, namely, the complete identification of the "people of God" with a concrete sociological entity. In the one case Islam, which included all the faithful of Allah and his Prophet, and in the other all Christians. The Ottoman authorities refused to recognize the existence of any differences of nationality in the Christian *millet* and contented themselves with approving the elections of the patriarch and the bishops. Inevitably this regime had a profound effect on the lives of Christians living under Turkish rule in the Near East.

1. It shut them up in a kind of ghetto from which they did not dare to escape, even though their situation was at times relatively prosperous and even when they were able to exercise a kind of effective control over the policies of the Porte. It was quite impossible for them to pursue any kind of missionary work. Even if they had been materially able to do so, such activity would have been regarded as a political crime against the state. Only the Russian Church was free to continue the work of Byzantium in this field.

2. As ethnarch of the Christians and an official of the Turkish Empire, the patriarch and his collabora-

[6] Before long these various signs of authority were adopted by the bishops too. But in Russia they were only introduced in the seventeenth century, under the Patriarch Nikon, when of course they had ceased to have any political significance.

tors necessarily had a share in the dreadful system of corruption by which the Empire was governed—albeit their implication was of an involuntary nature. Each new election entailed the payment of a large sum of money to the Turkish government, which was specified on each occasion by the sultan's *berat* of investiture. The sum was levied either on the patriarchal treasury—in which case the newly elect reimbursed the amount in the course of his patriarchate by means of corresponding assessments on the dioceses—or on the personal property of the new patriarch. To a lesser degree the same procedure was followed in the case of episcopal elections, which also required the *berat* of the sultan. Moreover, as the patriarchal throne was occupied and vacated rather frequently, according to the vagaries of Ottoman politics, the corruption developed into a kind of gangrenous evil. In the eighteenth century, one of the darkest periods in the annals of the Church of Constantinople, forty-eight patriarchs succeeded each other in the space of sixty-three years! Only saints could remain faithful to the ideals of their office under such conditions as these, and the survival of the Greek Church, under four centuries of Turkish rule, is no less than a miracle.

3. The patriarch's role as ethnarch of all Christians in the Turkish Empire enabled him to claim authority over other churches as well. The Bulgarian patriarchate of Trnovo was given to a Greek prelate in 1394, and then later was reduced to the status of a simple diocese of the ecumenical patriarchate. The autocephalous status of Ohrid was suppressed in 1776 by the Patriarch Samuel I, who also abolished the Serbian patriarchate of Pech. This tendency toward centralization was unfortunately also accompanied by measures regarded as particularly obnoxious by the Slavic nations, in that Greek bishops would be appointed to Slavic sees and then proceed to suppress

the use of Slavonic as a liturgical language. All opposition to such measures on the part of the local clergy was virtually impossible, for the patriarch exercised absolute civil as well as religious control over them in the name of the sultan. Nationalism, that bane of modern Orthodoxy, began to flourish everywhere under the Turkish regime. There was Greek nationalism which identified Orthodoxy with Hellenism and the Greek longing for independence, and Slavic nationalism which forced the restoration of autocephalous churches in the nineteenth century by means of threats of revolt and in an atmosphere of mutual distrust that can hardly be described as very Christian in spirit. Domestic quarrels of this kind were the disgrace of Orthodoxy during the dark years of the Turkish yoke. However, they did not prevent a number of new Christian martyrs from shedding their blood for Christ during outbreaks of anti-Christian fanaticism. The most famous of these was the ecumenical patriarch Gregory V, who was hanged by the Turks in 1821 on Easter Sunday from the great porte-cochère of his patriarchate in the Phanar, just after he had celebrated the solemn paschal liturgy.[7]

Owing to its liturgy and the works of the Fathers preserved in the monastic libraries, the Church managed nevertheless to get across the essential burden of its message. The communal prayer in the churches and the astonishing richness and symbolism of the Byzantine liturgical formulas enabled the Greeks and other nations in the Balkans and Near East to remain faithful to their Orthodox faith and assisted them to rally more closely than ever around a church that had been deprived of all schools, books, and a properly trained clergy.

Elements of Byzantine theological scholarship, how-

[7] The gate has remained closed to this day in memory of the martyrdom of St. Gregory V.

ever, continued to be maintained by a handful of outstanding churchmen. Some of these were self-taught; others studied in the West and frequently came under the influence of their Catholic or Protestant teachers. The ideas of the Reformation and Counter-Reformation thus made their way to the East. Deprived of a genuine Orthodox schooling, the theologians of the seventeenth and eighteenth centuries not infrequently used Roman arguments against the Protestants and Protestant arguments against the Roman Catholics. Politics also played its part in the continual seesawing back and forth of those years. The ecumenical patriarchs were not above making use of the Catholic ambassadors to the Porte (Austria, France) or their Protestant colleagues (England, Holland) in order to exert pressure on the Turkish authorities, and the foreign ambassadors were not above bringing pressure to bear to cause the dethronement or election of patriarchs.

As we have seen, the patriarchate established a kind of modus vivendi with the Turkish authorities in the fifteenth and sixteenth centuries, during the period immediately after the fall of Constantinople and before direct pressure began to be exercised in such a disgraceful manner. Councils could be held more or less regularly and the affairs of the Church settled. Some of these had to do with relations with the Latin Church. That of 1454, for example, under the Patriarch Gennadios Scholarios, officially repudiated the Union of Florence; and that of 1484, attended by the three other Eastern patriarchs, published a special ritual for the reconciliation of Roman Catholics with Orthodoxy.[8] Toward the end of the sixteenth century

[8] This ritual included the sacrament of Confirmation. However, in the Greek islands under Venetian rule it was not uncommon, until the eighteenth century, for Catholic and Orthodox clergy to observe communion *in sacris*. This state of affairs—which poses certain canonical problems for both sides

the first important contacts took place between Protestant theologians and the Orthodox Church. In 1573-
1574 a group of Lutheran theologians at Tübingen sent
to the ecumenical patriarch Jeremias II a copy of the
Augsburg Confession, which they had translated into
Greek, and asked him to express an opinion on it. The
long reply of the Greek prelate constitutes a very important document and does credit to its author, showing that an Orthodox theologian was capable of passing a proper judgment on Protestantism on the basis
of the Augsburg Confession *alone*. This judgment was
friendly but critical. It was followed by correspondence between the two parties, but nothing came of
these moves.[9]

Relations between Constantinople and the Western
powers assumed a less peaceful character in the seventeenth century. and were dominated in fact by the
tragic case of Cyril Loukaris. The latter was one of
the best-educated Greeks of the time, having spent
many years in Italy where he learned to write Latin
with great fluency and became familiar with the works
of Thomas Aquinas, and also kept up relations with
the German humanists Noeschel and Sylburg. First
elected patriarch of Alexandria (in 1602 at the age of
thirty), he then became ecumenical patriarch in 1620.
As the pupil, relative, and protégé of the outstanding
Meletius Pigas, who had preceded him on the throne
of Alexandria, it seemed that he was destined to have
a brilliant future since he had already won the grati-
tude of the Greeks for his attempts to raise the standard of education of his coreligionists and revive the
Greek pride in their national heritage. But at Constantinople he unfortunately came under the influence

---

—was due partly to the existing political situation and partly
to the desire not to recognize the schism as a *fait accompli*.

⁹ On the correspondence, see the work of E. Benz, *Witten-
berg und Byzanz* (Marburg, 1949).

of the Reformed theology, in the person of the Dutch ambassador Cornelius Haga, who obtained the necessary books for him from the West. In 1629 Loukaris published at Geneva, in Latin, his famous *Confession,* which completely reflects the strict Calvinist point of view. The basic purpose of Loukaris was to combat the influence and missionary zeal of Roman Catholics, but his Western training and numerous contacts with Calvinist circles had led him astray and caused him to embrace Protestantism. The *Confession* accepts, pure and simple, the Protestant doctrine of the *sola scriptura,* excludes the deuterocanonical books, rejects the real presence in the Eucharist, empties the Orthodox doctrine of the priesthood and holy orders of all meaning, and deplores the veneration of icons and the invocation of saints as forms of idolatry. Protestants were under the impression that they were about to witness the complete conversion of the Eastern Church to the doctrines of the Reformation in the person of the ecumenical patriarch. It is not surprising, therefore, that the *Confession* was published in four French translations, an English translation, and two German translations, beginning in 1629. In 1633 it also appeared in Greek, also at Geneva.[10]

The Catholic powers, France and Austria, were not slow to intervene, when the true state of affairs became known, and gave financial and political support to a group of Orthodox bishops who dethroned the patriarch. The latter, accused of plotting with the Russians, was arrested by the Turks and strangled. His body was thrown into the Bosporus, but was later recovered and buried on the island of Halki.

It is not difficult to imagine what a great stir was

[10] The original manuscript of Loukaris is preserved by the Library of Geneva and suffices to prove that the *Confession* is indeed authentic. Ancient and recent claims to question its authenticity are nothing more than pious attempts to save the good name of the patriarch.

caused in the East by the publication of this *Confession*. Six councils condemned it in succession: Constantinople in 1638 (three months after the death of Loukaris), Kiev in 1640, Jassy in 1642, Constantinople in 1672, Jerusalem in 1672, and Constantinople in 1691.

Under the influence of this anti-Protestant reaction, Peter Moghila, the metropolitan of Kiev, was also induced to compile his famous *Orthodox Confession* (1640), which he intended for use in his own province. Orphaned at the age of eleven, the son of a hospodar of Moldavia, Moghila (Rumanian Movila) studied in Poland and then became a monk, finally archimandrite of the great Laura of the Crypts in Kiev. Here he set up a printing press and founded a school that became famous and had a lasting influence on the Orthodox world as a whole. Moghila aimed primarily at raising the educational level of the Orthodox clergy as a means of preserving Orthodoxy from the encroachments of Uniatism, which had the support of the Polish kings. The case of Cyril Loukaris was particularly embarrassing to him because it seemed to prove the contention of Roman Catholic theologians that the Orthodox Church was riddled with Protestantism and was even about to embrace Protestantism as a whole! In order to remove this blot, Moghila was determined to give Orthodoxy as precise and clear a definition as Roman Catholicism and present it along the systematic lines of the various Latin catechisms. His *Confession* therefore amounts to little more than a copious borrowing from Roman catechisms then in use, especially that of Canisius. Certain disputed points with which the theologians of Kiev did not feel themselves sufficiently competent to cope, such as purgatory and the exact moment of the consecration of the eucharistic gifts, were referred to the patriarch of Constantinople for decision. Moghila himself resolved these questions in favor of the Latin view. There can be no doubt whatever that Moghila and his Kievan associates were insufficiently grounded in genuine Orthodox tradition and displayed what can only be described as a marked inferiority complex toward the formularies of the Counter-Reformation, thereby falling into the most elementary kind of Latinism. However, the *Confession* was approved at Kiev (1640), and then amended in certain important respects by the Council of Jassy (1642), at which time it was translated into Greek by the Greek theologian Meletios Syrigos. The original Byzantine position regarding purgatory and the words of institution in the Eucharist was thus restored. It was in this new form that the *Confession* was approved by the Council of Constantinople in 1643.[11] Even in its corrected form, however, the work is the most Latin-sounding document, both in spirit and form, that the Orthodox hierarchy has ever formally approved. Nevertheless, from then on it exercised great influence over the teaching of Orthodox theology, and only toward the middle of the nineteenth century when the Church began to experience a "return to the sources" did this influence decline.

Besides Peter Moghila, there was also another zealous defender of Orthodoxy who was engaged in the struggle against Protestant influence, namely, Dositheus of Jerusalem. Largely self-taught, Dositheus was eager to promote a knowledge of the Fathers in the East and published an important collection of Byzantine theological texts in Rumania, since the Eastern patriarchs had no printing presses of their own. His renown as a scholar came to the attention of a French diplomat, Nointel, whom Louis XIV had appointed as his ambassador to Constantinople and who was him-

---

[11] Schaff, *Creeds of Christendom*, Vol. II (New York, 1889), pp. 275-400.

self a student of theology, of Jansenist tendencies. The ambassador got in touch with him as well as with several other Orthodox prelates and requested him to give his opinion on the *Confession* of Loukaris. The result was a detailed and systematic refutation of the latter work, which Dositheus had approved by a council at Jerusalem in 1672. This document, known henceforth both as the *Confession of Dositheus* and the *Acts of the Council of Jerusalem,* is the most important Orthodox dogmatic text of this period. Its authority is undisputed. In the nineteenth century the celebrated Philaret of Moscow had the greatest respect for it. To be sure, Dositheus, under the influence of Moghila, occasionally makes use of a Latinized terminology, but his basic inspiration is much more fundamentally Orthodox than that of the metropolitan of Kiev. The Calvinism of Loukaris is firmly rejected in favor of the traditional sacramental realism of Orthodoxy, a doctrine of the priesthood and holy orders founded on the sacramental nature of the Church, and an Orthodox explanation of the veneration of the saints and holy images.[12]

The reaction of the Orthodox Church to the Reformation was therefore sufficiently clear, so that there could be no misunderstanding on this score. The *Confessions* of Moghila and Dositheus undoubtedly played a most important part in helping to strengthen the Orthodox position, regardless of their Latinizing tendencies. This Latinism is evidence, at least in the case of Dositheus, not of any particular sympathy for the Roman Church or for Latin scholasticism, but of the absence of an adequate theological training. But how could things possibly have been otherwise after

[12] The *Confession of Dositheus* may be found in Schaff, *op. cit.,* pp. 401-44. The most recent complete collection of Orthodox dogmatic texts is that of I. N. Karmiris (in Greek), *Ta dogmatika kai symbolika mnemeia tes orthodoxou katholikes ekklesias,* 2 vols. (Athens, 1953).

two centuries of the Turkish yoke and in the almost complete absence of proper schools and books?

A kind of instinct of self-preservation and unlimited faithfulness to the truth taught by the Church, as preserved by the liturgy—still a living force—and by the works of the Fathers, explains the reaction of the Orthodox to the temptations from the West, whether from Catholics or Protestants, both of whom were eager to enlist the Orthodox on their side in the great controversy dividing them. There can be no doubt that this was the primary motive inspiring the Western ambassadors in Constantinople to interfere in the internal affairs of the ecumenical patriarchate. The Protestants looked upon the Eastern Church as out of date and rooted in error, but they recognized that it had a long tradition of anti-Romanism which went back far beyond Luther and Calvin. Its consent to the principles of the Reformation was therefore worth obtaining, if possible. In spite of the generally bad reputation which Greeks enjoyed in the West, Catholics acknowledged that the Orthodox bishops were the successors of St. John Chrysostom and St. Basil. Latin missionaries in the East therefore were constantly vacillating between an extreme condescension toward and toleration of the Orthodox, even going so far as to maintain a *communio in sacris* with them, and an aggressive proselytism which aimed not only at bringing the Greeks back to union with Rome, but at Latinizing them in the process.

The reaction of the Orthodox Church to efforts of this kind was no less categorical. A synod at Constantinople in 1755, attended by the patriarchs of Alexandria and Jerusalem as well as by the ecumenical patriarch Cyril V, took up the question of the admission of Latins to the Orthodox Church. Modifying the decisions of the Council of 1484, the synod decreed that Latin and Armenian baptisms were invalid and that converts must be rebaptized according to the Byzantine rite of triple immersion before they could be admitted to the Church. Thus the strictest regulations regarding the admission of heretics to the Church were now applied to Roman Catholics and Monophysite Armenians.[13] This decision met with opposition on the part of some bishops, but it was adopted under pressure by the Greek population in Constantinople, which was violently anti-Latin. It remained in force in the Greek churches until the beginning of the twentieth century.

These various episodes in the life of the Church under Turkish rule add nothing of great importance to our understanding of the history of Orthodox theology, but they may serve as a sort of proof of the vitality of Greek Orthodoxy and the determination of the Orthodox to retain their identity under very trying circumstances. The fanatical attitude also displayed by some Greeks in their opposition to the West

[13] About this time the Russian Church, which until then had generally followed the practice of rebaptizing Latins, now decided to adopt a more liberal policy and ordered that only a profession of the Orthodox faith and penance were necessary before a Roman Catholic could be admitted to the Orthodox Church. This confusion among the Orthodox regarding the admission of converts from Roman Catholicism has its counterpart in similar hesitations on the part of the Catholics themselves: when Orthodox became Catholics in Hungary and Poland in the fourteenth century, they were customarily rebaptized (see our article "Le projet de concile oecuménique en 1367," in *Dumbarton Oaks Papers*, Vol. XIV [1960]) although *communio in sacris* was widely practiced in the Greek islands under Venetian rule until the eighteenth century (see especially W. de Vries, "Das Problem der 'communicatio in sacris cum dissidentibus' im Nahen Ostem zur Zeit der Union," in *Ostkirchlichen Studien*, No. 6 [1957], pp. 81-106). While on the Roman side these differences were ironed out in the nineteenth century, there are still variations on the Orthodox side between the more liberal Russian practice (penance) and that of the Greeks who have now returned to the canons of 1484 (Chrismation).

can be explained, at least in part, as a natural reaction against the outrageously aggressive acts of Latin missionaries. When the latter found what a difficult task it was to convert the Moslems, they turned their attention to the Orthodox Christians living in those parts, Greeks and Arabs, and thought nothing of depriving them of the sole remaining treasure which had been preserved to them: their Orthodox faith!

However, this fanaticism tended to die down and was less evident in works produced in the nineteenth century, giving way finally to a more moderate approach made possible by the reopening of schools and the appearance of publications of all kinds. It was in this atmosphere that the Orthodox patriarchs replied to several appeals from the popes during the nineteenth century, appeals that were hardly calculated to win their sympathy. In January 1848, just after he had ascended the papal throne, Pius IX addressed an appeal "to the Orientals" recalling them to reunion with Rome. The four Oriental patriarchs of Constantinople, Alexandria, Antioch, and Jerusalem replied with an encyclical to all the Orthodox, signed also by twenty-nine metropolitans. In it they defined "papism" as a heresy and then expressed the hope that Pius IX would himself be "converted" to the true Orthodox faith and return to the true Catholic Apostolic and Orthodox Church, for, as they declared, "no patriarch or council has ever been able to introduce any novelty among us, since the Body of the Church, that is, the people themselves, is the guardian of religion." This encyclical of 1848, the text of which seems to have been approved in advance by Metropolitan Philaret of Moscow, was given wide publicity and is still regarded today as an important, authoritative statement of Orthodox views on the Church.[14] The Church,

[14] Original Greek text in Karmiris, *op. cit.*, pp. 905-95; Russian translation, Moscow, 1849; French translation, Paris, 1850, etc.

which is the guardian of truth, forms a single body and no member, whether clerical or lay, is excluded from taking an active role in the common life of the whole.

To a new appeal addressed to the East by Leo XIII in his encyclical "Praeclara gratulationis" of 1894, the ecumenical patriarch Anthimos replied with another encyclical which stigmatized the dogmas of the Immaculate Conception and Papal Infallibility as "Roman novelties" and declared that reunion could be contemplated only on the basis of the undivided faith of the first centuries.[15]

Doctrinal fidelity and attachment to tradition: these are the two fundamental keynotes of Orthodox writers during this dark period, conditioning their thought even when an inadequate grounding in theological principles caused them to resort to the expedient of using Protestant arguments against the Catholics and Catholic arguments against Protestants. A few strove to make it possible for contemporaries to become better acquainted with the real sources of Orthodoxy, the Scriptures and the Fathers. One name in particular deserves special mention here, that of Nicodemus the Hagiorite (1748-1808), a monk of Mount Athos, who published at Venice in 1792, in collaboration with Macarius, Bishop of Corinth, an important collection of texts from the Fathers relating to prayer. The *Philocalia*, as this collection is called, has ever since been regarded as a spiritual classic by the Orthodox. The *Philocalia* was responsible for acquainting modern generations with the mystical tradition of the Greek Fathers. The work was translated into various languages, Slavonic, Russian, Rumanian, and others, and helped to start a real spiritual revival in certain coun-

[15] Text in Karmiris, *op. cit.*, pp. 932-46 (there are also many translations in French, Russian, English, and German).

tries.[16] Nicodemus, recently canonized by the Orthodox Church (1955), was also the author of several
other works on spirituality inspired by Western examples (Scupoli, Ignatius of Loyola), which amount
virtually to adaptations of the latter for the benefit
of Orthodox mysticism. He was also an advocate of
frequent communion in the Greek Church. Nicodemus
and his followers brought about a revival of interest
in the spirituality of the Desert Fathers, the monks of
Mount Sinai, and the Hesychasts of Mount Athos, the
effects of which are still being felt today.

Thus, in spite of various historical disasters, the
Orthodox Church has managed to survive in the Near
East. Its liturgical richness and its spiritual traditions have revealed their true worth under the most
trying circumstances. At times the latter have seriously
impeded the normal growth of the Christian cultural
tradition that was heir to Byzantium and prevented it
from bearing all the fruit that one might have expected under more favorable conditions. But a new
period began to dawn for the Orthodox world in the
nineteenth and twentieth centuries, as a result of the
overthrow of the Ottoman Empire, the final liberation
of the Slavic, Greek, and Rumanian nations in the
Balkans, the achievement of independence by various
Arab states, the establishment of a lay republic in Turkey, and the mass migration of Greeks from Asia
Minor. Further on we shall discuss the present status
of the Orthodox Church in these countries.

[16] A partial uncritical translation (from the Russian) is to
be found in Kadloubovsky and Palmer, *Early Fathers from the*
Philocalia, and *Writings from the* Philocalia *on the Prayer of
the Heart* (London, no date)

CHAPTER VI

THE RUSSIAN CHURCH
FROM ITS BEGINNINGS TO 1917

BYZANTINE missionaries first made their way to Russia in the ninth century, the century which witnessed the conversion of the Slavs. They prepared the ground for the later conversions of Princess Olga (955) and St. Vladimir of Kiev (988), which were followed by the "baptism of the Russians," that is to say the establishment of Christianity as the state religion in the principality of Kiev. The translation of the Bible and the liturgical books into the Old Slavonic language had already been largely completed for the benefit of the Bulgars and the Slavs of Moravia in the time of St. Cyril and St. Methodius (ninth century). The Russians therefore had but to avail themselves of this precious heritage. Thus it came about that the Slavic dialect which happened to be spoken in the neighborhood of Thessalonica—which Cyril and Methodius used in their translations—became Church Slavonic (or Old Slavonic), the common liturgical tongue of all the Slavs to this day.

Baptism enabled the principality of Kiev to enter full-fledged into the concert of civilized European states and to play a very important role at that time. Jaroslav, the son of Vladimir (1036-1054), built a cathedral in his capital dedicated to Hagia Sophia, the Divine Wisdom, and had it decorated by the best artists from Constantinople. He married his daughters to the ruling princes of Europe: Ann of Russia, for example, became Queen of France. However, the European destiny of Russia was rudely interrupted by the Mongol invasion (1240), which isolated the Russians from Europe for several centuries. It has been the curious fate of the Byzantine world to have had to bear the brunt of repeated attacks which have seriously disrupted the course of its organic development from the time of the ecumenical councils down to the present day. Such were the Arabic, Mongol, and Turkish invasions, which put an end, successively, to the spiritual influence of great centers like Alexandria, Antioch, Kiev, and Constantinople.

Until the fifteenth century, the metropolitanate of Kiev, erected under Vladimir, was canonically dependent on the patriarchate of Constantinople. With only a few exceptions, the metropolitans of Kiev were all Greeks who came from Byzantium, while the rest of the episcopate and clergy were chosen locally. The ecumenical patriarchate treated Russia as one vast, firmly centralized missionary diocese. This system was at the basis of the canonical and administrative tradition which made the metropolitan of Kiev—later the patriarch of Moscow—the unique head of the Russian Church, and all other bishops directly subject to his authority. The other Oriental and Balkan patriarchates, by contrast, were always divided into metropolitanates in accordance with ancient canonical custom and have therefore never known any such patriarchal autocracy. The Russian system nevertheless had certain advantages in that it enabled the metropolitan of Kiev, appointed by Constantinople and therefore relatively neutral with respect to local politics, to act as the supreme judge of the country.

The Mongols were generally tolerant in matters of religion and allowed the Church to enjoy the privileges which it had enjoyed under the old Kievan regime. The arbitrary nature of several khans, however, who demanded that the subject Russian princes perform certain pagan rites when they were invested with authority by the Golden Horde (near Astrakhan) resulted in a number of martyrdoms: thus St. Michael of Chernigov, his friend Theodore, and St. Romanis of Ryazan were put to death for their refusal to perform these rites. However, these were isolated instances. The prevailing attitude of the Mongols toward Russian customs was one of tolerant forbearance, a fact that was not slow to be appreciated. Thus we find that a grand prince of Novgorod—the only principality not conquered by the Tartars—St. Alexander Nevsky, had no compunctions about seeking an alliance with the khan, without detriment to his religious convictions, in order to be able to oppose the invaders from the West, whose avowed aim was to effect the submission of the "schismatics." The Russian prince was obliged successively to fight Swedish Crusaders (1240) and the Teutonic Knights (1242). In effect, the Western crusading spirit caused the Russians, as it later would the Byzantines, to prefer the yoke of the Asiatic to the imperialism of Roman Christianity.

Meanwhile, the Orthodox Church was free to expand and organize. It could boast, for example, of a number of remarkable missionary successes: there are numerous instances of the conversion of Mongols to Christianity, and in 1261 it was possible to establish an episcopal see at Sarai, the capital of the Golden Horde! Missionary monasteries—Valamo and Konev on Lake Ladoga, and Solovki on the White Sea—began the work of converting the Finnish tribes of the North. Finally, in the fourteenth century, a remarkable missionary, St. Stephen of Perm, translated the Bible and the liturgy from Greek, with which he was well acquainted, into the Zyrian language. Anxious at all costs not to seem to be forcing Russian ways on his new converts, he created for them a new alphabet and steadfastly refused the political support offered him by the grand prince of Moscow. He was also the first bishop of Perm, the capital of the Zyrian nation.

Dominated by the ideals of Byzantine spirituality, the Russian Church could hardly do otherwise than to allow monasticism to play the important role which it did quite generally throughout the Christian East. At the very time when the Christian foundations of Russia were being laid, St. Theodosius established the famous Monastery or Laura of the Crypts at Kiev. The numerous branches of this mother house served as spiritual foyers for the dissemination of the Gospel in the southern and western parts of Russia, which would later be known as the Ukraine. In the north, St. Sergius of Radonej founded the Laura of the Trinity (today Zagorsk), in the middle of the fourteenth century, while his disciples ranged far and wide through the northern forests. As missionaries, builders, colonizers, and scholars, the monks played an important role in the religious life of the times.

Kiev, the ancient and famous capital of Russia, was sacked several times by the Tartars. Eventually reduced to the status of an abandoned village, it ceased to be the residence of the metropolitan. After a brief sojourn in Vladimir, the primatial seat was transferred to Moscow under the Metropolitan Peter (1308-1326). This was an event of great historical importance. Moscow, hitherto a rather obscure principality, became the religious capital of all the Russias. Separatist tendencies at once made themselves felt in the south and west. The princes of those areas, subject to the authority of the king of Poland and the grand duke of Lithuania, demanded the right from Constantinople to have their own metropolitan and finally won their case in the fifteenth century when Moscow became autocephalous with respect to Byzantium.

The independence or "autocephaly" [1] of the Russian Church was proclaimed as a consequence of the acceptance by the then metropolitan, Isidore, a Greek, of the decisions of the Council of Florence (1439-1440). We have already briefly touched upon the conditions under which this unionist council was held and described how its decisions were quickly repudiated by the Greek Church at large. The Metropolitan Isidore, however, was a staunch advocate of the policy of reunion. In reward for his conciliatory attitude and for the part played by him at Florence, the pope had appointed him a cardinal priest immediately after the conclusion of the council. Upon arriving in Moscow in 1441, he celebrated a solemn liturgy in the cathedral of the Dormition, mentioned the pope's name in the course of the service, and proclaimed the reunion with Rome. After pondering the matter for three days, the Grand Duke Basil had Isidore arrested and imprisoned for some months in a monastery, and then allowed him to escape to Lithuania.

After much hesitation and a prolonged correspondence with Constantinople—where the Union of Florence had not yet been officially proclaimed—the Russians decided to enthrone a new metropolitan themselves. It was thus that Jonas was appointed to the see of Moscow in December 1448. Constantinople was simply informed of the *fait accompli*. The step was taken partly as a precautionary measure to forestall trouble with the ecumenical patriarchate in the

[1] According to Orthodox canon law the term "autocephaly" stands for the right, enjoyed by a group of dioceses, of electing their own primate. The boundaries of the various autocephalies often coincide with the frontiers of a state, although this is not always true.

future, for it was widely assumed that the Union of Florence would not last long there. In fact, as soon as Constantinople fell, in 1453, the Greeks repudiated the Council of Florence. However, Moscow now had its own metropolitan and was not disposed to give up what circumstances had enabled it to usurp.

These events also had their psychological aftermath, for, beginning in the fifteenth century, we find the first serious traces of a profound popular distrust of the Orthodoxy of the Greeks on the part of the Russians. Had the Greeks not betrayed the true faith at Florence, had they not been deservedly punished by God, who had handed over their empire to the Turks? Moscow was henceforth the "Third Rome." Ancient Rome was now heretical, the New Rome was groaning under the yoke of the Turks, the Third Rome alone remained intact. The theocratic ideal of a universal Christian empire thus found its last refuge in Moscow. Before long the grand dukes adopted the title of "czar" (a Slavic version of Caesar) and considered themselves henceforth as the legitimate successors of the rulers of Byzantium. In the purely ecclesiastical sphere this theory was never pushed to its logical conclusion, however, for the see of Moscow, in spite of its great power and wealth, never formally claimed to supplant the ecumenical primacy of Constantinople. There were always men in Russia who saw things in a more humble and realistic and less romantic light than the partisans of the Third Rome.

Thus it came about that, in the course of the sixteenth century, the Russian clergy and indeed all of Russian society were divided by a violent quarrel over the way in which the religious future of Russia was to be envisaged. One party, headed by the learned abbot Joseph of Volock, was completely dedicated to the idea of a new Christian Muscovite empire: they were the partisans of a close alliance between Church

and state in the Byzantine manner, and demanded in
return that the state allow the Church and the monasteries to keep the enormous domains which they possessed and which were used for charitable, educational, and social purposes. They firmly believed in the
urgency of building here and now a City of God, of
which Moscow was to be the center. The other party,
on the contrary—whose spokesman was the austere
monk of the northern forest, Nil Sorskij—preached
the virtues of monastic poverty, independence with
respect to the state, and canonical loyalty to Constantinople. They foresaw that a wealthy and "naturalized"
Church would more easily become a prey to state
control. In the end the Church finally recognized that
there was an element of truth in the claims of both
sides: both Joseph and Nil were canonized. However,
apparent victory lay with the party of Joseph, in the
sixteenth century. The Church retained its properties
and allied itself with the Muscovite state. But history
has shown that Nil was, to a large extent, right. The
Byzantine Middle Ages were well over by the sixteenth century and the further development of the
Russian Empire along the lines of a secularized modern state, which in the eighteenth century was destined
completely to subject the Church to its will and con-
fiscate its property, justified the misgivings of Nil and
his party a posteriori.[2]

Having achieved an autocephalous status, the Russian Church proceeded to develop its own religious
literature (lives of the saints, liturgical texts) in the
course of the fifteenth and sixteenth centuries. Russian

[2] On the sixteenth-century controversies and their consequences, see also our study *Une controverse sur le rôle social
de l'Église.—La querelle des biens ecclésiastiques au XVI*
siècle en Russie* (Chevetogne, 1956 [articles appearing in
Irénikon, 1955 and 1956]). Cf. W. K. Medlin, *Moscow and
East Rome. A Political Study of the Relations of Church and
State in Muscovite Russia* (Geneva, 1952).

art (iconography), ever faithful to its Byzantine masters, attained a high degree of perfection with the work of Andrew Roublev. A great council, held at Moscow in 1551 (Stoglav, "Council of the Hundred Chapters"), introduced a number of reforms in the Russian Church aimed at curbing the influence of sects and the spread of Western forms of piety and religious thought. A considerable number of Russian saints were canonized. The Third Rome thus gave evidence that it intended to live up to the new title which was being attributed to her. The Russians were particularly pleased when the ecumenical patriarch Jeremias II visited their country and consecrated the first patriarch of Moscow and all the Russias, Job (1589). The new patriarchate, however, was only accorded fifth place in the hierarchy of Oriental sees and even today occupies the same place, after Constantinople, Alexandria, Antioch, and Jerusalem.

The theory of the Third Rome suffered still further blows under the pontificate of the great patriarch Nikon (1652-1658). As soon as he had been elected this very authoritarian-minded prelate decided on a twofold policy for his pontificate: he intended to establish the supremacy of the spiritual over the temporal power and to reform the Russian Church in accordance with the liturgical norms then prevailing in the four other Oriental patriarchates. The close friendship between Nikon and Czar Alexis—the second of the Romanovs—enabled him to attain his first objective. For some years the Russian czar was the obedient son of the patriarch. However, Nikon was lacking in the tact and patience necessary to profit by this favorable situation, and his power did not last. His second objective resulted in a schism which separated millions of the faithful, who had taken the theory of the Third Rome seriously, from the mother church. Why, these critics asked, should minor customs (like making the sign of the cross with two fingers, singing the Alleluia twice, etc.) be reformed, when our fathers had been saved by observing them? Why accept as a criterion in these matters the corrupt Greeks whom God had punished for their infidelity? This was childish reasoning, of course, but it nevertheless contained a certain logic, all the more so in that the reforms were introduced by violence and intolerance, and certain measures—for example the requirement that the clergy wear their hair long—were not justified by the ancient practice of the Byzantine Church but were merely modern Greek customs dating from the time of the Turkish occupation. Nikon was finally deposed and condemned by a synod (1666-1667). The very Oriental patriarchs whose spokesman he had been took part in the synod and confirmed the deposition. The patriarch's reforms, however, were not abolished, and the schism ("raskol") of the Old Believers lasted for centuries.[3]

The claim of the Patriarch Nikon to dominate the czar haunted the mind of the young Peter the Great, who ended by imitating the impetuosity of the proud prelate but along entirely different lines. After the death of the Patriarch Hadrian (1700), the czar forbade the holding of elections for a new patriarch for twenty-one years, and then in 1721, promulgated his famous *Spiritual Regulation*, compiled by Theophanes Prokopovich, bishop of Pskov, which abolished the patriarchate and placed a collegiate body at the head of the Church, the Holy Synod, consisting of bishops and two or three priests. In accordance with the new regulations, a lay procurator, appointed by the czar, was required to take part in all discussions (without formally being a member of the Synod) and gradually

[3] On Nikon and the Raskol, see the monumental thesis of P. Pascal, *Avvakum et les débuts du Raskol* (Paris, 1938).

became the head of the administrative organization of the Church.

This system, influenced by the ecclesiastical regimes found in the Protestant states of Central Europe, did not formally regard the czar as the head of the Church (documents referred to him merely by the ambiguous title of "Supreme judge of the present college"), but Peter subjected the Church to the state in a way that neither Byzantium nor Russia had ever dreamed of before his time. Called upon to approve the new arrangement, the other Orthodox Eastern patriarchs finally gave their consent, after Dositheus of Jerusalem—whose efforts on behalf of Orthodoxy we have mentioned above—protested in vain against the whole of the czar's reforms.

Politically separate from Moscow, the provinces that later formed the Ukraine (in Russian, Ukraine signifies "frontiers") experienced an altogether different, and at times quite tragic, fate. After the election of Jonas to the see of Moscow, Isidore retained at least nominal authority over the diocese of Kiev in Polish and Lithuanian territory. He resigned in 1458. His successor was appointed by Rome and consecrated by the Uniat patriarch of Constantinople (resident in Rome). The new incumbent was Gregory Bolgarin, who for twelve years maintained the communion of the Ukrainian Church with Rome. Then, in 1470, he returned to Orthodoxy and recognized once more the authority of the ecumenical patriarch at Constantinople (under Turkish rule). The latter, after Bolgarin's death in 1472, appointed an Orthodox prelate to succeed him.

From this date the Russian dioceses of Poland and Lithuania, although canonically dependent on Constantinople, led a practically independent life and were constantly subject to pressure on the part of the

Catholic kings of Poland. This pressure was exercised particularly by means of the "right of patronage" which enabled the kings and certain nobles to appoint candidates for the priesthood and the episcopate and to administer some of the property of the Church. Opposition to Latinism was fostered especially by various confraternities of Orthodox laymen, who sometimes succeeded in buying up the right of patronage over their churches, published works defending Orthodoxy, and supported Orthodox schools. Undoubtedly it was these laymen who were mainly responsible for saving the Orthodox faith in the Ukraine, and not the apathetic clergy, who were subservient to the king and corrupt.

In 1596 the metropolitan of Kiev, Michael Ragoza, and the majority of Ukrainian bishops signed an act of reunion with Rome at Brest-Litovsk. This was the origin of the "Uniat" Ukrainian Church. However, the majority of the faithful led by two bishops and an exarch of the ecumenical patriarch, the Archdeacon Nicephorus, remained faithful to their Orthodoxy. When the two Orthodox bishops died (1607-1610), the faithful were without any pastors for ten years and were governed by the Uniat bishops whom the king of Poland imposed on them. In 1620, however, Theophanes, patriarch of Jerusalem, paid a visit to Kiev and re-established an Orthodox succession. At first more or less secretly, then openly, this hierarchy was finally recognized by the (Polish) state.

These events, the conditions under which the union with Rome had been imposed, excesses of all kinds, kept alive for centuries a fierce hatred among the Orthodox faithful toward the authority of Rome, which, in these parts, became identified with that of the Polish kings.

Forced to live under these difficult conditions, the Orthodox Church nevertheless had the good fortune to be governed by a number of distinguished prelates, notably the Metropolitan Peter Moghila (1632-1647). Famed for his *Confession,* which we have mentioned above, Moghila founded a school at Kiev in which the teaching was largely according to Latin methods of instruction. He reformed the liturgy and church government, endeavoring thus to overcome the inferior position in which the Orthodox found themselves by comparison with their Latin neighbors.

Finally in 1686, as a result of Russian victories over Poland, the Ukraine was annexed to the Muscovite empire of the Romanovs and the metropolitanate of Kiev was attached to the patriarchate of Moscow with the formal approval of the patriarch of Constantinople. Many Kievan theologians now moved to Moscow and served as invaluable assistants to Peter the Great, who was intent on introducing pro-Western reforms into Russia. They also brought along with them Latin methods of instruction and Latin ways of thought, which had a lasting effect on Russian theology.

As for the Uniats, a large part of them returned to Orthodoxy following the partition of Poland (three bishops and many faithful in 1839, at Polotzk). However, the major part of their church in Galicia, at first under Austrian, then under Polish sovereignty, remained faithful to Rome until 1946. There is evidence that the recent return of this unfortunate church to Orthodoxy was effected under conditions rather similar to if not worse than those under which it was formerly united with Rome.

The synodal period of Russian church history (1721-1917) is not viewed with a kindly eye today and is frequently cited as a classical example of the worst that can happen when a church is enslaved by the state. In actual fact, however, religion remained very much alive in Russia during this period and in many respects was even productive of exceptionally good results, so that it would be inaccurate and misleading to dismiss too summarily the rather artificial system under which it labored. Contemporaries themselves recognized the uncanonical nature of the new ecclesiastical regime, but they were powerless to do anything except tolerate it. The system of state control imposed on the Church, like a dike, left the Church's awareness of itself intact. It restricted some of the church's activities and resulted in the creation of deplorable conditions—the clergy, for example, became a social caste—but it did not corrupt church life fatally.

We shall dwell here briefly on three positive aspects of the Russian Church during this period: Russian spirituality, education, and missionary efforts.

The Christian East has always had a particular respect and even affection for the monastic life, as we have seen. The monasteries of Byzantium were the recognized centers of spiritual life in the city and Empire. In this respect, the Russians were the faithful disciples of the Greeks. During the synodal period, moreover, their loyalty to the monastic ideal was highly important because it was largely this which made possible the survival of Russian spirituality by acting as a counterweight to the process of statism, the attempt of the state to make over the Church in its own image and reduce it to the role of a mere servant. It was in the monasteries that the great Russian saints of the period made their appearance and carried on their apostolate.

In the eighteenth century, for example, a bishop of Veroneje, St. Tykhon (1724-1783), spent the remaining sixteen years of his life in the monastery of Zadonsk and there devoted himself to the contemplative life and the writing of spiritual works. Dostoevsky was inspired by his example to create a character with the same name in his *The Possessed.*[4] Tykhon soon acquired a great reputation as a spiritual adviser. Under the influence of German pietism, he advocated a complete renunciation of worldly things. The excessive nature of his teaching on this point illustrates better than anything else the typical reaction of many Russian Christians to the arrogant secularism of the reforms of Peter the Great. The conflict between the new political realism and the spiritual traditions of the past came to a head only during the Russian intellectual and spiritual renaissance in the nineteenth century.

A revival of interest in patristic spirituality was heralded by the publication of a Slavic translation— the work of Paisij Velickovskij, a monk from Athos who founded the monastery of Neamt in Moldavia— of the *Philocalia* of Nicodemus (St. Petersburg, 1793). From now on the Russians possessed in their own language a collection of the important texts of the Fathers on prayer, asceticism, and mysticism. Before long, the greatest modern Russian saint, Seraphim, had become famous in the monastery of Sarov, and the *startsi* of Optino were being chosen as the favorite spiritual advisers of the Russian intellectual élite.[5] Gogol, Dostoevsky, Alexis Khomiakov, and Vladimir Soloviev all found the ultimate source of their inspiration in the Russian Church and the spiritual traditions of Orthodoxy. On the very eve of the Revolution, the conversion of noted Marxist intellectuals (Struve, Frank, Bulgakov, Berdiaev) seemed to place a seal

[4] N. Gorodetzky, *St. Tikhon Zadonsky, Inspirer of Dostoevsky* (London, 1951).

[5] On this movement as a whole, see especially E. Behr-Sigel, *Prière et sainteté en Russie* (Paris, Éditions du Cerf, 1950); I. Kologrivof, *Essai sur la sainteté en Russie*, ed. Beynaert, (Bruges, 1953); V. Zenkovsky, *A History of Russian Philosophy*, 2 vols. (New York, 1953).

on the reconciliation of Spirit and Matter under the sovereignty of Christ. Unfortunately, this reconciliation, achieved on the purely intellectual level, was insufficient in itself to arrest or alter the great tide of events which had been preparing for such a long time as a result of so many social and economic factors.

If these spiritual movements as a whole appeared to take place on the fringes, as it were, of the official state Church—the reforms of Peter the Great resulted in the division of Russian society into a closed caste system (nobility, clergy, peasantry)—the official Church nevertheless did contribute to the intellectual life of the country, particularly by creating a system of church-run schools which attained a remarkably high standard of excellence in the nineteenth century.

Toward the end of the seventeenth century a theological academy was founded at Moscow. This term henceforth became traditional in Russia as the designation for a graduate school of theology or what in the West would be called a major seminary. In spite of doubts about their orthodoxy, it was the Latinizing theologians of Kiev, the former pupils of Peter Moghila, who were called upon to work out the curriculum and define the methods of instruction to be used in the new school. Throughout the eighteenth century the future higher clergy of the Russian Church studied in Latin from manuals compiled in accordance with the approved methods of Latin scholasticism. The system was only modified in 1808, but some of its features remained in effect until 1867, while its influence of course lasted much longer. Though alien in spirit, from the viewpoint of Orthodox tradition, these Latin methods nevertheless produced tangible results in the purely educational field, especially after the founding of three other academies (St. Petersburg, 1809; Kiev, 1819; Kazan, 1842) in addition to the one at Moscow. The students who attended these higher institutes were chosen from among the ablest pupils in the seminaries (secondary schools for the clergy), founded in many Russian dioceses in the course of the nineteenth century. By 1914, the Russian Church had a total of fifty-eight seminaries with 20,500 pupils, of whom only a certain portion went on to be ordained. The majority of the others became lay teachers, for the Church also controlled a part of the country's elementary school system and furnished professors of religion who taught in the secular schools. In all, there were 40,150 schools of all kinds dependent on the Church in 1914.[6]

Gradually overcoming the defects which they had when founded in the eighteenth century, the church-directed schools turned out an appreciable number of the able theologians, historians, and liturgists in the nineteenth and twentieth centuries, whose works— unfortunately little known in the West where only a few Slavic scholars were able to read Russian—were and still are authoritative in a number of fields. In the field of patrology, for example, special attention was paid to the translation of the original texts. More works of the Fathers and related texts have been translated into Russian than into any other European language.[7]

Thus by 1914 the Russian Church represented an imposing body of nearly a hundred million faithful, divided into sixty-seven dioceses.[8] The sixty-seven bishops in office were assisted in their work by eighty-two auxiliary bishops, 50,105 priests, 15,210 deacons,

[6] *La Documentation française,* No. 1931 (Oct. 9, 1954), *Le Problème religieux en U.R.S.S.,* Vol. II, p. 5.
[7] See C. Kern, *Les Traductions russes des textes patristiques, Guide bibliographique* (Chevetogne, 1957).
[8] Ever since the time of the Middle Ages, when Russia consisted of only one missionary metropolitanate dependent on the patriarchate of Constantinople, the number of Russian dioceses has traditionally been very small.

21,330 monks, and 73,299 nuns. The number of monasteries for men came to 1,025, that of convents for women to 473.[9]

During the synodal period, moreover, the Russian Church continued its missionary advance toward the East. We have seen that in the Mongol period Russian missionaries began the evangelization of several ethnic groups living in European Russia. Progress continued in the fifteenth and sixteenth centuries, facilitated by the capture of Kazan (1552) and Astrakhan (1556), and by the gradual conquest of Siberia. The missionary activity of several archbishops of Kazan (St. Gurius, St. Barsanuphius, St. Germanus) resulted in the establishment of a solid core of Christian Tartars around this city in the sixteenth century. Philotheus, metropolitan of Tobolsk (1702-1727), dispatched missionaries to the Kamchatka (1705) and to Iakutsk, in eastern Siberia (1724). He was the first to extend his missionary efforts beyond the confines of the Russian Empire by sending a mission to China (1714), where there had been a Christian Orthodox colony in the suburbs of Peking ever since the year 1689, consisting of Sinicized Russian Cossacks. Toward the end of the eighteenth century, monks from the monastery of Valamo on Lake Ladoga proceeded to Alaska—then a Russian possession—and established an Aleutian-speaking mission.

In the nineteenth century the Archimandrite Macarius, a Hebrew specialist and one of the most successful translators of the Bible into Russian, founded a mission at Altai in western Siberia in 1830, and translated the Bible and the liturgy into the various

[9] N. Zernov, *The Russians and Their Church* (London, 1945), p. 143; *Pamiatnaia Knizhka* (Government Annual) (1916), pp. 466-72. Cf. J. S. Curtiss, *The Russian Church and the Soviet State* (Boston, 1953), pp. 9-10 (citing the official figures for 1914).

dialects of the region. By 1903, 25,000 of the local inhabitants had become Christians and had a complete liturgy in their own language. Eastern Siberia also had its apostle in the person of John Veniaminov, who, first as a priest (1824-1840) and then as a bishop (1840-1868), labored indefatigably with a group of helpers, for the conversion of the Eskimos and the Indians of Alaska, the Aleutian Islands, and the Kurile Islands, and the Yakuts of Siberia. Appointed metropolitan of Moscow in 1868, he founded in the capital an "Orthodox Missionary Society" for the purpose of centralizing all the missionary activities of the Russian Church. After thirty years of labor, the Society could congratulate itself on the conversion of some 124,200 pagans to the Gospel.

The whole missionary effort of the Russian Church was given a new direction toward the middle of the nineteenth century, when a center for missionary studies was founded at the Academy of Kazan. The heart and soul of the new center was a lay professor, I. I. Ilminsky, a remarkable linguist, who was perfectly acquainted both with the Biblical languages (Hebrew, Greek), Arabic, and with the various languages of Central Asia. In order to counteract the rapid progress of Islam among the Tartars, Ilminsky and his group conceived the idea of translating the Biblical and liturgical texts, not into the literary language which was very little understood by the people, but into the various spoken dialects. Thus a veritable Orthodox library was created for the benefit of the Tartars, Yakuts, Buryats, Tungus, Votyaks, Mordvinians, Cheremiss, Ostyak-Samarovs, and Kirghiz. By the year 1903, the liturgy of St. John Chrysostom was being celebrated in more than twenty languages in the region of Kazan. In 1899 the diocese of Samara had 128 clergy (74 priests, 17 deacons, and 37 lectors) who were able to speak Chuvash, and of this number 47 priests, 12 deacons, and 20 lectors were of Chuvash origin.

Beyond the Russian frontiers the Japanese mission was by far the most important. It is still active today, as we shall see later on.[10]

Orthodox missionary activity in Asia from the fifteenth to the nineteenth centuries, on the whole— though with notable exceptions, especially in Japan —followed the colonial expansion of the Russian Empire. But this was equally true of Western missionary efforts, Catholic and Protestant, in Africa and Asia, which in general coincided with the colonial occupation of those areas by European countries. The success of the Orthodox missions, particularly in Islamic regions, is at least partly attributable to the time-honored Byzantine custom of translating the liturgy into the various local spoken languages, and partly to a certain cleverness on the part of the Russians in being able to adjust themselves to and identify themselves with the life of the subject peoples.

In any case, the story of these missions is sufficient to refute an erroneous impression regarding the dullness and ineffectiveness of Russian church history during the synodal period. While remaining outwardly a part of the governmental machinery, the Church was nevertheless still capable of producing saints and apostles who testified to the remarkable vitality of Russian Christianity during these years.

[10] Regarding the Orthodox missions, see especially the monumental works of J. Glazik, *Die russisch-orthodoxe Heidenmission seit Peter dem Grossen* (Münster-Westfalen, 1954); *Die Islammission der russich-orthodoxen Kirche* (Münster-Westfalen, 1959), who cites many Russian sources. Cf. also E. Smirnoff, *Russian Orthodox Missions* (London, 1903), and S. Bolshakoff, *The Foreign Missions of the Russian Orthodox Church* (London, 1943).

CHAPTER VII

THE ORTHODOX CHURCH AND
THE COMMUNIST STATE

THE EARLY decades of the twentieth century were
fateful from every point of view and the Christians of
Russia were destined to find themselves in the very
midst of the great transformations then taking place.
The part played by them in these events and above all
the remarkable survival of religion in Russia prove
that the Russian Church was by no means, as so
readily assumed, a mere cog in the wheel of the
czarist government. Throughout the nineteenth century farsighted individuals constantly looked forward
to the day when the Church could be modernized by
means of adequate reforms, and especially, to the
imperative necessity of achieving greater independence with respect to the state. At the time of the 1905
revolution, when Nicholas II granted a constitution
guaranteeing almost complete freedom of movement
and speech in Russia, a wave of intellectual and
social unrest broke over the Church. Russian religious publications in this period (1905-1917) are filled
with passionate discussions of the reforms that were
deemed necessary in the Church. The Holy Synod
agreed to the holding of a national synod of the Russian Church—not since the time of Peter the Great

had it even been possible to contemplate such a step—
and established a Pre-conciliar Commission charged
with the responsibility of preparing the agenda. The
Russian bishops were invited to suggest a program of
reforms: their replies to this inquiry constitute one
of the most interesting documents of the period. On
the whole they were in favor of widespread reforms
in the Church which would enable it to carry on its
mission in a more effective way and with less control
by the state. A decided majority was in favor of the
re-establishment of the patriarchate.

Thus the Church was better prepared than is generally supposed for the events which were now about
to take place. The Provisional Government of Kerensky allowed the Church to summon the council, which
had been in preparation for twelve years. The body
which met at Moscow in August 1917 included 265
members of the clergy and 299 laymen. Elected by
indirect voting in the dioceses, the council was representative of the ecclesiological tendencies prevalent
in the Russian Church in the nineteenth century, and
in accordance with these principles laymen were permitted to share with the episcopate responsibility for
the affairs of the Church at all levels of church government. The council sat until August 1918 and drew up
a new constitution for the Church, which provided
for the re-establishment of the patriarchate, the
election of bishops by the dioceses, and the representa-
tion of laymen on parish councils, on diocesan councils, and in the higher administration of the patriarchate. On October 31, 1917—six days after the
overthrow of the Provisional Government by the Bol-
sheviks—Tykhon, metropolitan of Moscow, was elected
patriarch. Episcopal elections could not be held in
all the dioceses; however, in Petrograd the popular
Bishop Benjamin was elected metropolitan by the
clergy and faithful in the very midst of the revolu-

tionary turmoil. Thus, far from seeming to uphold the *ancien régime*, the Church on the one hand boldly asserted its right to independence from the state, and on the other showed that it was disposed to allow the people to elect their own ecclesiastical heads.

However, most members of the council of 1917-1918 and the majority of Russians at large lacked any clear ideas on what the proper relations between the Church and the new Russian state should be. During the brief reign of Kerensky, there was an intense longing on the part of church leaders for some form of independence, but this longing was not identified with any particular theory regarding the exact nature of future Church-state relations. The Church leaders first of all spoke out on behalf of what they regarded as the national interest, by demanding material support from the Provisional Government for the Orthodox faith as the dominant religion of the new republic, by appealing to the army to continue the war against Germany, and later, by solemnly condemning the Treaty of Brest-Litovsk, which had been concluded by Lenin. These acts clearly showed that the Church did not at first envisage the necessity of having to separate itself completely from the state and that this separation, once it had been brought about through force of circumstances, did not mean that the Church intended to remain silent with regard to the acts of the government and refrain from passing judgment on them. The Church had reformed itself internally, but its attitude toward the various phases of the Russian Revolution was determined pragmatically by the mental outlook and conscience of its rulers, especially by that of its head, the Patriarch Tykhon.

The Communist Party, an intensely active and well-disciplined minority, triumphed with relative ease and unexpected suddenness in the midst of the frightful political confusion in the country at the time. The

Church thus found itself confronting a government resolved to combat all religion as such, for Marx had
defined religion as the "opium of the people."

The attitude of the Soviet state toward religious
beliefs in general, and toward the Orthodox Church in
particular, has been remarkably the same over the
years, as far as theory or doctrine is concerned.
Equally remarkable are the various tactics it has
adopted over the same years in dealing with the religious opposition.[1] It seems that this fact is to be explained not by any deliberate Machiavellianism on the
part of the party leaders in the field of religious policy,
but by certain misconceptions which have vitiated
their analysis of the religious situation in Russia.
Marxist dogma, in effect, was laid down in the West
and under different conditions from those prevailing
in the Russia of 1918: "Christianity," wrote Engels,
"has become more and more the apanage of the ruling classes and is used by them as a bridle by which
to control the lower classes." [2]

According to this doctrine it was enough merely to
create a classless society to bring about the disappearance of religion. But in Russia the Orthodox
Church was a popular church—the ruling classes, on
the contrary, had been largely secularized since the
eighteenth century—and it had just provided itself

[1] "Marxism is materialism. As such, it is without mercy for
religion," wrote Lenin (Works, 3rd ed. [Leningrad, 1935-1937],
Vol. 4, p. 70). "All religious doctrine," wrote P. Kasirin,
"serves to camouflage the interests of the exploiting classes,"
The Reactionary Essence of Religious Ideology (in Russian)
(Moscow, 1951), p. 29. The Soviet press still frequently regrets
that "all Soviet citizens are not yet emancipated from the
vestiges of former times, particularly the traces of religion." See,
for example, M. Persitz. "The Legislation of the October Revolution on the Freedom of Conscience" (in Russian), in Questions of History of Religion and Atheism, Vol. V (1958), p. 63.

[2] See the collection entitled Thoughts of K. Marx and F. Engels on Religion (in Russian) (Leningrad, 1929), p. 31.

with an even more "democratic" constitution in the council of 1917-1918, by accepting fundamental reforms in its structure and its administration. The antireligious measures of the government therefore struck not at the "ruling classes" of the former regime, but at a popular clergy and the great mass of believers, who by and large did not identify their cause with the political and military counterrevolution, and did not represent, therefore, except for their religious convictions, any deep threat to the new government. In order to impose its will in this matter the government did not hesitate to have recourse to force and considerable bloodletting, and thus succeeded in transforming the Orthodox Church into a martyred church. Frightened by the consequences of its own actions, the government made several tactical retreats—it tried, for example, to win over to its side a part of the clergy, with a limited amount of success, and thus divide the Church. Finally, after many years, it arrived at a kind of modus vivendi with the reunified Church, a rather unstable arrangement by the terms of which both sides, Church and state, appear to be staking all on the future.

We shall first briefly touch on the restrictive measures of the government in the field of religion, and then analyze the reaction of the Church and the ensuing conflict.

On January 20, 1918, the Council of Commissaries of the People approved the famous decree regarding the "separation of Church and State and the separation of the schools from the Church," which was promulgated on January 23.[3]

This decree forbade all participation by the Church

[3] An account of the history of this decree, as well as a photographic copy of the original with the autograph corrections of Lenin, has recently been published in the periodical *Questions of History of Religion and Atheism,* Vol. V (Moscow, 1958), pp. 50-63.

in the life of the state and all religious instruction in
public or private schools. It proclaimed complete freedom of conscience for all citizens. The freedom envisaged, however, was not the same kind as that which
existed in "bourgeois" countries, for religious groups
were no longer regarded as juridical persons capable
of enjoying juridical rights. Such groups were deprived of the right to own property (paragraph 12);
their property was declared nationalized; only places
of worship (according to the autograph correction of
Lenin in the original text) might be made available
to them by the state, as the result of a special decision by the authorities (par. 13). Worship was not
allowed except where it did not interfere with public
order (par. 5), the authorities alone being the sole
judge in the matter since the Church as a religious
group had no juridical rights. The new government
was not only separated from the Church; it placed
the latter completely "outside the law." The publication of the decree was accompanied by numerous
antireligious disturbances, inspired and carried out by
local Communist officials or by undisciplined revolutionary groups. The most notorious of these outbursts
was the one that resulted in the murder of the metropolitan of Kiev, Vladimir (January 25, 1918). These
governmental acts, radical and brutal by their very
nature, were clearly designed to break down the resistance and organization of the Russian Church.
The latter, however, remained hopeful of being able
to come to some kind of an understanding with the
Soviet government. On two occasions (November 4-8,
1917, March 15, 1918), a delegation from the Church
Council—which continued to sit in Moscow—went
to the Kremlin to try to reach an agreement on the
relations between Church and state. But each time,
while the tone of the conversations was correct, no

results were forthcoming. The government had decided on unilateral action.

When the great famine of 1921-1922 was raging throughout the length and breadth of the land, especially in the Volga region, the Patriarch Tykhon addressed an appeal to the Russian Church (August 1921), as well as to foreign churches, to collect funds for the starving. An ecclesiastical committee was set up to centralize and distribute the help. But the government was afraid of the moral prestige that might accrue to the Church if it succeeded in providing help on a massive scale, and confiscated what had already been collected. A new decree dated February 26, 1922 went even further: it ordered the confiscation of all valuable objects in the churches (metals or precious stones), declaring that they were needed to alleviate the sufferings of the starving. Such valuables, in fact, were already the property of the state by the decree of 1918.

By its laws and its arbitrary acts the government indicated clearly enough its intention to build in Russia a society in which there would no longer be any place for the Church. For the Christians of Russia, therefore, it was no longer merely a question of recognizing the social reforms introduced by the Soviets —the collectivization of the land, the nationalization of industry—as just or unjust, but of defending the very existence of religion in Russia and of finding the best way to do this. A part of the clergy chose the simplest path: they sided with the White armies fighting the Reds in various parts of the country. The patriarch, however, and the majority of the clergy who were in territory controlled by the Soviets could not avoid defining their attitude toward the new state of affairs in a more realistic manner. And they did so as Christians. Their witness to the truth and the moral

and physical sacrifices which they were obliged to
endure constitute the best guarantee for the future
of religion in Russia. The figures at our disposal show,
more eloquently than anything else, the enormous
risk which they incurred by remaining faithful to
their vocation. Between 1923 and 1926, some fifty
bishops were either shot to death or died following
deportation. In the years 1921-1922 the business of
confiscating church valuables cost the lives of some
691 secular priests alone. A much greater number of
priests were forced to submit to rigorous governmental
measures of all kinds and were subject to various harassments, including that of being deprived of all civil
rights.[4]

Three months after the October Revolution, in response to the unbelievably crude and violent initial
attacks on the Church, the Patriarch Tykhon launched
a sentence of excommunication against the "open or
disguised enemies of Christ" from his residence in
Moscow:[5]

> By the authority which God has vested in me,
> we forbid you to approach the Mysteries of
> Christ; we anathematize you, provided you still
> bear the name of Christian and belong, by birth,
> to the Orthodox Church. . . . As for you, faithful
> sons of the Church, I appeal to you to defend our
> holy Mother, outraged and oppressed. . . . And

[4] The Constitution of 1918, par. 69. See M. Pol'skij, *New
Martyrs of Russia* (in Russian) (Jordanville, U.S.A., 1949),
pp. 168-80; cf. N. Timascheff, *Religion in Soviet Russia* (London, 1943), p. 89; A. A. Bogolepov, *The Church under Communist Power* (in Russian) (Munich, 1958), pp. 16-17. It is
obvious that the figures cited by these *émigré* authors cannot be controlled materially, the sole criterion being their prob-
ability. However, the latter is beyond question for the period
we are studying. The ecclesiastical trials and deportations were
frequently and fully reported in the Soviet press.

[5] Complete English translation in P. Anderson, *Church and
State in Modern Russia* (New York, 1944), pp. 65-68.

if it becomes necessary to suffer for the cause of Christ, we appeal to you to follow the path of suffering. . . . And you, my brother bishops and priests . . . organize religious groups as quickly as possible, appeal to them to form an alliance of spiritual combatants determined to oppose to physical force the power of the Spirit. We firmly believe that the enemies of the Church of Christ will be defeated and dispersed by the power of the Cross, for the promise of Him who bore the Cross is unshakable: "I will build my Church and the gates of hell shall not prevail against it."

In spite of the passionate nature of this appeal, the patriarch refrained from expressly mentioning the government among the "enemies of Christ"—hoping no doubt that the latter would not carry to extremes the violence unleashed by the revolutionary spirit—and did not call upon the faithful to resist the governmental measures by force, but only by "spiritual" means. Thus while the head of the Church made no pretense of remaining "outside politics"—in March 1918 he condemned the Treaty of Brest-Litovsk—he nevertheless refrained from pronouncing any judgment on the social reforms of the new regime. From this moment, under his guidance, the Church refused to identify itself with the old regime and made it clear that it intended to exercise its own right to proclaim the Gospel to the Russian people. In October 1918, Tykhon addressed a new message directly to Lenin:[6]

It does not pertain to us to judge the earthly power; all power permitted by God shall have our blessing bestowed on it, if it truly shows itself the "servant of God, for the good of the governed"

[6] This appeal of the patriarch may be found in all books devoted to the Russian Church after 1917.

(Rom. xiii.4). . . . As for you, we address to you this admonition: celebrate the anniversary of your assumption of power by releasing prisoners, by ceasing to shed blood, by abandoning violence and placing restrictions on the faith; cease to destroy, in order to organize order and justice, give the people the respite they are longing for. . . . Otherwise, all the just blood that you have shed will cry out against you and you will perish by the sword, you who have taken the sword (Matt. xxii.52).

This letter to Lenin did not mean that the patriarch was now contemplating supporting the counterrevolutionary forces. In a new appeal issued in September 1919 he called upon the faithful to refrain from any act which might arouse the suspicions of the Soviet authorities and to obey all the regulations provided they were not opposed to the faith and true piety. Several other bishops issued similar appeals to their flocks. Thus, when the Metropolitan Benjamin learned in Petrograd that a plan was afoot to profane the relics of St. Alexander Nevsky, he sent a delegation to Zinoviev, the president of the local soviet, asking him to revoke the order, and solemnly promised to suspend any cleric under his jurisdiction at once if any gave assistance to the Whites.[7]

This attitude, revealing that the Church was prepared to be critical and obdurate on moral issues but politically loyal, won it a certain amount of respect. In the midst of the unbelievable turmoil into which Russia had been plunged—revolutionary excesses of all kinds, civil war on several fronts, foreign intervention—the Orthodox Church appeared as a solid bastion and haven of hope, materially shaken, but spiritu-

[7] Mentioned by *Izvestia*, Sept. 20, 1919, cited in J. S. Curtiss, *The Russian Church and the Soviet State* (Boston, 1953), p. 339.

ally purified by the martyrdom of many of its sons. The most serious blow which it had to face during these years was the confiscation of valuable objects.

As we have seen, the government had forbidden the Church to organize relief for the starving in its own name and then decreed in February 1922 the confiscation of all valuable objects in the churches. The patriarch thereupon issued a circular letter permitting the church authorities to hand over nonconsecrated objects (the ornaments on icons, ex-votos, candelabra, and the like), but forbidding the surrender of items used in the liturgical services (sacred vessels, sacerdotal vestments). As an alternative, he proposed that the faithful organize a drive and pay the authorities the equivalent of the objects that could not be handed over. He would certainly have gone even further, if he could have been sure of exercising the least control over the actual use of the confiscated objects. The patriarch's circular resulted in a wave of persecutory acts of unusual violence, and provided the government with a valuable propaganda weapon to use against the clergy. The patriarch and bishops, it was maintained, were refusing to come to the relief of the starving! In many towns there were violent clashes between the governmental authorities and the faithful. For the first time, the government dared to try some of the church leaders publicly. In Moscow, forty-four persons—priests and laymen—were dragged before the courts and eleven were condemned to death. In Petrograd the Metropolitan Benjamin himself, in spite of his repeated declarations of loyalty and disposition to come to some kind of understanding over the question of valuable objects, was condemned to death and executed along with several of his assistants.[8] The controversy over valuable objects had

[8] Several of the present leaders of the Moscow patriarchate then formed part of the entourage of Metropolitan Benjamin.

another outcome: it led to schism in the Church group. One group of priests publicly declared that it was opposed to carrying out the instructions of the hierarchy. Such statements were of course given wide publicity and readily received the support of the government. This was the origin of the Living Church.

The Patriarch Tykhon, who had come to Moscow during the trial of the "forty-four" to attempt to protect the accused by his authority, was not arrested himself until May 9, 1922. The offices of the patriarchate were then invaded by representatives of the Living Church, who claimed to be the "Provisional Government of the Russian Church." Supported by the government, the schismatics were soon able to claim the allegiance of part of the clergy and even of some of the bishops. To an already deplorable and tragic situation there was now added a new element, that of schism. The ecclesiastical revolution[9] was led by a group of secular priests, members of the so-called "white" clergy, as opposed to the "black" or regular clergy. Because the "white" clergy were married they were excluded from the episcopate according to the traditional norms of Orthodox canon law, and there was therefore a certain long-felt animosity among them toward the monks who governed the Church. The Living Church, which would soon also allow bishops to marry, permitted priests to marry a second time, and therefore it was natural that it should derive its main strength from the circles of the married clergy. It also gained some adherents among intellectual circles, anxious at all costs to work out a modus vivendi

---

The present patriarch, Alexis, was his auxiliary and succeeded him in the government of the diocese. The Metropolitan Gregory of Leningrad (†1957), then a priest, was sentenced, in the same trial, to a long term of forced labor.

[9] The movement later became split into several groups, the most important of which were the Living Church and the Renovated Church.

with the government. Some of the reforms introduced by this body are not devoid of interest, notably in the liturgical field, but the whole movement was vitiated from the start by the decidedly fraudulent way in which it seized power, by the favor which it curried with the government, by the calumnies which it spread against the patriarch, and finally by the flagrantly uncanonical acts of which it was guilty. Before long, the moderate party of schismatics, called the Renovated Church, was given permission by the government to use the majority of churches, but it never won the widespread support of the faithful. It was the same with the other schisms, particularly that in the Ukraine, where a group of priests had unsuccessfully petitioned for the restoration of an autocephalous Ukrainian Church and then in 1921 determined to go ahead with their plans anyway in spite of the opposition of the patriarch and the bishops. Consecrating certain "bishops" themselves, they formed another schismatic group which in some cases received the support of the government, anxious as always to promote the disintegration of the Orthodox Church.

The first setback to the increasing trend toward schism occurred when the patriarch was suddenly released in June 1923, after having signed an official statement acknowledging his past "faults," specifically his condemnation of the Treaty of Brest-Litovsk, his excommunication of the communists, and his circular letter on the question of church valuables.[10] After a year's imprisonment, Tykhon thus agreed, in effect, to pass no further public judgment on the acts of the Soviet government. In appeals to the faithful he defined his new attitude as "apolitical": "Let monarchists abroad and in the country know that I am

[10] The text of this statement was published by *Izvestia*, No. 141 (June 27, 1923); quoted in Curtiss, *op. cit.*, pp. 159-60, 347.

not the enemy of the Soviet government," he proclaimed.[11]

While adopting a conciliatory attitude toward the
government, the patriarch nevertheless remained obdurate toward the schismatics. As soon as he was released he formally condemned them, and certain well-
known figures among the Renovated did solemn penance before him.[12] Tykhon died in Moscow on April
7, 1925. After his death the newspapers published
his testament in which he once again called upon the
faithful to recognize the new regime with a sincere
conscience, to oppose its enemies, and to regain the
confidence of the government, which, in turn, would
then permit the religious instruction of children, the
functioning of a number of theological seminaries, and
the publication of books and newspapers.[13] The patriarchal Church remained faithful to this testament,
without, however, having obtained even to this day
all the advantages which the patriarch hoped for, notably in the fields of religious education and publications.

The next stage in the life of the Russian Church
covers the period from 1927 to 1943. Patriarch Tykhon
foresaw that it would probably be impossible to hold
a regular election for a new patriarch and therefore
designated three possible *locum tenentes* to succeed
him: the Metropolitans Cyril, Agathangelos, and Peter.
Since the first two were imprisoned at the time of
Tykhon's death, the third, Metropolitan Peter of Krutica, was recognized as *locum tenens* of the patriarchate. Eight months after his installation, on Decem-

[11] *Izvestia*, Nos. 147, 149 (July 4, 6, 1923); quoted in Curtiss,
loc. cit.

[12] Among them was Sergius, then archbishop of Jaroslavl,
the future patriarch.

[13] *Izvestia* (April 15, 1925); quoted in Curtiss, *op. cit.*,
pp. 176-77, 349.

ber 23, 1925, he too was arrested and exiled to Siberia, after appointing as his successor in the office of "deputy *locum tenens*" the Metropolitan Sergius of Nizhni Novgorod. It was with this strange title—which many refused to recognize—that Sergius took over the direction of what remained of the patriarchal Church, and governed it from 1927 until 1943. Only a few bishops were still at liberty, while the majority of the churches were in the hands of the Renovated Church. Sergius himself was arrested in December 1926. Following his release (March 30, 1927), he published a series of declarations affirming his loyalty to the government in stronger terms than ever: "We wish to be Orthodox," he proclaimed, "while at the same time recognizing the Soviet Union as our country. We wish its joys and successes to be our joys and successes and its defeats to be our defeats." [14] Moreover, he officially appealed to the NKVD (People's Commissariat for Internal Affairs) requesting it to "legalize" the existence in Moscow of a patriarchal Synod (until then the government had not even admitted that Metropolitan Sergius resided in Moscow). The latter demand appeared to many to be going too far in the way of accommodation, for government "legalization" necessarily implied an unspecified amount of government control. Many of the bishops, in exile or at liberty, protested against the new attitude of Metropolitan Sergius. One group of bishops, exiled to Solovki on the White Sea, including Hilarion Troickii, a well-known theologian and former right arm of Patriarch Tykhon, sent an appeal to Sergius which also professed complete loyalty toward the state, but demanded instead an unprejudiced application of the

[14] The text of this statement may be found in *Le Patriarche Serge et son héritage spirituel* (in Russian) (Publications of the Moscow Patriarchate, 1947).

law on the separation of Church and state guaranteeing the internal freedom of the Church.[15]

But these protests were in vain. Metropolitan Sergius acted in accordance with his conscience, in the
hope of being able to re-establish some form of administrative machinery for the Church, then virtually
nonexistent, and thus safeguard the embryo of a
church, as it were, for the future. In spite of the humil-
iating declarations it was obliged to make particularly
on the subject of religious persecutions, which even
at the beginning of the Revolution were allegedly
purely political in nature, in spite of the obviously in-
correct information it was obliged to give out regarding the existence of "religious liberty" in Russia, the
patriarchal synod, established by Sergius, continued
in fact to be attacked by the press and its members
were often arrested and exiled. Antireligious legislation became more and more oppressive as successive
modifications were made in the Constitution of the
Soviet Union. The Constitution of 1918 had guaranteed to citizens "religious freedom" and "freedom of
religious and antireligious propaganda" (par. 13).
This paragraph was modified in 1929. From then on
it was a question merely of "freedom of religious confession and antireligious propaganda." The Constitution of Stalin of 1936, still in force, merely confers on
citizens the "freedom of religious worship and antireligious propaganda" (par. 124).

During World War II, however, the Soviet government made a sudden about-face in its tactics toward
religion.

After issuing a patriotic message to the Russian people on the very day of the German invasion (June 22,

[15] The existence and authenticity of this message from Solovki
is admitted by all. The text was circulated clandestinely in
Russia and also outside the country.

1941), Metropolitan Sergius and his church were granted a certain amount of freedom of movement and action. A few bishops were released from exile. On September 4, 1954, Sergius and two other metropolitans (Alexis of Leningrad and Nicholas of Kiev) were received by Stalin, and obtained official approval for the holding of a patriarchal election. The synod, consisting of only eighteen bishops—many of the others were still imprisoned—duly met and elected Sergius patriarch. This resurrection of the Church coincided with the prompt liquidation of the schism of the Renovated Church, which, lacking any popular support, was in full decline. The patriarchate obtained the right to use the religious edifices hitherto reserved largely to the schismatics. It was permitted, also, to proceed with the reorganization of the Church, establish theological seminaries, and publish an ecclesiastical periodical.

Whatever judgment one may feel inclined to pass on the policy of Patriarch Sergius, it is undeniable that the reappearance in Russia in 1943 of a traditional church, faithful in all respects to Orthodox canonical norms and rites, amounted to a veritable miracle, and constituted a kind of rebuff to the antireligious campaign and the materialist ideals with which the government had tried for so long to indoctrinate the Russian people. Wholly excluded from the schools and from the press, religion had nevertheless resisted the unprecedented assault made on it by the organs of propaganda. On the eve of the war, in its May 1941 issue, the periodical *Antireligioznik* stated that the antireligious publications issued that year by the government press included sixty-seven titles of books and pamphlets totaling 3,505,000 copies, and two periodicals and a newspaper with a total of 5,880,-000 copies.[16] In addition to this, of course, all text-

[16] Cited by Curtiss, *op. cit.*, pp. 280, 363.

books and all teaching in the schools had to be slanted in an antireligious direction.[17]

It was after surviving trials of this kind that the Russian Church was able to celebrate in 1958 the fortieth anniversary of the election of Tykhon as patriarch, in the presence of numerous foreign Orthodox prelates. To be sure, the conditions at the time of his election and the different aspects of his patriarchate were soft-pedaled or glossed over; nevertheless the Church felt that it was celebrating the memory of one who had worthily borne witness for Christ and thus prepared the way for the survival of the Orthodox faith in Russia.

But the state of course had and has no intention of abandoning its antireligious program. Its attitude was given concrete expression in the decisions of the Central Committee of the Party, dated November 10, 1954, and signed by the secretary, N. Khrushchev, printed in *Pravda* on November 11, 1954. "The Communist Party," the document asserts, "relying on the only truly scientific conception of the world, the Marxist-Leninist, and on the theoretical foundation of the latter, dialectical materialism, cannot adopt an indifferent or neutral attitude toward religion, since the latter is an ideology wholly alien to science." The Party, consequently, "will assist every believer finally to get rid of his religious errors." The text of the document then goes on to state the classical doctrine that religion is essentially nothing but a means employed "by the exploiters in their struggle against the workers." Consequently, "after the victory of socialism and the liquidation in the USSR of the exploiting classes, the social roots of religion will find themselves cut off and the basis which served for the sup-

[17] On the effectiveness and nature of this propaganda, see especially P. B. Anderson, *People, Church and State in Modern Russia* (New York, 1944); cf. the same author's *Russia's Religious Future* (London, 1935); see also Curtiss, *op. cit.*

port of the Church will no longer exist." The existence
of believers in Russia is therefore merely a survival
from the past, allowed by the Constitution to the extent that the exercise of religion is limited to "worship"
(par. 124) and "the servants of the Church, in the
vast majority of cases, today adopt a loyal attitude toward the Soviet authorities." Therefore, the Committee condemns "administrative measures and harassments directed against believers and the clergy"; these
measures "cannot but be harmful, by strengthening
religious prejudice." The struggle against religion
should therefore be viewed from the purely ideologi-
cal level. It should consist above all in the education
of the workers according to materialist principles. An
editorial in the periodical *Questions of Philosophy*
(1959, No. 8) recently declared that religion will
gradually lose its influence over the masses "when
socialism shall become stronger, as the level of material and cultural life rises, as technical progress is
made, and as the government is able to exercise more
pressure through its attack on religion."

We must realize therefore that the situation of the
Orthodox Church in Russia today is far from being an
easy one. Obliged, in theory, to be politically neutral,
and in effect to support the government, it does not
receive anything in return for this attitude. Restricted
in its activity to religious "worship," it must nevertheless seek to oppose as best it can an active antireligious campaign directed against all religion. In the
following chapter we shall attempt to analyze the
present situation in Russia and speculate briefly on the
prospects for the future.

The establishment, after the Second World War, of
"popular democracies" in various countries of Eastern
Europe with largely Orthodox populations took place
under conditions totally different from those which

witnessed the triumph of communism in Russia. The new rulers were able to profit by the experience of the Russians. Thus it happened that when they seized power, they were careful to avoid the violent persecutions, public trials, and other harassments which might have served as an excuse to make martyrs of the faithful. Without attempting to impose a uniform pattern for the separation of Church and state everywhere, they maintained a tight control over all the activities of the clergy, neutralizing certain prominent individuals and curtailing, wherever possible, the apostolic efforts of the Church. Faithful to the doctrine of the eventual disappearance of religion in a classless society, they preferred to rely principally on time and communist re-education of the masses to achieve their objective. Administrative measures were aimed—and still are—against all those who show too openly their opposition to the regime or official propaganda. On the whole, the Orthodox hierarchy in these countries models its attitude on that of the patriarch of Moscow. Disassociating itself from all connection with the former regimes, it is careful to express its loyalty to the new by taking part in semiofficial organizations such as the "Partisans for Peace."

At first glance, the legislative attitude of the popular democracies appears to be more favorable to religion than that of the Soviet Union. The latter, as we have seen, forbids "religious propaganda" and only allows "antireligious propaganda" (Constitution of 1936, par. 124). The Bulgarian (par. 78), Rumanian (par. 84), and Hungarian (par. 54) constitutions simply mention freedom of "conscience" and of "religious worship." The Czechoslovak Constitution (par. 15) is even more explicit and guarantees the freedom of "acts connected with religious profession," while the Polish Constitution, by far the most liberal, admits that the Church and religious groups "may perform their religious functions" (par. 17).[18] These constitutional guarantees, however, are limited by special laws regarding religious bodies, and by the new constitutions which the latter were obliged to adopt. On the whole, such laws and constitutions are designed to permit the state to establish a tight control over all the activities of the Church. Activities such as preaching and the publication of religious works are allowed far more freely than in the USSR. However, in all the popular democracies, with the single exception of Poland, the Church is carefully excluded from the field of education of the youth. It is here, ultimately, that the real battle between Christianity and the new Marxist orthodoxy will be fought. Will religion, reduced to mere "worship," gradually disappear from the new society, along with the other traces of capitalism? Only the Christians fated to live in those countries can supply the answer to this question, and the future alone will reveal the advantages or disadvantages of the present attitude of the hierarchy. In our brief discussion of the present situation in each of these countries, in the chapter that follows, we shall see that this attitude has varied considerably and that it is more flexible than is commonly supposed.

[18] See A. Bogolepov (in Russian), *The Church under Communist Power* (Munich, 1958), pp. 80-81.

CHAPTER VIII

THE ORTHODOX CHURCH TODAY

IT IS NOT very easy to deal with the subject of religion in terms of pure statistics, because statistics involve numbers, and cannot adequately describe such phenomena as religious experience or religious practice. Now it is impossible to estimate the real strength of a religious group without adequate information about these fundamental factors. For more than forty years— that is, ever since the Russian Revolution—it has been impossible to give any adequate statistics for the whole of the Orthodox Church, even with respect to numbers alone. According to a very approximate estimate based on religious practice, the number of Orthodox Christians today who participate more or less regularly in the sacraments of the Church comes to roughly 100,-000,000. About 50,000,000 of these are in the Soviet Union. However it seems quite certain that the number of *baptized* Orthodox must be much higher, for reception of the sacrament was obligatory in Russia before the Revolution and even today there are many families who still have their children baptized but who otherwise remain aloof from the life of the Church. Therefore, it is reasonable to conclude that the above

figure of 100,000,000 is not really representative of
the actual strength of Orthodoxy among the various
Christian confessions. The totals for Roman Catholics
(450,000,000) and Protestants (250,000,000), as they
are usually given, are based on baptismal records, but
it is recognized that these do not reflect actual religious practice.[1]

The Orthodox Church is at present a decentralized
organization, based partly on centuries-old traditions
going back to the ancient Oriental patriarchates and
partly on more modern conditions. It consists of a
number of local or national churches, all enjoying an
"autocephalous" status, that is to say, possessing the
right to choose their own heads, the bishops (Greek
auto-, "self," *kephale,* "head"). Some of these churches
are contained within the boundaries of one state and
are, in effect, national churches. Others, especially in
the Near East, possess more traditional boundaries
and include faithful belonging to several nationalities.
Canonically speaking, the boundaries of all the local
churches are not national but territorial in nature, and
correspond to former metropolitan provinces; that is,
they form groups of dioceses whose bishops meet regularly in synod and elect their own primate, who bears
the title of patriarch, archbishop, or metropolitan.
Bound together by observance of a common canonical
tradition, these churches give expression to their communion of faith by holding general councils from time
to time, as the need arises. As we have seen, councils

[1] Of the 450,000,000 Roman Catholics in the world (or
nearer 500,000,000 according to recent statistics), some 200,-
000,000 are in South America, but it is admitted even by
Catholic authorities that the number of practicing Catholics in
Latin America does not exceed 10 per cent of the nominally
Catholic total population. The same situation obtains—by per-
centage—in certain nominally Protestant countries of Europe,
particularly in Scandinavia.

including all or some of these autocephalous churches were frequently held, even after the close of the medieval period.

The relations of these autocephalous churches with each other are determined by a kind of hierarchy of honor, headed by the "ecumenical" patriarch of Constantinople as *primus inter pares*. The order of precedence among the three other Oriental patriarchates (Alexandria, Antioch, Jerusalem) was fixed in the fifth century. In spite of its great size and importance, the patriarchate of Moscow, established in 1589, is accorded only fifth place in this hierarchy. Other autocephalous churches are assigned a place in accordance with the date when they became ecclesiastically independent.

This system, which is theoretically nothing more than an adaptation of ancient canon law to modern conditions, undoubtedly has the great advantage of being very elastic. It permits autocephalous churches to be founded, abolished, then re-established again in the course of history without affecting the entire organization of the Church. Moreover, the absence of any binding centralized authority permits the various hierarchies of the churches today to adopt different political attitudes without rupturing the doctrinal and sacramental bonds of unity. When conditions become more propitious, the leaders can once more re-establish cordial relations, without too much difficulty. The disadvantages of the system, however, are equally obvious. Independent by right and in fact, the autocephalous churches are too inclined to live in isolation from each other, they are unable to take any common action effectively, and they lack a common system for the training of the clergy. The effects of nationalism, that disease which ravaged eastern Europe in the nineteenth and twentieth centuries, can be overcome in the ecclesiastical sphere only with great difficulty.

The Church often comes to be regarded as nothing more than a mere adjunct of the nation, a mere instrument useful in helping to preserve the language and customs of the people. Because the missionaries from Byzantium everywhere rendered the sacred liturgy in the languages of the people and transplanted to Slavic soil not only the religion of Byzantium but the Byzantine theory of the Christian state, a fertile ground was prepared for the development of the modern, essentially secularized, form of nationalism. Everywhere in Eastern Europe the Orthodox Church has remained an essentially popular church. This is one of the important factors enabling it to survive the Turkish and Mongol yokes, and this is what holds in check today the Marxist theory of religion as an "instrument in the hands of the exploiting classes." But these very factors are also the source of a certain weakness, because they make it difficult for the Church to bear witness, *in action*, to the universal and transcendent nature of the Truth. However, the historical age in which we live has forced us to distinguish between the absolute and the relative, between Church and state, between Christ and the nation. And thus it is compelling the Orthodox world today to make a choice between mere human traditions and Revelation, and to retain only what constitutes the essential of the Christian message. From numerous signs, which will be noted in our brief survey of the present situation of the several churches, it would seem that an entirely new age appears to be dawning in Orthodox history.

1. The Ecumenical Patriarchate of Constantinople

The second and fourth ecumenical councils gave the Church of Constantinople "equal privileges" to those of the Roman Church, while reserving to the latter its

traditional primacy of honor. Since the schism between West and East the patriarch of Constantinople
enjoys a primatial status in the Orthodox Church. His
title is "archbishop of Constantinople-New Rome and
ecumenical patriarch." [2] As diocesan bishop of Constantinople (which is known today as Istanbul) he
exercises direct patriarchal authority over four metropolitan sees in Turkey, the miserable remains of the
once flourishing Greek Christian communities in Asia
Minor, which became mere titles when the Greek
population left as a result of the Greek-Turkish War
(1922). To give him added prestige, however, the
Greek Church and government agreed to leave under
the patriarch's authority the dioceses of the Greek
islands, and in a purely nominal way, those of northern Greece also. Moreover, the patriarchate exercises
jurisdiction over a certain number of dioceses of Greeks,
Russians, and Ukrainians belonging to the Orthodox Diaspora (in Western Europe, North and South
America, Australia, and New Zealand) and over the
Orthodox Church in Finland.[3] Since the last war his
jurisdiction over the Baltic countries has been taken
over by the patriarch of Moscow.

Thus the patriarchate which once exercised authority over vast stretches of the Orthodox world, as we
have seen, under the Byzantine Empire and under the
Turkish yoke which followed, has now been reduced
to a very small image of its former self. The various
Orthodox Churches in the Balkans obtained their
autocephalous status in the nineteenth century and the
Greeks in Asia Minor left the territory of the patriarchate in the twentieth. It is only with the help of

[2] The title of ecumenical patriarch goes back at least to 588
and therefore long antedates the schism.
[3] We shall have more to say in detail further on with regard
to the situation of the Orthodox Church in the West.

has been able to survive the various trials which he has been through and has continued to maintain his headquarters in the Greek quarter of Constantinople known as the Phanar. The ecumenical patriarchate owes its prestige today, therefore, not to the fact that it exercises ecclesiastical jurisdiction over less than two millions of the faithful (nearly half of whom are in America), but to the primacy of honor which it traditionally has among the various autocephalous churches.

Basically, his authority consists of the right of initiative, which the other patriarchates acknowledge as belonging to the ecumenical patriarch in matters of common concern. The ecumenical council of Chalcedon (451) also granted him the important right to hear appeals from other churches (Canon 17) and placed under his jurisdiction the missionary areas (in "barbarous" countries) which lay beyond the Roman dioceses of Thrace, Asia, and Pontus (Canon 28): in the fifth century this meant essentially the regions of Eastern Europe and the Caucasus. Some modern canonists tend to interpret this canon more liberally and would grant to the ecumenical patriarch jurisdiction over the entire Orthodox Diaspora (which he already possesses in part).

The patriarch of Constantinople is elected by the metropolitans of the patriarchate.[4] A synod of twelve bishops assists him in running ecclesiastical affairs and appoints the bishops for vacant sees. There is a patriarchal seminary on the island of Halki, in the Princes Islands, which receives students from nearly all the Near Eastern countries.

The present occupant of the ecumenical see is His Holiness Athenagoras I, who was elected in 1948.

---

[4] Until 1922 the patriarch, who was then also political head of the Greeks in Turkey, was elected by a somewhat larger body, including laymen.

Also under the jurisdiction of the ecumenical patriarchate is the world-famous monastic republic of Mount Athos, an important spiritual center and remarkable survival of medieval Byzantine monasticism. Dating from the tenth century, the monasteries of Athos have survived in spite of all kinds of trials and still had 2,700 monks in 1952. In the seventeenth and eighteenth centuries Athos went through a critical period and the number of monks greatly declined. It increased again in the nineteenth century, owing particularly to a large influx of Russian novices, so that, by 1913, Mount Athos had a population of 6,345. Since then, however, as a result of the generally unfavorable conditions prevailing in the Orthodox world, this number has steadily declined, and the situation is likely to remain precarious until better days return.

Isolated from the rest of the world on their Chalcidic peninsula, living under conditions which have not varied essentially since the Middle Ages, the monks of Athos are grouped into twenty monasteries, distributed over the area of the peninsula, and by means of their representatives govern the region. The land belongs by right to the Kingdom of Greece, but enjoys an international status. Of the twenty monasteries, seventeen are Greek (though sometimes with monks from other countries), one Russian, one Serbian, and one Bulgarian. There was also, formerly, a Georgian monastery, and in the Middle Ages there were even Latin monasteries. Scattered over the peninsula of Athos there are also a great many hermitages, the *skiti* and *kellia,* in which monks of various origins live in accordance with different rules. Certain *skiti* are actually large monasteries, while others are mere anchoritic cells.

As a unique example of a monastic republic which, in former days, once gave a number of great theologians and doctors to the Church, Athos can still claim to be a spiritual center for all the Orthodox. However, it suffers under certain disabilities at the present time. The monks are recruited almost exclusively from the rural Greek countryside, they are intellectually isolated (this being sometimes wrongly regarded as an ascetic virtue), and they receive almost no new vocations today from any countries other than Greece—these are the important reasons contributing to their decline. To remedy the situation, in part, at least, the ecumenical patriarch established a theological school on Athos in 1953. Recently, the international situation has improved sufficiently to enable a number of new monks to arrive from Yugoslavia, but Athos should really be opened to novices from all countries, if it wishes to recover its former glory.

2. The Patriarchate of Alexandria

At the time of the great Christological controversies in the fifth and sixth centuries, the greater number of Egyptian Christians refused to recognize the authority of the Council of Chalcedon (451) and formed the Monophysite or Coptic Church, which "Orthodox" is still the largest Christian body in Egypt. By contrast, the Orthodox constituted only a small minority and were known as Melkites (the "King's people"). They were Greek-speaking (whereas the Copts adopted the native Egyptian language for their liturgy) and were long regarded as foreigners in the land. Their numbers declined to such a point that from the sixteenth to the eighteenth century the Orthodox patriarch of Alexandria almost never resided in Egypt but remained in Constantinople. It was only toward the beginning of the twentieth century that the Greek Orthodox population began to increase, owing to the immigration of Greeks and Syrians. However, the number of the Orthodox in Egypt has never amounted to more than 200,000. The Greek community in Egypt has a number of hospitals and schools. Owing to the present political and economic situation in Egypt, it is rapidly decreasing.

Although his flock is rather small in Egypt, the patriarch of Alexandria has jurisdiction over all the Orthodox in Africa.

Candidates for the patriarchate are elected by a council or synod of thirty-six clergy and seventy laymen, which draws up a list of three names, one of whom is then chosen by the Holy Synod. Until the beginning of 1959, there were eight metropolitans (Tripoli, Ismailia, Port Said, Tanta, Addis Ababa, Johannesburg, Khartum, and Tunis). Three new sees have just been established (Accra, Central Africa, and East Africa) as a result of the missionary activity of the patriarchate. The patriarchal see of Alexandria is occupied at the present time by His Beatitude Christopher II, who was elected in 1939.

3. The Patriarchate of Antioch

Antioch on the Orontes was once the third largest city in the Roman Empire, after Rome and Alexandria. It is today no more than a small village on Turkish soil. The patriarch, whose jurisdiction goes back to a once glorious past, resides in Damascus. The Church over which he presides, and which includes about 400,000 faithful in Syria and Lebanon, consists of the largest group of Arabic-speaking Christians there is. Important groups are also found in Iraq and in America (more than 100,000).

From 1724 until 1899 the patriarch and all the bishops were Greek prelates, appointed because of the preponderance of Greek influence which the Phanar was able to exercise under Turkish rule. Since then, in part owing to Russian influence, Arabs have been

elected to the see of Antioch. The procedure for patriarchal elections, which takes place in several stages,
has recently been modified to allow the laity to play a
greater role. The patriarch is not assisted by a permanent synod, but the metropolitans meet once a year,
after Easter, in accordance with ancient canonical custom. There are ten metropolitan sees in all (Aleppo,
Sheikh Tabba, Beirut, Homs, Hama, Latakia, Zahle,
Tripoli, Tyre and Sidon, and Baghdad). Three other
bishops, responsible to the patriarch, govern the faithful in North and South America.

Although possessing only a few educated clergy, the
Arab Orthodox in Syria and Lebanon have nevertheless experienced something of a revival since World
War II, thanks to the Orthodox Youth Movement,
founded by enterprising young university graduates.
The movement interests itself in a variety of activities:
preaching, the establishment of schools, the publication of a remarkable periodical in Arabic (*An-Nur*),
sending members abroad to study theology and thus
provide new ranks for the clergy, and the founding of
monastic communities (Deir-el-Harf on Mount Lebanon, for example). There are thus great hopes for the
future.

The patriarchal see is occupied at present by His
Beatitude Theodosius VI.

4. The Patriarchate of Jerusalem

Established as an independent patriarchate by the
Council of Chalcedon (451), the see of Jerusalem,
especially after the Arab conquest, devoted itself
primarily to protecting the Holy Places. Its present
constitution is also largely oriented toward this need.
A kind of monastic order, the Confraternity of the
Holy Sepulcher, sees to this responsibility. The bishops and church officials are chosen from among its

members. The patriarch himself is the head of the body, which consists of a hundred members, all of whom are Greeks. The faithful, by contrast, are all Arabs. The Orthodox of Jerusalem have suffered considerably as a result of recent events in Palestine and today amount to no more than about 50,000, many of whom are emigrating to Syria or Lebanon.

In addition to the patriarch, there is a Holy Synod composed of six titular archbishops (Sebaste, Mount Tabor, Diocaesarea, Philadelphia, Eleutheropolis, and Tiberias). The lower clergy is entirely Arab in origin. A mixed council—including Arab laymen—was created in 1911, but friction between Greeks and Arabs is frequent, particularly when there is a patriarchal election. The different statutes of the patriarchate have gradually made allowance for greater participation by the Arab clergy and faithful in the affairs of the patriarchate.

The Laura of Mar-Saba, an ancient high place of Oriental monasticism, is today inhabited by only twenty monks. It lies within the jurisdiction of the patriarchate. The Russians formerly came in droves on pilgrimage to Jerusalem and still have two convents of nuns there.

Since 1957 the see of Jerusalem has been occupied by His Beatitude Benedict I.

5. The Patriarchate of Moscow

Until the fall of 1959, it was possible to maintain that the Russian Orthodox Church had reached a relatively stable point in its relations with the state, as a result of events during the last war. However, the events of the last two years have shown that this stability is quite precarious. During the period of stability (1946-1959), it was still extremely difficult to obtain reliable information concerning the number of the faithful.

The reason for this was given by the Patriarch Alexis himself, in an interview granted to the Reuters Agency in 1948: "Because of the separation of Church and state, and also because of religious freedom, we do not now have at our disposal a list of all the faithful, as was formerly the case in Russia." [5] This very revealing statement means that the Church on the one hand no longer is in a position to compile accurate statistics, the latter being the monopoly of the state, and, on the other, that the drawing up of lists of the faithful, which could be used for various purposes of control, would be regarded as an infringement of the liberty of the individual faithful, which he now enjoys, since religious conviction and practice are not a matter of official record. Because of this dearth of statistics, we are therefore obliged to resort to generalizations and estimates, based on sparse official information and accounts which frequently appear in the press. The estimate of roughly 25,000 parishes for the whole country, substantiated by various trustworthy sources,[6] seems to be reliable. Since witnesses unanimously report that the churches are always extraordinarily full and several of them could hold several thousand of the faithful, it does not seem unreasonable to conclude that the number of the faithful per church is about 2,000. Using this figure as a basis, we thus arrive at a total of about

[5] Quoted in *Le Problème religieux en U.R.S.S.—II: Données et documents sur l'organisation actuelle des différentes églises et associations religieuses,* in *La Documentation française,* No. 1931 (Oct. 9, 1954), p. 4. This study (Nos. 1624 and 1931 of the *Documentation*) contains very complete information on the status of religion in Russia.

[6] See especially A. Serguéenko, in *Messager du patriarchat russe en Europe occidentale,* No. 2 (1957), p. 13. G. Karpov, an official of the Soviet government, in charge of the Council for the Affairs of the Orthodox Church, mentioned, in 1949, the figure of 22,000 parishes (*U.S.S.R. Information Bulletin* [Washington, January, 1949], pp. 54-56). The difference of 3,000 between the two figures can be explained by the existence of "prayer houses," to which A. Serguéenko also refers.

50,000,000 practicing Orthodox in the Soviet Union, or about 25 per cent of the population of the Soviet Union at the present time. This number could possibly be even higher.[7]

In spite of the violent persecution to which it has been subjected, and in spite of forty years of Marxist propaganda, the Orthodox Church has therefore retained the allegiance of about half its membership.[8] As, moreover, the practice of religion in Russia today still exposes the individual (and families) to discrimination of one kind or another—he may find it difficult to be promoted in his job or may acquire a bad political or professional reputation, factors which in large part explain why the churches are filled with so many women and old men—it is virtually certain that the hidden influence of religion is much greater still. The most serious problem confronting the Church in Russia remains that of education. While it is still capable of attracting large numbers of the faithful, it does not possess the means of instructing them in any way except through the liturgy and by sermons inside places of worship. Yet, rich as the liturgical tradition of the Orthodox Church is in suggestive imagery, this alone

[7] The city of Moscow today has a population of 6,000,000, with only 55 churches open (compared with 657 before 1917). The method we have employed to calculate the number of the faithful (2,000 per church) would only allow about 110,000 practicing Orthodox for Moscow, but this number seems to be much too small, since according to a statement of Fr. Kolchitzky, an important official of the patriarchate, 50 per cent of all infants born in the capital are baptized (*Le Problème religieux en U.R.S.S.*, p. 4). In the country, the proportion would of course be even higher.

[8] In 1914 there were officially 98,500,000 Orthodox in the Russian Empire. If all the infants born of Orthodox parents were instructed in the faith of the parents the normal rise in the populations would have brought the number of Orthodox today to 130 or 140 million (see *Le Problème religieux en U.R.S.S., loc cit.*). Among non-Christian religions, Islam has the next greatest number of adherents in the USSR, with nearly 30 million (nominal).

cannot, except to a very limited extent, make up for the complete absence of religious publications and schools other than those intended for the training of the clergy.

The following table illustrates these various aspects of the present situation rather graphically, namely, the miraculous revival of the Church between 1941 and 1947, but its almost complete impotence in the field of education.[9]

Almost totally nonexistent in 1941, the machinery of church government was re-established in 1943 when Metropolitan Sergius was elected patriarch, and especially by the council of 1945 which, in the presence of two Oriental patriarchs (Christopher of Alexandria and Alexander of Antioch), a delegate from the ecumenical patriarch of Constantinople and several delegates from other churches, proceeded to elect the present patriarch, Alexis,[10] and approved new

[9] The table is taken—with some slight modifications—from *Le Problème religieux en U.R.S.S.*

	1914	1941	1947
Churches	54,457	4,255	22 to 25,000
Chapels	25,593	?	3,500
Priests at their posts	57,105	5,665	33,000
Monasteries and convents	1,498	38	80
Theological academies	4	none	2
Seminaries	57	none	8
Various religious schools	40,150	none	none

[10] Born in 1877 in Moscow of a family of aristocratic origins, the present patriarch (whose secular name is Sergei Vladimirovich Simanski) received a brilliant general education and then embraced the ecclesiastical state. In 1913 he was consecrated a bishop. He gained some prominence because of his political activity, oriented toward the right. As auxiliary to Benjamin, metropolitan of Petrograd, when the latter was tried and condemned to death in 1922 (cf. above p. 136), he took charge of the see. During the difficult years (1922-1941) he adhered without fail to the conciliatory policy of Sergius as metropolitan of Leningrad.

statutes for the Orthodox Church. In contrast to
the Statutes of 1917-1918, the government of the
Church is now centralized in the hands of the patriarch, who, with a synod of six bishops, exercises almost autocratic authority, particularly in the matter of
the appointment and frequent transfer of bishops
from one diocese to another. Laymen, theoretically,
are members of the national council which elects the
patriarch, but the Statutes do not specify the way in
which they are to be chosen. This unusually brief
document was adopted without debate. Its incomplete
nature shows that the Church continues to live under
conditions which it is unable to control in all respects.[11]

The Russian Church now has seventy-three dioceses
inside the Soviet Union[12] and several exarchates or
missions abroad. The clergy is given preliminary
training in seminaries and the most promising students are then sent on to one of the two theological
academies or graduate schools (Zagorsk near Moscow, and Leningrad). The exact number of students
attending these institutions is only partially known.
The numbers increased rapidly during the years after
the war. The Seminary and Academy of Zagorsk
jointly had 108 students in 1947, 320 in 1951-1952, and
396 in 1953.[13] In January 1961, for the first time, the
Journal of the Moscow Patriarchate, published in Moscow, gave the number of graduating students in June

[11] Complete French translation of the Statutes in *Le Problème religieux en U.R.S.S.*, pp. 13-15. In connection with recent
antireligious policies of the state, the Statutes were recently
(1961) modified. They now give an increased power of control to laymen on the parish level.

[12] The number of Russian dioceses has been traditionally
small since the Middle Ages. There were only sixty-seven in
1914 for 100 million Orthodox. There are approximately the
same number in Greece for 6 million inhabitants. *Le Problème
religieux en U.R.S.S.* gives a list of the present Russian bishops
and some biographic details about each.

[13] *Le Problème religieux en U.R.S.S.*, p. 9.

1960: forty-three students graduated from both academies and 185 from the eight seminaries. Of the latter, 119 were ordained and received parish assignments, while sixty-six were sent to do graduate work in the academies. It hardly needs to be pointed out that these numbers are ridiculously small when compared with the needs of some fifty million faithful! This graduation took place before the recent measures aimed at restricting theological education, which will be mentioned below. Considerable difficulty has been encountered in the recruitment of competent professors, since the ranks of personnel trained in the pre-Revolutionary institutions have greatly dwindled. To judge by certain articles appearing in the *Journal of the Moscow Patriarchate* and from personal contacts which now become possible, however, it seems that the academic level is now beginning to rise appreciably. Russian theologians still suffer a great deal from their enforced isolation from the rest of the world. They have so far been forbidden to publish any books or manuals,[14] and current theological literature can be

[14] The few publications of the patriarchate are concerned with the liturgy (calendars, special liturgical offices) or are in the nature of propaganda. In the latter category must be reckoned the above-mentioned *Journal of the Moscow Patriarchate* (a monthly periodical in Russian, which always includes articles on political themes, especially on the movement of the Partisans for Peace) and several collections of the sermons of Patriarch Alexis and Metropolitan Nicholas of Krutica, in which articles or sermons of a strictly spiritual or theological nature are always accompanied by others with a definite political slant. The Bible, and the New Testament separately, were recently published in Russia for the first time in forty years, but the number of copies printed did not exceed 50,000—and most of these were sold abroad. The apostolic value of this output is therefore very slight. The patriarchate has no Slavonic press. The liturgical books used by the Church date either from before the Revolution or are imported from Czechoslovakia. Some photographic reproductions of old editions have appeared recently in Russia. No work of a theological nature or indeed on Christianity at all has been published since 1918.

obtained from the West only with the greatest difficulty. The publication of a Russian theological periodical, long announced, took place in 1960. Only one issue
has appeared so far.

The Statutes adopted in 1945 clearly refer to the
control which the government intends to exercise over
the religious activities of the clergy. The government's
"authorization" is required before a synod of bishops
can be summoned—such an assembly has been held
as a matter of fact only twice since 1918—and a national council (comprising clergy and laity) may be
summoned, curiously, "if this is externally possible"
(par. 7). Paragraph 11 stipulates, moreover, that "for
questions requiring the consent of the government of
the USSR, the patriarch will communicate with the
Council of Affairs of the Orthodox Church of the Council of Ministers of the USSR." The personal signature
and seal of the patriarch (par. 16), the bishops (par.
26), and parish curates (par. 48) must be registered
with the civil authorities, which thus gives the latter the
formal right to control the nominations to all ecclesiastical appointments. The Council of Affairs of the Orthodox Church attached to the Council of Ministers is
a government office with ramifications throughout the
Soviet Union. All requests for the use of places of
worship, which by law belong to the state, have to be
made to it and may be granted under certain conditions (pars. 39, 41, etc.). Moreover, the patriarch of
Moscow never fails to publish solemn declarations,
signed by the patriarch and bishops, approving the
position of the Soviet government on all major questions of international politics, such as the Korean war,
the problem of nuclear disarmament, French-English
intervention in Suez, the Hungarian revolt, and so
forth.

It would be simplifying the problem, however, to
consider the patriarchate of Moscow a mere political

tool in the hands of the Soviet government. Its humil-
iating status of subservience to the latter on all questions relating to international affairs is, in effect, the
price which the Church must pay for its continued
existence inside the USSR. Yet, curiously enough, far
from being considered the friend of the government
there, it finds itself constantly the butt of repeated
attacks.

Since the fall of 1959, the government has appar-
ently decided upon a new wave of measures hostile
to the Church, in a manner which reminds one more
and more of the prewar days. In December 1959, the
newspapers and the radio gave wide publicity to the
statement of a former Orthodox priest, Ossipov, a professor of theology in the Leningrad Academy, who
left the Church and then violently attacked all religious belief and the system of theological education re-
established by the patriarchate in particular.[15] Simul-
taneously, new impetus was given to the antireligious
campaign in various publications.

This new and direct challenge gave the patriarchate
an opportunity to show that it was not a mere tool of
the government. A decision of the Holy Synod was
published in Moscow in the official *Journal of the
Moscow Patriarchate*,[16] excommunicating Ossipov and
two of his followers for having "publicly blasphemed
the Name of God." The patriarch himself, invited to
speak in February 1960 at a conference on disarmament in Moscow, courageously proclaimed: "The Savior himself predicted that there would be attacks
against Christianity and promised that the Church
will remain unshaken and that the gates of hell will
not prevail against it." [17]

[15] *Pravda*, Dec. 6, 1959, No. 340 (15099).
[16] 1960, No. 2, Feb., p. 27.
[17] *Messager de l'exarchat du Patriarche russe en Europe Occidentale*, Nos. 33-34 (January-July, 1960), pp. 8-10.

The government intensified its attacks on the Church. Job, the archbishop of Kazan, was publicly tried and sentenced to three years in prison for "illegal traffic in candles." Although widely publicized in the Soviet press, the trial was not mentioned in the official journal of the patriarchate. In December 1961, Andrew, archbishop of Chernigov, was sentenced to *eight* years of prison under a similar pretext. Finally, the government carried out a number of administrative measures calculated to have far-reaching effects, by closing two of the eight seminaries allowed to be open, and more than five hundred churches and several monasteries.

Nothing could be more paradoxical, therefore, than the present situation of the Russian Church. As the loyal ally of the Soviet government in international affairs abroad, it is treated inside Russia as a "vestige of capitalism," and the government-controlled press is continually proclaiming that materialism is incompatible with "religious prejudices." But this paradoxical situation also applies to the Soviet government itself, for it is obliged to reconcile with Marxist principles the fact that church dignitaries are present at official receptions, and is powerless to deny that there are some fifty million practicing Christians in Russia today after forty years of "socialism." The fact that this paradoxical situation still exists is a sign of hope for the future. Externally the Church seems strong enough to be able to resist material liquidation. However, there are temptations of a subtler nature which it must face. The clergy controls rather large sums of money —the voluntary contributions of the faithful who crowd the churches—but has no means of spending them. The temptation may be simply to raise the standard of clerical life, without making any attempt to improve the effectiveness of the Church's mission. Is this not precisely the very aim of the Communist Party?—to transform the Church into an opulent vestige of the departed past, and then to compromise it in the eyes of the people. It seems that this was actually the purpose of the recent trial of the archbishops of Kazan and Chernigov.

Fortunately, there is continual evidence in the Soviet press of the purely spiritual influence which the Russian Church can still wield over large sections of the population and which gives hope that Russian Orthodoxy will be able to surmount its present difficulties.

6. The Serbian Orthodox Church

St. Sabbas, the brother of St. Stephen the "First-crowned," was consecrated as the first Serbian archbishop at Nicaea in 1220. From that time until the Turkish conquest the Serbian Church experienced a rather prosperous period within the cultural orbit of Byzantium, while at the same time being virtually independent of the ecumenical patriarchate ecclesiastically. Its autocephalous status was only suppressed by Constantinople in 1766.

Several Serbian autocephalous churches were formed in the nineteenth century in parts of the Balkan Peninsula not subject to Turkish rule. These were:

1. The *Church of Montenegro,* with a metropolitan resident at Cetinje.

2. The *Patriarchate of Karlowitz* (*Sremski Karlovci*), founded in 1848, which included all the Orthodox Serbs in the Kingdom of Hungary.

3. The *Metropolitanate of Czernowitz* (*Chernovtsy* or *Cernauti*), which included both Rumanians and Serbs, and to which two dioceses in Dalmatia (Zara and Kotor or Cattaro) were added in 1873. In effect, this church had under its jurisdiction all the Orthodox in the Austro-Hungarian Empire.

4. The *Serbian Church of the Kingdom of Serbia,* autonomous since 1832, then autocephalous (1879).

5. The *Church of Bosnia-Herzegovina,* which was formed in 1878 in provinces annexed by the Austro-Hungarian Empire but never became completely autocephalous with respect to Constantinople.

These five churches were united in 1920, under a primate residing in Belgrade, to form the Serbian Church, and included all the Orthodox in the new state of Yugoslavia. The ecumenical patriarch approved the new arrangement on March 9, 1922 and recognized the head of the Church as patriarch. Before the last war the Serbian patriarch also had jurisdiction over the Rumanian Banat of Temesvar and the diocese of Mukacevo (in Czechoslovakia), as well as over certain Orthodox parishes in Hungary. Today there are a total of thirty-one dioceses on Yugoslav soil.

Until 1940 the Church possessed five seminaries and a theological faculty. Now, after the separation of Church and state, it has only two seminaries, one at Belgrade and the other at Prizren, and the faculty which has been detached from the University and is called the Patriarchal Faculty. There were about 7,500,000 faithful in 1950, with 3,101 priests and 2,864 parishes.

During the last two decades the Serbian Church has gone through a series of trials, which began in 1941 and which have not been very fully reported in the West. Patriarch Gabriel and Nicholas, the bishop of Ohrid, were arrested by the Germans as soon as the latter occupied Yugoslavia, and deported to Dachau. The Serbian faithful, whose clergy often gave support to the resistance movement, were treated with unheard-of severity, not so much by the Germans as by the fascist authorities of the state of Croatia, which was supported by the occupiers of the country. These

Croatians were in large measure Roman Catholics, but it is difficult to say exactly what motives—religious, political or national—were primarily responsible for the frightful massacres that took place during the occupation. In the majority of cases, however, the real excuse for the executions appears to have been the fact of belonging to the Orthodox Church. Thus the Orthodox bishop of Planski, Sabbas, was executed along with 137 of his priests (only five priests remained alive in the diocese). Bishops Plato of Banja Luka and Peter of Sarajevo were also executed along with many of their clergy. Serbian sources, corroborated by the present Yugoslav government, estimate the total number of victims at about 700,000.[18]

The moral prestige of the Serbian Orthodox Church was therefore very high at the end of the war. Patriarch Gabriel returned from Dachau to face at home a "popular democratic" form of government, one of whose first acts was to decree the separation of Church and state. The majority of bishops were outspokenly anticommunist. In this respect the Serbian hierarchy differed decidedly from the Orthodox bishops in other Balkan countries. While anxious not to create any new martyrs—one bishop (Joannice of Montenegro) and several priests, however, were executed—the government of Tito nevertheless treated certain prelates very harshly. A series of notorious trials took place: Barnabas of Sarajevo (consecrated bishop in 1947) was condemned in 1949 to eleven years of forced labor; Joseph of Skoplié was arrested in 1950, at the time of the patriarchal election (he was the most likely candidate for the office); Arsenius of Montenegro was arrested and sentenced in July 1954.

[18] See the official documents pertaining to the trial of Cardinal Stepinac. See also the book *Persecution of the Serbian Church in Yugoslavia*, published by the Serbian Orthodox Church in the United States (Chicago, 1954).

The situation seems to be somewhat improved at the present time, owing to a more conciliatory attitude on the part of the Patriarchs Vincent (1954-1958) and Germanus (elected in 1959). The Holy Synod, however, has refused until now to recognize the activities of the government-sponsored Association of Priests, and opposes all efforts aimed at restricting its authority. These efforts—openly supported by the government—have to do principally with the creation of churches independent of the patriarch in the various constituent parts of the republic. A compromise solution recently put an end to a dispute of this kind relating to Macedonia: the Church there will enjoy a certain amount of ecclesiastical autonomy, but the Holy Synod in Belgrade retains canonical authority over the Macedonian Church as such.

The heroic struggle of the Serbian clergy has thus won for them an unquestioned moral prestige both in Yugoslavia and abroad. It is uncertain, however, whether they will be able to meet the challenge of the new society now being molded. In Yugoslavia, as elsewhere, the Church finds itself largely deprived of the means of assuring the religious education of the youth and the training of the future clergy. Since Tito's break with the Comintern, however, Yugoslav Orthodox are now less isolated from the rest of the world than their brethren in the other communist-dominated countries. Contacts with Greece, Constantinople, and the Near East have now become quite frequent, as we can see, for example, by the recent trips to those countries of Serbian prelates, particularly Patriarchs Vincent and Germanus.

7. The Rumanian Orthodox Church

Two autocephalous Rumanian-speaking churches were established in the nineteenth century: one in

Transylvania, in the Austro-Hungarian Monarchy; the other, by act of the ecumenical patriarch in 1885, in the newly independent state of Rumania. Many Rumanian-speaking Orthodox were also subject to the Serbo-Rumanian metropolitan of Czernowitz or Cernauti (see above). Like the Serbian patriarchate, the present Rumanian Church thus was formed from a coalescence of various groups which took place in 1925, when the title of "Patriarch of the Rumanian Church" was adopted by the archbishop of Bucharest.

With nearly 12,000,000 faithful, the Orthodox Church of Rumania is today the largest of the autocephalous Orthodox churches after that of Russia. After being closely tied to the old monarchy—the Patriarch Myron once presided over the Council of Ministers—it too has had to face the brutal shock of a change in regime. The attitude adopted by the present government authorities toward the Rumanian Church differs considerably from that prevailing elsewhere. Paradoxically the new communist state has never published a decree separating Church and state, but in August 1948 a law recognized the "general regime of religion" in the popular democratic Republic of Rumania. This law abolishes the role that the Church once played in the state and in education, but preserves the control which the state always exercised over the Church. The paradoxical situation which exists in all the communist-dominated states is thus written into the very text of the constitution in Rumania. Although regarded as a lay republic, Rumania possesses a constitution which mentions the Orthodox Church and defines it as a "unified church with its own head." Though inspired by Marxist principles, the state pays the salaries of the clergy and supports Church-run schools. Bishops must swear an oath of allegiance to the state before the Minister of Religion when they are installed ("As a servant of God, as a

man and a citizen, I swear to be faithful to the People
and to defend the Popular Rumanian Republic against
its enemies both internal and external. . . . So help
me God")!

By acquiescing in this state of affairs the Rumanian
hierarchy runs the risk of appearing in the eyes of its
own faithful, and in those of the world at large, as a
mere body of officials at the beck and call of the government, whose ultimate and avowed aim is the
destruction of all "religious prejudices." In fact, however, what we know about the religious situation in
Rumania before 1959 seems to suggest that the Church
has gained certain advantages in exchange for this
formal government control—the Church had 8,326
parishes, 10,153 priests, 182 monasteries, and 11,506,-
217 faithful, and was able to retain a part of its property. Two theological institutes were functioning, with
thirty professors, one at Bucharest (290 students) and
the other at Sibiu (338 students); the Church published about a dozen religious periodicals, one of
which, the review *Studi Teologice,* is by far the best
Orthodox theological publication appearing behind
the Iron Curtain. Religious instruction may not be
given, officially, to youths who are under eighteen—
as in all communist countries—but this serious gap was
made up partially by the existence of six "schools of
cantors" where students remained for three years and
received a general religious education (there were
759 in 1959). Moreover, the revival of monasticism
constituted until recently one of the brightest spots for
Orthodoxy in Rumania. Orthodox monks in Rumania
in 1959 totaled more than 7,000.[19] In order to raise

[19] See on this subject D. I. Doens, "La Réforme législative
du patriarche Justinien de Roumanie. Sa Réforme et sa Règle
monastique," in the Belgian periodical *Irénikon,* Vol. XXVII,
No. 1, pp. 51-92; supplementary note in No. 3, pp. 331-51; and
information in Vol. XXXIV, 1961, p. 199; for the spiritual and
intellectual life in the monasteries, see Un Moine de l'Église

the intellectual level of these institutions, to make them veritable spiritual centers for the whole Church and thus refute the charge of the government that they were "unproductive institutions," Patriarch Justinian (elected in 1948) published a common Rule for Rumanian monks, based on the traditional principles of Oriental monasticism but also incorporating certain features of the Benedictine Rule. Liturgical and private prayers, particularly the Prayer of Jesus, were accorded their accustomed place, but, on the other hand, greater emphasis was given to manual work and to intensive intellectual labor, which could serve to justify the existence of the monasteries "socially" and enable them to respond, in an original and creative way, to the challenge of the socialist regime by integrating the monasteries in the new economic life of the country. The Rule provided for the establishment of monastic seminaries, of which three were actually in existence: a seminary for monks in the monastery of Neamt, founded by the Staretz Paisij Velickovskij, the translator of the *Philocalia* in the eighteenth century (38 students); and two others for nuns at Agapia and Hurezu (124 novices in all). The monastic revival has been aided by the publication of a number of spiritual works, particularly a Rumanian translation of the Fathers of the Church (*Philocalia*).

Unfortunately, this entire development was brought to an end by the severe measures taken by the government beginning in July 1958. Many church leaders, including—temporarily—Patriarch Justinian himself, were arrested and several hundreds of monks and priests were reduced to the lay state. Among those condemned to a long imprisonment were several noted professors of theology, in particular Father Stanilooe, the learned editor of the Rumanian *Philocalia*. During

orthodoxe de Roumanie, "L'Avènement philocalique dans l'Orthodoxie roumaine," in *Istina*, Nos. 3 and 4 (1958).

the latter half of 1960 more than 4,000 Orthodox monks and nuns were reported to have been arrested.[20]

The Rumanian Church at present has a total of twelve dioceses, which form three metropolitan provinces. The patriarch and a Holy Synod have supreme control over all ecclesiastical affairs. Approximately 10,000 priests are now (or were) serving the faithful.

The future of the Church in Rumania as well as the other countries of Eastern Europe depends largely on the effectiveness of the antireligious propaganda being aimed at the youth. The measures available to the Church for counteracting this poison are very limited indeed and are practically reduced to the personal witness that individual practicing Christians can make in the new materialist world which the government leaders are trying to build.

8. The Bulgarian Orthodox Church

The Bulgarians were baptized in the ninth century by Byzantine missionaries in the time of the great patriarch Photius and at his instigation. Ecclesiastical independence was soon attained, but again abolished when the Byzantines conquered the country in the tenth century, then re-established once more in the thirteenth century with the restoration of the patriarchate of Trnovo. Under the Turkish regime it was abolished once again in favor of the supremacy of the Phanar. The question of independence was long a sore point in the nineteenth and twentieth centuries, for the Bulgarians were governed by Greek bishops who, especially in the towns, sought to suppress the Slavonic liturgy and generally Hellenize the Church. There was great longing for ecclesiastical autonomy and feelings ran high on both sides. Several of the

[20] *Irénikon,* Vol. XXXIV (1961), p. 199.

ecumenical patriarchs tried to satisfy the legitimate claims of the Bulgarians in the course of the nineteenth century, but they always failed because of the hopeless way in which the two populations were mixed up with each other in the Balkan area. In Constantinople itself they lived side by side, but the Bulgarians, inspired by nationalist feelings, demanded the establishment of a genuine national church without any precise territorial limits and with jurisdiction over all their compatriots, in default of which they wished to have equality between Greeks and Bulgarians in the administration of the ecumenical patriarchate. In 1860 a few Bulgarian bishops caused a schism at Constantinople. Finally, in spite of conciliatory moves by the patriarch Gregory VI, the Bulgarians obtained a "firman" (decree) from the sultan authorizing the establishment of an independent Bulgarian exarchate.

The Patriarch Anthimus VI then held a synod in Constantinople in the presence of the patriarchs of Alexandria and Antioch (1872) and launched a sentence of interdict against the Bulgarian exarch, condemning at the same time the sin of "phyletism," that is to say, nationalistic rivalries and quarrels between different nationalities within the Church of Christ.

Actually, the Bulgarians were not the only ones guilty of phyletism. The wrongs were also shared by the other side, as the history of the schism shows. But formally speaking, canonical right was on the side of the Phanar. The Bulgarian Church remained under patriarchal interdict until 1945, when the ecumenical see finally recognized the autocephalous status of the Bulgarian Church *within precise territorial limits,* and after the Bulgarians had officially requested the lifting of the interdict.

The Bulgarian Church has about 6,000,000 faithful today. In 1940 there were 2,742 parishes, 2,381 priests, and eleven dioceses. Until May 10, 1953, the metropolitan of Sofia bore the title of Exarch, but he has now assumed the title of Patriarch.

As a state church closely tied to the former regime, the Bulgarian Church could not expect any leniency when the change of regime occurred in 1944. The new government took the same measures with respect to it that were taken by the popular democracies in other countries: all religious instruction in the schools was abolished (January 1946), some of the clergy were arrested, including Bishop Cyril of Plovdiv (the present patriarch), support was given to an Association of Priests which forms part of the present "Patriotic Front," and finally the separation of Church and state was decreed (Constitution of 1947).

The Exarch Stephen and the bishops followed the example of the Russian bishops and swore that they were loyal to the new state. But to avoid all possible misunderstandings, the Holy Synod forbade priests to take part in the Patriotic Front. In June 1948 it received a circular letter from the Minister of Cults, Iliev, declaring that "since every Bulgarian ought to belong to the Patriotic Front, all pastors and priests ought to do likewise" and ordering the heads of the Church to join in the fight against anticommunist propaganda.[21] The Holy Synod replied that it would ignore the circular. In September of the same year the Exarch Stephen was obliged to resign and the Holy Synod gave the necessary permission.

The period from 1948 to 1953 was particularly difficult for the Bulgarian Church. In 1949 the government unilaterally published a law on "religious associations,"[22] establishing strict control over the various ramifications of the Church. This control is exercised

[21] Text in R. Tobias, *Communist-Christian Encounter in Eastern Europe* (Greenfield, Ind., 1956), p. 358.
[22] English translation of the law in Tobias, *op. cit.*, pp. 371-76.

particularly with respect to the laws of the Church (article 6), religious services held out of doors (art. 7), the Church budget (art. 13), the encyclicals and other decrees of the bishops (art. 15), the training of the clergy (art. 14), and their appointment to various posts (art. 13), and so on. In 1951 a new constitution for the Church went into effect. The hierachy had obtained a number of benefits from its conciliatory attitude: the number of copies of religious journals allowed has increased, taxes on Church property have been eased, and above all, the Holy Synod received permission in 1955 to dissolve the Association of Priests, which the government had used until then to bring pressure to bear on the hierarchy.

For the training of the clergy the Bulgarian Church at present has at its disposal the Academy of St. Clement of Ohrid (the former theological faculty of the University of Sofia, now separated from the university). It is able to publish at least four religious periodicals, including an interesting theological review (the Annual of the Academy), a number of textbooks for students and even some illustrated books for children. The hierarchy faithfully follows the policy of the patriarchate of Moscow in approving the movement known as the Partisans for Peace and in issuing rubber-stamped statements on international affairs at the proper times.

9. The Church of Greece

Shortly after the achievement of Greek independence in 1833 a synod of Greek bishops proclaimed the autocephalous status of the Greek Church within the boundaries of the new state. This unilateral act was motivated particularly by the fact that the ecumenical patriarch was regarded by the Greeks as being too subject to Turkish control to be able to function effectively as the supreme head of a Greek Church in the newly independent state. After protesting in vain, the Phanar finally acquiesced in the inevitable and recognized the *fait accompli* in 1850. Since then the Greek Church has been governed by a Holy Synod, under the presidency of the archbishop of Athens. The constitution of the Church, and especially the relations between Church and state, have undergone several changes between 1850 and 1959. While the system adopted in the beginning was directly inspired by the Regulation of Peter the Great and envisaged a strict subordination of the Church to the state, the tendency since then has been to give the hierarchy much greater freedom. In 1959, however, an internal dispute among the Greek bishops caused the government to tighten its grip again. Greece therefore is today the only country where the Orthodox Church remains a state church and plays a dominant role in the life of the country.

With a total of more than 8,000,000 faithful, the Greek Church has eighty-one dioceses, forty-nine of which are in the so-called "new" provinces in northern Greece (added to the kingdom in 1913) and nominally subject to the jurisdiction of the ecumenical patriarch. However they are represented in the Synod at Athens. Among all the Balkan countries Greece has the greatest number of dioceses, but also the smallest in size. There were formerly 120, but this number was reduced in the nineteenth century. A further reduction has recently been decided upon. This multiplicity of dioceses goes back to the period of the primitive Church, when each important community had its own bishop. But in those days bishops were elected by the faithful and were irremovable, and there was no tendency for them to form a bureaucracy or to think of the episcopate as a career. Measures have recently been

proposed aimed at eliminating these evils in the modern Greek Church.

Since the main facts about the Church in Greece are
rather well known, we shall confine ourselves here to
a few general remarks about the situation of religious
education in the country and to the activities of the
various groups engaged in an internal apostolate.

Two theological faculties, which form parts of the
universities at Athens and Thessalonica, offer higher
instruction in theology. Most graduates prepare for
careers as teachers of religion in secondary schools
and remain laymen. However, a certain number enter
the ranks of the regular clergy and in this way become
candidates for the higher posts in the Church. Only a
small number join the ranks of the married parish
clergy. Parish priests are trained in minor seminaries.
In general, lay theologians enjoy a more important
status in Greece than in other Orthodox countries. The
majority of professors of theology and many preachers
are laymen. One of the most interesting features of
religion in modern Greece is the extraordinary development of various missionary movements directed
toward an internal apostolate in the Greek Church
itself. The most important of these is the Association
known as Zoe ("Life"), founded in 1911 by Father
Eusebios Matthopoulos, which is a kind of monastic
order of a new type. The Association has only about
130 members, of whom only thirty-four are priests,
but all—with very few exceptions—have a higher degree in theology. They practice the three traditional
monastic virtues but spend only one month each year
in communal life in their mother house. The rest of
the time, the brothers are dispersed throughout the
country, preaching, teaching, or presiding over the
various missionary or catechetical efforts in which the
Association is engaged. Since they have vowed to oppose any tendency toward careerism, they have stead-

fastly refused to accept episcopal appointments and consider themselves wholly and solely dedicated to evangelical work. They are advocates of a more meaningful performance of the liturgy (and hence favor reading the eucharistic canon out loud), of a more genuine participation in the sacramental life of the Church (and hence favor frequent communion), and of a deeper knowledge of the Bible on the part of the faithful. Because of these attitudes, they have contributed materially to a spiritual revival in the Greek Church. The organizations which they control are numerous and varied. As examples, we may cite the Christian Union of Men of Science (an association of Christian intellectuals), the Christian Union of Students (with 2,400 members), the Women's Association *Eusebia,* the Christian Union of Teachers, and the Christian Union of Young Workers (with 2,000 regular members and 6,000 associates). Zoe even runs a school of engineering. Some idea about its extensive influence may be gained from the extraordinary number of publications which it edits (in view of the present size of the Greek population). The periodical *Zoe*—a weekly periodical of eight pages containing only articles of a religious nature—has a circulation of 170,000 copies and thus has the largest circulation of any Greek-language periodical today. The monthly review *Aktines* (the organ of the Union of Men of Science) is published in 15,000 copies. A dozen or so other periodicals—some of them illustrated for children—have a comparably wide circulation. Particular attention is paid to distributing copies of the Bible among the Greek people. The pocket edition of the New Testament published by Zoe is in its thirty-second edition and 650,000 copies have been printed.

In addition to Zoe there are other organizations, such as the Orthodox Unions, which pursue the same objectives. They owe their existence to private initiative but they carry on within the traditional framework of the Church (dioceses and parishes) and have the blessing of the hierarchy. The latter, however, tends to view with some suspicion movements that it does not directly control. It would obviously prefer that they were more closely tied in with the official machinery of church government. It realizes, however, that it would be unwise to attempt to bring this about through administrative measures. Instead, it has established, under its own auspices, an organization known as *Apostoliki Diakonia* (Apostolic Service), which performs much the same sort of work as Zoe (preaching, publications, youth work). These various Greek missionary endeavors therefore are more concerned with emulating each other than with rivalry. They are all directed toward one common objective, the preservation of the Orthodox faith among the Greek people. Their success in this field is apparent, particularly as regards the religious education of youth. Nearly 500,000 Greek children attend the 7,800 catechetical schools of the Church (of which 2,000 are controlled by Zoe). For some years now these movements have taken a keen interest in the ecumenical responsibilities of the Church. Students from Uganda, Ethiopia, and Korea attend Greek institutes and seminaries, and various Greek youth movements are affiliated with *Syndesmos* (the World Association of Orthodox Youth Movements). A Committee for the Promotion of Foreign Missions has recently been formed with the approval of the hierarchy.

10. The Church of Georgia

One of the most ancient branches of the Christian Church, the Georgian Church was founded at the beginning of the fifth century by a woman apostle, St. Nino, who converted Mirian the king of Georgia to Christianity. Since Georgia lay within the ecclesiastical sphere of the patriarchate of Antioch, although remote from that capital, the Georgians long received their bishops from there. Later they came under the jurisdiction of Constantinople. Their church achieved autocephalous status even in medieval times and was governed by its own Catholicos.[23] In 1801 Orthodox Georgia sought the help of the Russians against the Persians and found itself annexed to the empire of Alexander I. The old autocephalous status was abolished, and, from 1817, the Church was governed by a Russian exarch, who was a member of the Synod of St. Petersburg. At the time of the Russian Revolution, the Georgians recovered their autocephalous status, but this was not formally recognized by the patriarch of Moscow until 1943.

The Church was destined to go through a tragic period during the Revolution. Kirion, the first Catholicos to be restored to the throne, was assassinated. His successor, Ambrose, was tried and sentenced to ten years' imprisonment (1923). The relative freedom gained by religion as a result of the last war also benefited the Georgian Church, but its present situation seems to be rather weak. Officially there are fifteen dioceses (as against twenty-eight in the eighteenth century), but nine of these are vacant. A new Catholicos, Ephrem, has recently been elected by the national synod, following the death of his predecessor, Melchizedek. A church calendar is published at Tiflis (Tbilisi). Information with regard to the existence of a seminary is uncertain.[24] Georgia at present has 2,500,000 inhabitants, who were all Orthodox before 1917. Statistics regarding religious practice are unobtainable today.

[23] This title was often borne by the heads of autonomous churches situated outside the borders of the Byzantine Empire.
[24] See *Le Problème religieux en U.R.S.S.*

11. The Church of Cyprus

The Council of Ephesus (431) proclaimed the independent status of the archbishopric of Cyprus, which
until then had been dependent upon Antioch. Since
that time this ancient church had had a rather turbu-
lent history. The island was conquered by the Arabs
in the seventh century, reconquered by the Byzantines,
and then seized by Richard the Lion-Hearted in 1191
on his way to the Third Crusade. Cyprus remained
under Latin rule for several centuries, first under the
house of Lusignan (1191-1489), then under Venice
(1489-1571). It was conquered by the Turks in 1571
and occupied by the British in 1878. In spite of all
these different rulers, however, the Cypriots remained
faithful to their Orthodox faith, though during the
centuries of Latin rule they were obliged to submit
to a Latin archbishop. Several massacres of the Orthodox clergy by the Turks took place after the de-
parture of the Latins. The Turkish minority on the
island, in fact, is a vestige of the former Ottoman occupation.

When the British occupied Cyprus they preserved,
to a large extent, the political situation which had existed under the Turks. As we have seen, it was the
Turkish custom to hand over to the Orthodox clergy
both civil and religious control over their faithful, and
the archbishop of Cyprus continued to be viewed as
the ethnarch ("national head") of the Greek Orthodox under the British.

The Orthodox population of Cyprus today amounts
to about 450,000 and there are some seven hundred
priests. The faithful are governed by a Holy Synod
consisting of the archbishop and three metropolitans
(Paphos, Kition, and Kyrenia), all elected by the faithful in accordance with a rather elaborate system in
several stages. The present archbishop, Makarios,

elected in 1950, has achieved world-wide fame as a result of his part in the Cypriot struggle for union with Greece. He has been chosen as president of the new Republic of Cyprus. The role which he has played in recent events is entirely in accordance with the traditions of the Cypriot Church, which for many centuries was the rallying point for the Greek population under so many foreign rulers.

12. The Archbishopric of Sinai

By a special privilege, the head of the monastery of St. Catherine built by Emperor Justinian I in the sixth century near the spot where Moses is said to have received the Tables of the Law, enjoys the rank of an archbishop and the monastery has the status of an autonomous church. The archbishop-abbot is elected by the chapter of monks but receives episcopal consecration at the hands of the patriarch of Jerusalem. He only has jurisdiction over the monastery and the Bedouins who live in the neighborhood. The present archbishop of Sinai, Porphyrios III, generally resides in the *metochion* (priory) of his monastery in Cairo.

The monastery of Sinai possesses a very rich library of ancient Greek, Georgian, and Slavic manuscripts and an interesting collection of icons.

13. The Albanian Orthodox Church

In 1944 the Albanian population consisted of 688,000 Moslems, 210,000 Orthodox, and 104,184 Roman Catholics. Only after political pressure had been brought to bear did the ecumenical patriarch finally consent to recognize the autocephalous status of the Albanian Orthodox Church in 1937, a minority in the country, practically without schools or traditions of its own. Despised by the Italians, the Albanian Orthodox had

still more to suffer as a result of the antireligious acts
of the new communist-dominated government in 1945-
1946. Two bishops were arrested toward the end of
1948, and in August 1949 the archbishop of Tirana,
Christophoros, was deposed and imprisoned for "activities considered harmful to the Albanian people and
the Church." His successor, Paissios, elected under
dubious conditions, was recognized by the patriarch
of Moscow but not by Constantinople.

14. The Polish Orthodox Church

Within the Polish frontiers, as these were defined at
the end of World War I, there was a large population
of 4,000,000 Byelorussian and Ukrainian Orthodox
forming several dioceses which until then had been
subject to the Russian Church. In 1924 these dioceses
were combined by the ecumenical patriarch to form
an autocephalous church. In 1939 the Polish Orthodox
Church had five dioceses, 1,624 parishes and two
seminaries (Vilna and Krzemieniec with a total of 500
seminarians), as well as a theological faculty at Warsaw (150 students).

In 1939 the Soviet Union occupied the part of
Poland inhabited by the majority of the Orthodox,
and gained still further territory as a result of World
War II. Canonically, these regions were again attached to the patriarchate of Moscow, while only
some 350,000 Orthodox remained on Polish soil. The
situation of the latter was aggravated by the fact
that the patriarch of Moscow had not recognized
the act of 1924 which confirmed the autocephalous
status of the Polish Church. In 1948, therefore, three
Polish bishops, including the Metropolitan Dionysius,
had to do penance before Patriarch Alexis and received a new autocephalous act *from him*. Metropolitan Dionysius was forced to retire. In 1951 a new

head was provided for the Church in the person of a Russian bishop, Makarios Oksiusk, the former bishop of Lvov and former professor (before 1917) of the Kiev Theological Academy. The independence of the Polish Church with respect to Moscow is therefore of a very relative nature. Metropolitan Makarios died on March 1, 1961. A successor, Timothy, archbishop of Bialystok, was canonically elected.

There are at present five Orthodox dioceses in Poland: Warsaw, Bialystok, Lodz, Wroclaw (Breslau), and Gdańsk (Danzig).[25] The number of parishes is about 160.

15. The Orthodox Church of Czechoslovakia

Between the two world wars the Orthodox Church presented a rather heterogeneous picture in Czechoslovakia. It was composed of two originally separate groups of faithful, amounting to about 250,000 persons in all. First of all, a group of Czech Orthodox were provided with a head in 1923 by the ecumenical patriarch in the person of Bishop Sabbatios. In 1925 a more important group of priests and faithful constituting the Czechoslovak National Church, which had separated from Rome, joined the Orthodox Church. They were provided with a head by the Serbian patriarch, who consecrated for them Bishop Gorazd. The latter therefore presided over a certain number of Orthodox faithful of the Latin rite. In 1930, 200,000 Carpatho-Russian Uniats also returned to Orthodoxy and the patriarch of Belgrade formed the diocese of Mukacevo for them. Finally a small number of Russian parishes

[25] It should be remarked that two of these dioceses are on former German territory, thus implying, on the part of the Orthodox authorities, full recognition of the western frontiers of Poland. As is well known, the Vatican has to this day refused to appoint Catholic bishops to this region on the grounds that a peace treaty has not yet been signed between Poland and Germany.

remained throughout this period subject to a Russian bishop who recognized the authority of Metropolitan Eulogios of Paris.

These four groups were united by the patriarch of Moscow in 1947 to form one church, the Serbian Church giving its consent to the arrangement. In 1950, finally, two dioceses of Byzantine rite in communion with Rome (Prešov and Mikailov) returned to Orthodoxy.[26] The Orthodox Church in Czechoslovakia therefore today has about 250,000 faithful. There are four dioceses (Prague, Olomouc, Prešov, and Mikhailov) and in 1951 its autocephalous status was confirmed by the patriarch of Moscow. Its first head, Eleutherios (who resigned in 1958), and its present head, Metropolitan John, are both Russian bishops. The independent status of the new church has recently been recognized by the patriarch of Constantinople, after the death of Sabbatios, whom the ecumenical see continued to recognize as archbishop of Prague.

An Orthodox seminary was opened at Karlovy Vary in 1948 and another is functioning, it seems, at Prešov. The Church publishes a theological review and has a Slavonic press which prints liturgical books, largely for export to Russia, where the Church has no means of publishing anything of the kind.

16. The Orthodox Church of Finland

When Finland won its independence from Russia in 1918 one of the first acts of the Finnish Orthodox— for the most part Karelians converted from paganism in the Middle Ages by the monks of Valamo on Lake Ladoga—was to remove the stigma of being called

---

[26] Their union with Rome dated from 1649 and was brought about as a result of pressure exercised by the Austrian government. It must, unfortunately, be acknowledged that their return to Orthodoxy has been brought about under conditions hardly any better, if at all.

"Russians" by the vast majority of Lutheran Finns, who tended to view Orthodoxy as a "Russian faith." So under the leadership of Archbishop Germanos Aab, in 1923, the Church of Finland placed itself under the jurisdiction of the ecumenical patriarch of Constantinople. Moscow protested against this situation, but finally in 1958 recognized the autonomous status of the Finnish Church.

About 70,000 Orthodox faithful live in the midst of an overwhelming majority of some 4,000,000 Lutherans. Nevertheless the Orthodox Church is considered to be the second state-church of Finland. The Orthodox had much to suffer when the Soviets annexed part of the country in 1939 (Finnish Karelia, annexation confirmed in 1945). Most of them in fact lived in this part of the country contiguous to Russia. They were obliged to retire to the interior of the country and are today found scattered all over Finland. Their church has two dioceses (the archbishopric of Kuopio and the bishopric of Helsinki), a seminary which has been transferred from Sortavala, in Karelia, to Helsinki, and there are plans for the creation of a theological faculty. Since the Orthodox youth are eager to promote international and ecumenical contacts and anxious to show that they belong to the Western European world, while at the same time clinging to their Orthodox traditions, it is possible that the Finnish Church is destined to play an important part in manifesting the spirit of Orthodoxy to the West.

17. The Orthodox Missions, the Orthodox in Western Europe and America

In the nineteenth and early part of the twentieth century Russian missionary activity extended far beyond the eastern limits of the Empire. The Orthodox colonies in China, Korea, Japan, and Alaska are evidence of this fact to this day.

The Chinese Orthodox mission goes back to the end of the seventeenth century, when a group of Cossacks from the Russian outpost of Albazin were hired as a personal bodyguard by the Chinese emperor in Peking. Although completely Sinicized, their descendants retained their Orthodox faith and formed the nucleus of an Orthodox colony in the capital. This nucleus in turn became the basis for an important mission established at Peking in the nineteenth century, which had numerous branches and some twenty schools. However, the number of converts does not seem ever to have exceeded ten thousand. The number of Orthodox faithful in China increased after the Russian Revolution, when many refugees, including clergy, fled from Siberia. After the triumph of communism following the victories of Mao Tse-tung, the Orthodox Church, like all other Western Churches, had to rid itself of its Western personnel. The Russian clergy in charge, as representatives of the patriarch of Moscow, were not privileged in this respect and had to leave the country. In 1950 a Chinese priest, Simeon Dou, was consecrated as bishop of Tientsin in Moscow, and later transferred to Shanghai. In 1957 another Chinese priest, Basil Yo Fuan, was consecrated as bishop of Peking (Peiping). Three other dioceses remain without bishops. Two monasteries and a catechetical school are functioning in Peking.

Toward the end of the nineteenth century a Russian mission was also sent to Korea. The Orthodox faith there has managed to survive through all the recent turmoil and the mission was recently taken over by the Greek Archdiocese in the United States. It operates under the supervision of two Korean priests and has a school and a hospital.

Orthodox missionaries were even more active in Japan, thanks particularly to Father Nicholas Kassatkin, one of the most remarkable missionaries of all time. He arrived in 1861 as chaplain to the Russian consul in Hakodate but soon gave up his diplomatic tasks to devote himself exclusively to missionary work in Japan. His first efforts were directed toward translating the New Testament and essential liturgical texts into Japanese. In 1872 the first Japanese Orthodox priests were ordained by a Russian bishop at Hakodate. In 1880 there were 6,099 Orthodox in Japan; by 1891 this number had climbed to 20,048 and there were twenty-two priests with 219 churches and chapels. The same year saw the completion of the imposing Orthodox cathedral of Tokyo, which remains today the most conspicuous religious edifice in the capital. The Japanese have always called it "Nicolai-Do" ("House of Nicholas"). Consecrated as bishop of Tokyo in 1880, Nicholas was extraordinarily successful in winning the confidence of the country where he was laboring on behalf of the Gospel. During the Russo-Japanese War of 1904-1905, for example, he was able to move about freely, and celebrated Te Deums for the victory of the Japanese armies. Even today, the truly native character of Japanese Orthodoxy is a well-recognized phenomenon and is a sign of hope for the future.

The Japanese Orthodox Church has about 36,000 faithful, one bishop, and thirty-eight priests, all Japanese. A seminary has recently been opened with some twenty seminarians, who sometimes go abroad to complete their studies. After a period of decline between the two world wars the prospects for Japanese Orthodoxy are now beginning to brighten once again.

Russian explorers discovered and occupied Alaska in 1741. Monks from Valamo (on Lake Ladoga) undertook missionary work there in 1794 and opened the first school for the Eskimos. An unusually capable missionary—John Veniaminov—labored for many long years in this arduous vineyard (1822-1852), as missionary, the author of a grammar of the Aleutian language, the translator of the Gospels and the Byzantine liturgy into the same language, and then as bishop of an immense territory embracing the Kamchatka, the Kurile Islands, Aleutian Islands, and Alaska. From 1841 until 1858 there was a seminary in operation on one of the Aleutian Islands. Veniaminov was provided with an auxiliary bishop in 1858. Finally in 1868 Russia sold Alaska to the United States. The Russian mission was made an independent missionary bishopric comprising the Aleutian Islands and Alaska. In 1872 the seat of the bishop was transferred to San Francisco, and in 1905 to New York. An auxiliary bishop remained in Alaska.

Such were the humble origins of American Orthodoxy. But the situation is far different today. During the latter years of the nineteenth century quite a few Uniat Catholic groups made up of emigrants from Carpatho-Russia returned to Orthodoxy and placed themselves under the jurisdiction of the Russian diocese in America. Groups of Greeks, Serbs, Albanians, and Bulgarians also organized parishes under its jurisdiction. In 1904 an auxiliary bishop was provided for the Syrians and Lebanese in Brooklyn, New York. With the blessing of the Holy Synod in Russia, Archbishop Tykhon (the future patriarch) authorized the publication of an English translation of the liturgy. Thus an American Orthodox Church began to take shape.

The Russian Revolution and internal dissensions in the Russian Church helped to retard the process of unification. Between 1917 and 1923 the American diocese was without any effective leadership (until Metropolitan Plato was appointed as the new bishop by

Patriarch Tykhon) and it broke up into a number of separate units, each national group forming its own diocese. The steady influx of new immigrants, moreover, made it extremely difficult to organize and integrate the new arrivals in a single church.

Hence today, besides the original Russian diocese, the United States has a large Greek Orthodox archdiocese, an archdiocese dependent upon the Arab-speaking patriarchate of Antioch, Serbian, Rumanian, Bulgarian, and Albanian dioceses. The Synod of *émigré* Russian bishops under Metropolitan Anastasius likewise moved its headquarters to the United States. Some of the autocephalous Ukrainian clergy[27] also established parishes there. While all these groups have begun to work more closely with each other, their union alone will truly assure the future progress of Orthodoxy in America.

The total number of Orthodox in the United States is about 3,000,000. More or less numerous groups are also found in Canada and South America. All national groups in the United States, with the exception of the Greeks, are gradually adopting English more and more as the liturgical language, a factor which will help the process toward unification. Whenever an Orthodox community is able to rise above its own ethnic and nationalist limitations it soon reveals that it is capable of exerting a missionary influence. Thus about a third of the clergy serving the Syrian diocese—under the jurisdiction of the patriarch of Antioch—consists of converts which have come to Orthodoxy from other Christian confessions. St. Vladimir's Seminary, in New

[27] An autocephalous Ukrainian Church was established, as we have seen, during the Russian Revolution, but its status was uncanonical. At first it was without apostolic succession when no bishops would join it; then, later, apostolic succession was obtained, but under dubious circumstances. Consequently this body does not enjoy communion with the rest of the Orthodox Church.

York, receives students from all the Orthodox communities in the United States and is one of the principal centers working for the unification of American Orthodox. A Greek Orthodox theological school is active in Brookline, Massachusetts, and there are four other schools belonging to the various jurisdictions where instruction in theology is given. There are numerous religious publications in English.

Until very recently only three "major" religious confessions were officially recognized in the United States: Protestantism, Catholicism, and Judaism. But by decision of most of the states the Orthodox Church has now been added to this number.

Between the two world wars the number of Orthodox increased very considerably in Western Europe. A Greek exarchate, headed by the titular archbishop of Thyatire, was established at London in 1922. The bulk of Russian refugees from this time on tended to settle especially in France. In 1922 Patriarch Tykhon named Metropolitan Eulogios to look after the new parishes. When the ecclesiastical authorities in Moscow finally asked him to submit a written statement of loyalty to the Soviet state, Eulogios appealed, in 1931, to the ecumenical patriarch and became the latter's exarch for the Russian parishes in Europe. His long faithfulness to Moscow (1922-1931) and his appeal to Constantinople got him into trouble with the *émigré* Russian bishops who had fled to Yugoslavia and established an independent Holy Synod there, but whose canonical status was not recognized by the other Orthodox Churches. As mentioned above, this synod has now transferred its headquarters to the United States and has jurisdiction over a certain number of *émigré* parishes.

Paris quickly became the chief intellectual center for the Russian emigration. Nicholas Berdiaev, Sergius

Bulgakov, and many other leading thinkers helped
to acquaint the West with the thought, spirituality,
and traditions of the Christian East. The Theological
Institute of St. Sergius in Paris, under the guidance of
Metropolitan Eulogios and a group of capable and
talented professors, has trained more than 150 Orthodox priests and has taken very active part in promoting ecumenical discussions over the years. Owing to
the presence of Russian *émigrés,* but without any efforts at proselytism on their part, a number of Western
Orthodox communities began to be formed in France
and Germany. Both in Europe and in America, communities of Western rite have also joined the Orthodox Church and were received as such by the
hierarchy. We are therefore confronted today by the
gradual emergence of a Western Orthodoxy, a welcome
phenomenon, which will assist the Orthodox youth
who have adopted the language, culture, and customs
of the countries where they were born, and are to all
intents and purposes as Western as their Latin brothers, to preserve their Orthodox faith. On the spiritual
and intellectual side, it is also important for the Orthodox to manifest their *presence* in the great movements which are gripping Western Christianity at this
time: the return to Holy Scripture and to the true
Christian Tradition of the Church, the movement toward reunion, the revival of patristic studies, a greater
awareness of social responsibilities, and the liturgical
movement. In all these areas the Orthodox not only
feels very close to his Catholic and Protestant brethren
but is often aware that he has much to learn from
them. The principal task of Western Orthodoxy should
be to show *by deeds* that these various remarkable
currents and trends in Western Christianity can be
given new strength and presented as a more coherent
whole in the light of Orthodox truth.

We shall conclude this long section on the Orthodox Diaspora and missions by mentioning a recent development which may have important consequences for the future, namely, the appearance of a new Orthodox Church in Africa, which had thus far escaped the attention of Orthodox missionaries. In 1932 a group of Christians in Uganda left the communion of the Anglican Church and were admitted to the Orthodox Church by the patriarch of Alexandria. Under the supervision of an African-born priest, Father Spartas, this group now numbers about 20,000 faithful. Recent information indicates that this church has experienced a phenomenal growth and is receiving more and more active help from the Greek Orthodox Church. Several Negro seminarians from Uganda are pursuing their studies at the patriarchal college in Cairo and at the theological faculty in Athens. A new bishop has just been appointed for East Africa. It seems certain that the rapid rise of this church is due not only to the attraction of the Orthodox faith itself, but also to the fact that its missionaries are not considered to be identified with colonialism. It is greatly to be hoped that the Orthodox authorities will be able to guide the movement wisely and can profit from the great advantage of not being identified with European colonial policies of the nineteenth century.

CHAPTER IX

ORTHODOX FAITH AND
SPIRITUALITY

WE MENTIONED earlier the great spiritual legacy which the Orthodox Church has inherited from its medieval forebear, the Byzantine Church. This legacy embraces the prayers, hymns, and other formulas of our liturgical services, the canonical organization and discipline of the churches, our spiritual tradition, and the dogmatic system of the Orthodox faith. Yet, while it is perfectly true that the Orthodox Church claims to be *the true Church of Christ,* the one and only Catholic Church, the Orthodox theologian, nevertheless, is under a strict obligation to distinguish carefully in this heritage between that which forms part of the Church's Holy Tradition, unalterable and universally binding, received from the past, and that which is a mere relic of former times, venerable no doubt in many respects but sometimes also sadly out of date and even harmful to the mission of the Church. All modernism of the wrong kind is of course to be condemned, as exemplified recently by the Renovated Church in Russia, but also all narrow conservatism like that of the Russian Old Believers, which tends to canonize the past as such. These two tendencies, unfortunately, are always present in most local Orthodox churches and soon make themselves felt. We need to be continually on guard against them. But this can be done only by persons who have received a sound training in theological principles, who are prepared to show a genuine respect for tradition, and who are disposed at all times and in all things to be guided by revealed Truth.

It is not possible within the limits of this book to offer the reader anything like a full systematic account of Orthodox doctrines.[1] He will undoubtedly have been able to gather from the preceding pages what the main Orthodox positions are on a number of points, and further dogmatic questions will be taken up in the chapter which follows. It is our purpose here merely to give a general survey of the mysteries of the Christian faith as the Orthodox Church sees them, to describe the Orthodox attitude toward them, and finally to dwell somewhat on the Orthodox conception of man's communion with God. The Orthodox faith is expressed, jointly, by its spiritual tradition and the declared dogmas of the Church, by the lives of the saints, and by the doctrines of its teachers (the Fathers of the Church and other theologians). It is both the *lex orandi* and the *lex credendi* of the Church. According to V. Lossky:

> Eastern tradition has never clearly distinguished between mysticism and theology, between a personal experience of the divine mysteries and the dogmas declared by the Church. . . . The dogma which expresses a revealed truth and appears to us like an unfathomable mystery, must be lived in such a way that, instead of assimilating the mystery to our manner of understanding it, we must, on the contrary, strive to bring about a pro-

[1] The best systematic account of this kind is still that by S. Bulgakov, *The Orthodox Church* (London, 1935; 2nd. ed., New York, 1960).

found change, an inner transformation of the soul,
so that we will be more receptive toward the
mystical experience. Far from being opposed to
each other, theology and mysticism mutually support and supplement each other. One is impossible without the other. If mysticism is the application by the individual of the content of the
common faith to his own experience, theology is
the expression of that which can be experienced
by each one for the benefit of all.[2]

The new reality made available to the world by
the Incarnation of the Word and made effective in the
Church through the operation of the Holy Spirit is
not a mere sum of knowledge, but a New Life. It is
not imposed on us like an external proof, but is a
transformation, a transfiguration of our being. We do
not achieve it simply by reading the Word of God
or through a knowledge of dogmas, but by dying and
rising again with Christ in Baptism, by receiving the
seal of the Spirit in Confirmation, by becoming members of the actual Body of Christ in the Eucharist, and
finally by making progress in ever greater knowledge,
until we attain the "stature of the man made in Jesus
Christ" (Eph. iv.13). This sacramental nature of the
true life in the Spirit presupposes the existence of a
visible Church with a hierarchy possessing special
functions and a charisma to teach, but it also means
that the *saints* are authentic witnesses of the actual
presence of God in the midst of his people. By means
of its hierarchic and sacramental structure, the Church
expresses the *permanence* and *reality* of the union
brought about, in Christ, between the human and the
divine. The Ascension of Jesus does not mean the end
of his presence but the glorification of human nature,
which is now deified and seated on the right hand of

    [2] *The Mystical Theology of the Eastern Church* (Napierville,
Ill., Allenson, 1957).

the Father. It presupposes Pentecost and the sending of the Holy Spirit by the Father to the Church. The Spirit builds the Body of Christ in history, confers the sacraments, establishes the Church in truth, and guarantees its permanence and its infallibility. It operates through various charismas, including those of teaching and pastoring which are proper to the bishops, but it does not impose itself, magically, on the inner freedom of the individual which constitutes the very basis of the human person. Each one of us receives, through the sacraments, a seed of sanctity, but it is up to us to make it bear fruit. The Church as an "institution" is therefore not opposed to the Church as an "event," but the one presupposes the other, as grace presupposes our personal efforts to make it effective. Since the age of the Fathers the Orthodox Church has always upheld the doctrine of *synergeia,* that is, the collaboration between divine grace and the free will of man on his way toward God. We are *all* saints by grace, but we must *become* saints by our acts and in our whole being.

God, in his very Being, his Providence, his Incarnation, his presence in the Church, and his manifestation of himself at the end of time, is the unique Object whom the saints know and whom theologians seek to express by their formulas. Two aspects of the conception of God appear to be particularly important if we wish to understand Orthodox theology as a whole. These two aspects—going back of course to the Greek Fathers—are the absolute *transcendence* and the *trinitarian,* that is, the personal, *nature* of the Divine Being.

God's transcendence is a logical consequence of the Biblical account of creation *ex nihilo.* This is one of the essential traits of Biblical religion. The Bible clearly affirms that the world is not an emanation of the divine nor a reflection of a pre-existent reality, much less an extension of the Divine Being, as the result of any natural necessity. God, says St. Paul, "sends his call to that which has no being, as if it already was" (Rom. iv.17). The world did not exist before the divine Fiat, but it began to exist, thus giving birth to the quantity we call "time." To be sure the Fathers spoke of "ideas" existing in the divine Mind before the creation of the world, but these ideas had only dynamic and intentional character. The appearance of created beings from nothing means that these creatures belong to an order of existence essentially different from God, an order called by the Fathers, beginning with St. Athanasius, the "natural" order, created by the *will* of God and existing by his will alone. Between God and the created world there can be no "interdependence," there can only be a total "dependence" of the creature on the Creator.

The abyss between the Absolute and the relative, the Uncreated and creatures, is a theme constantly recurring throughout the New Testament, and is what Christian theologians and mystics mean by the "transcendence" and "unknowability" of the divine Essence. Creatures can know each other, among themselves, but when it comes to knowing God they are crushed, as it were, by their total dependence on him and by their virtual nonexistence. Their only resource is to assert that God *is not* what they conceive him to be, that he is not like any creature, that no image or word can express his Being.[3] Unknown in his essence, God has however revealed himself as Father, Son, and Holy Spirit: the Son became man and the Spirit descended on the Church. The Christian God there-

---

[3] This is what is meant by the term "negative theology" or "apophatic theology," the two greatest exponents of which in the East were St. Gregory of Nyssa and the anonymous author of the fifth century who hid his real identity under the pseudonym of Dionysius the Areopagite, the disciple of St. Paul at Athens.

fore is not the "unknown God" venerated by philosophers, but a living God who reveals himself and *acts*.
This is the meaning of the Orthodox doctrine concerning the divine *energies* or actions, which are distinct
from the unknowable essence, as formulated by St.
Gregory Palamas in the fourteenth century.[4] The Old
Testament has much to say about the divine intervention in the history of the Chosen People, but with
Christianity we have a fullness of divine action in history: the Son of God "dispossessed himself, and took
the nature of a slave, fashioned in the likeness of men,
and presenting himself to us in human form; and then
he lowered his own dignity, accepted an obedience
which brought him death, death on the cross" (Phil.
ii.7-8). Henceforth the divine acts affect not only the
external man, but their very Source has assumed human nature, which is now deified in Jesus Christ. We
are no longer limited to acknowledging the transcendence and omnipotence of God, but we may also accept
the salvation which he grants us and assimilate the divine grace which he gives us. This is what the Fathers
meant by "deification": God became man that we
might become God.[5] This deification is realized when
we become members of the Body of Christ, but also,
and especially, by the unction of the Spirit when the
latter touches each one of us: the "economy of the
Holy Spirit" means precisely this, that we are able to
enjoy communion with the one and truly deified humanity of Jesus Christ throughout history from the
time of the Ascension to the final Parousia:[6] "God has

[4] See our *Study on Gregory Palamas* (London, Faith Press,
1963), and *Saint Grégoire Palamas et la mystique orthodoxe,*
Coll. "Maîtres Spirituels" (Paris, Éditions du Seuil, 1959).

[5] St. Athanasius of Alexandria, *The Incarnation of the
Word,* 54, PG 25.192 B.

[6] Cf. O. Clément, *Transfigurer le temps.—Notes sur le temps
à la lumière de la tradition orthodoxe* (Paris, Neuchâtel, 1959).

sent out the Spirit of his Son into our hearts, crying out in us, Abba, Father" (Gal. iv.6).

This "personal" emphasis of Orthodox theology and mysticism is intimately connected with the way in which the Fathers interpret the transcendence of God; that is, God remains unknowable in his unique essence, but he has revealed himself as a Trinity of Three Persons. The God of the Bible therefore is known to the extent that He is a living and acting Deity, the One to whom the prayers of the Church are addressed, the One who has sent His Son for the salvation of the world. This particular emphasis of the thought of the Eastern Fathers distinguishes them— without opposing them, however—to the way in which their Latin brothers preferred to think of God first as a unique essence, and then only as a Trinity.[7] These two different attitudes would later give rise to two schools of Trinitarian theology. In Latin theology, the divine Persons were considered as the simple inner relations of the unique essence of the Godhead: hence, if the very existence of the Spirit is determined by its relations to the Father and the Son, the doctrine of the *Filioque*—or procession of the Spirit from the Father and the Son—becomes a logical, dogmatic necessity, for the Spirit cannot be said to be distinct from the Son if he does not proceed from him.[8] Eastern theologians, on the other hand, remained faithful to the old "personalism" of the Greek Fathers. The doctrine of the *Filioque* appeared to them, consequently, as

[7] See on this point T. de Regnon, *Études de théologie positive sur la Sainte Trinité*, Vol. I, p. 433; G. L. Prestige, *God in Patristic Thought* (London, 1952), pp. 242 ff.

[8] The doctrine of the *Filioque* has been debated at two recent meetings of Catholic and Orthodox theologians; the minutes of the debates were published in the *Eastern Churches Quarterly*, Vol. VII (1948), Suppl. issue, and in *Russie et Chrétienté*, Nos. 3-4 (1950).

Semi-Sabellianism (to use an expression of Photius).[9] Consubstantial with the Father and the Son, because proceeding from the Father, the unique source of the Deity, the Spirit has his own existence and personal function in the inner life of God and in the economy of salvation: his task is to bring about the unity of the human race in the Body of Christ, but he also imparts to this unity a personal, and hence diversified, character. It is with a prayer to the Holy Spirit that all the liturgical services of the Orthodox Church begin, and with an invocation of his name that the eucharistic mystery is effected.

While remaining absolutely transcendent and incomprehensible, God has revealed himself in Jesus Christ, "in whom the whole plenitude of the Deity is embodied" (Col. ii.9). In this way the true Life which comes from God was communicated to men, who, until then and ever since the sin of Adam, had been subject to death, a kind of hereditary, cosmic corruption, the consequence of his revolt against God.

The drama of sin, described in the first chapters of Genesis and explained by St. Paul and the ancient Fathers of the Church, provides a key to the mystery of suffering and death as found in man, both in the past and today. Adam and Eve sinned and this sin involved their death, as well as the death of all their descendants. This doctrine of original sin, which has played such an important part in Western theology ever since the time of St. Augustine, is interpreted to mean that countless generations of men have been affected by the consequences of Adam's sin, who were not responsible, it would seem, for the original fault.

[9] *Mystagogia*, 9, PG 102.289 A B; Sabellianism is a heresy dating from the second century attributed to a certain Sabellius, who taught that the divine Persons are simply "modes" or "aspects" of a unique God.

In their eagerness to reconcile this fact with a certain conception of the divine "justice," Western theologians have always insisted on the *joint guilt* of all men for the sin of Adam: punishment for sin could not affect all humanity unless all men had sinned "in Adam" and had therefore merited the divine wrath. This interpretation seemed to be confirmed by the Latin translation of a particular passage in the Bible— it may even have had its origin there—which speaks of the "transmission" of Adam's sin (Rom. v.12: *in quo omnes peccaverunt*). But, as a matter of fact, this is an inaccurate rendering of the original Greek.[10] The Eastern Fathers who read St. Paul in the original Greek never attempted to prove the *joint guilt* of all the descendants of Adam for the sin of their ancestor: they merely observed that all men have inherited corruption and death by a process of inheritance and that all have committed sins. They preferred to interpret the state of affairs inherited from Adam as a slavery to the Devil, who exercises a usurped, unjust, and deadly tyranny over mankind since the sin of man's Progenitor. On the other hand God, throughout the history of Israel, sought to steer men toward salvation by preparing them gradually to receive the Promised Messiah freely and sincerely. In the fullness of time this Messiah, the true Word of God, became incarnate of the Virgin Mary and the Holy Ghost—therefore outside the corrupt inheritance

[10] The Latin text, by translating the Greek *eph'o* as *in quo*, implies that "all have sinned in Adam." But this is impossible grammatically. The two possible translations would read: "Death passed to all men, from the fact that all have sinned"; or, "Death, on account of which all have sinned, has passed to all men." The latter version finds confirmation in several of the Greek Fathers. In the first case, St. Paul would be referring to the personal sins of men committed by them on their own responsibility and meriting punishment like that which Adam suffered; in the second case, *mortality*, transmitted to the whole race of Adam, would be the origin of their personal sins.

of Adam—triumphed over the Devil on the Cross, rose again on the third day, and has given back to mankind access to life.

It goes without saying that these fundamental mysteries of the Christian faith are of the very essence of true doctrine and have their consequences for Christian spirituality. Doctrinal differences will necessarily entail certain variations in spiritual emphasis. Thus, the Christian East has remained a stranger to the juridical conceptions of salvation which have been dominant in the West since medieval times (the doctrines of the "merits" of Jesus Christ and indulgences) and which have so profoundly affected Western spirituality. The doctrine of original sin, moreover, as the Greek Fathers understood it, excludes the dogma of the Immaculate Conception of Mary in the form in which this was proclaimed by Pope Pius IX in 1854.[11] This dogma assumes that original sin consists of a "sin" committed "in Adam" and meriting punishment, and that the Virgin Mary could not have any share in this, for, from the moment of her conception, she was chosen and purified in view of the divine maternity. The choice that was made of her for this end is, in fact, irreconcilable with the divine anger associated with sin. But this reasoning no longer holds good if we adopt another interpretation of original sin. According to Orthodox tradition, slavery to the Devil, mortality, and corruption, transmitted by way of natural heredity, were the consequences of Adam's sin. The Virgin Mary was of course holy and pure from her conception, but she was born of Joachim and

[11] "We declare . . . that the doctrine which holds that the most blessed Virgin Mary at the first instant of her conception, by a singular grace and privilege of Almighty God, in virtue of the merits of Christ Jesus, Savior of the human race, was preserved immaculate from all stain of original sin, has been revealed by God . . ." (text in Denzinger, *Enchiridion Symbolorum,* No. 1641).

Anna in the same way that all other men have been
born, and like them she was mortal: Adam's legacy
was not passed over except in the case of her divine
Son, who was born of the Holy Spirit. The Byzantine
liturgy is certainly far from sparing in its praise of the
"Mother of God": it recognizes her exceptional role in
salvation—by her *Fiat* to the Archangel, Mary, the
New Eve, is the origin of the new human race which
shares in the life of God—and also extols the corporal
glorification of the *Theotokos* after her death; it sees
in her the goal and perfection of all creation, ready at
last to receive the Savior—but it is Jesus Christ, and
not Mary, whom the Church adores as the Prince of
Life, Savior, and Redeemer, and it is he alone who
benefited from an Immaculate Conception in her
womb. Mary is the Mother of God, the one who, in
the name of all mankind, received God the Redeemer.

Thus, in spite of the opposition of Orthodox theologians to the Roman dogma of the Immaculate Conception and their reservations regarding the new
dogma of the Assumption of Mary—to the extent that
this *could* imply that Mary did not die because of her
Immaculate Conception—in spite of these differences,
I say, which basically do not concern Mary herself
but the doctrines of original sin and the Redemption,[12]
East and West vie with each other in extolling the
virtues and grace of her "whom all generations shall
call blessed."

The Redemption which God granted in Jesus Christ
is available to us through the Church and by means of
the Church: both the whole corporate and personal
life of each Christian is thus determined by the histori-

[12] The Orthodox point of view in relation to these problems
has been well stated by G. Florovsky and V. Lossky in the
articles which they contributed to *The Mother of God*, ed. by
E. L. Mascall (London, Dacre Press, 1949). For the doctrine
of the Byzantine theologians, see our *Study on Gregory Palamas*.

cal fact of the death and resurrection of Christ. We
share in this resurrection in Baptism and we "commemorate" it in the Eucharist. Finally, it determines
our rule of prayer.

We mentioned above the very important part
played by the liturgy in the life of the Orthodox
Church, a living, drama-filled liturgy, which has
served as a unique source of inspiration for theological thought and a last refuge for the faithful during
particularly difficult periods, and has even revealed
itself capable of keeping alive the essential truths of
the Christian faith. Regardless of the age in which he
lives or his status in life, when the Orthodox Christian
enters a church he feels instinctively that he is in the
presence of Heaven, that the Kingdom of God is already here; he knows that Christ is there in the spiritual communion of his Body and his Blood, in the
Gospel read by the priest, and in the prayers of the
Church.

This sacramental conception of the Christian life
has been evident in Orthodox spirituality from the
beginning and pervades it. Extreme tendencies toward
an individualistic, personal form of piety all find themselves integrated in a coherent whole as a result of
this conception, which does not regard personal forms
of piety as something opposed to the corporate liturgy. This is especially true of Hesychasm, a mystical
movement which goes back to the Desert Fathers and
which has played such an important part in forming
the spiritual tradition of the Christian East. It was
actually in connection with the theological controversies over the question of Hesychasm in the fourteenth
century that the Orthodox Church came to define
its doctrine on grace and its conception of the relations
between God and man. These doctrinal definitions

therefore gave a permanent and lasting value to a spiritual tradition, whose methods and practical features, by contrast, are only of relative significance.

It was in the deserts of Syria, Palestine, and Egypt in the fourth century that we find the first Hesychasts (from the Greek *hesychia*, "solitude," "contemplation"), the first exponents of continual prayer. Alone with God in their solitary habitations, the Christian hermits saw in St. Paul's commandment: "Pray without ceasing" (1 Thess. v.17) the most effective way for remaining in direct contact with the grace of Redemption. Some of them were accustomed to recite the Psalter in an endless round, thus inspiring the *lectio continua* of the Psalter in our liturgical offices. Others were devoted to a monologic or pure form of prayer consisting of the constant repetition of a short prayer stressing the Divine Name. Had not the Old Testament revealed that a more than ordinary significance was to be attached to the Divine Name? Did the Bible not teach that we must constantly "glorify the Name of the Lord" and did Christ not send his disciples to baptize people "In the Name of the Father and the Son and the Holy Spirit"? The perpetual invocation of God's Name was the most appropriate means for monks to communicate with the Divine. The form of monologic prayer often varied—sometimes it consisted of a simple *Kyrie eleison* (Lord, have mercy)—but the essence of the practice was the continual repetition of a set formula.

Occasionally, the earliest doctors of Hesychasm, and especially Evagrius of Pontus († c. 400), a great ascetic who had studied Origen and Neo-Platonism, were inclined to envisage prayer as a means of dematerializing the self in order to attain to the world of the mind, as the "highest intellection of the intellect," as an ascension of "the immaterial toward the Immaterial." In part it was a question of mere terminology. The Greek Fathers were fond of expressing Christian truths in the language of the day and this language was permeated with the conceptions of Hellenism. But sometimes the Greek spirit also got the upper hand over Biblical doctrine, particularly in the matter of anthropology. The Bible never taught that man is a spirit imprisoned in matter, like Plato. The Word became flesh in order to save all mankind, the whole of mankind, and it should be the aim of Christian spirituality therefore to realize this salvation in its totality. Christian prayer, which Evagrius tended to conceive of as a kind of de-materialization and described without any reference to Christ, God incarnate, ought to bring the *entire man* face to face with God. Gradually these Origenist and Evagrian distortions were corrected by ecclesiastical tradition. A work by an anonymous author of the fifth century, who hid his true identity under the name of St. Macarius of Egypt, and many other works by spiritual writers of the time, were instrumental in bringing this about.

With St. Diadochus of Photice (fifth century) and St. John Climacus († 650) the "intellectual" prayer of Evagrius has been transformed into the "prayer of Jesus." Jesus henceforth will be the Divine Name incessantly invoked by ascetics, and Christ, the God become man, will be regarded as the sole mediator between the created world and the Divine. Their prayer will no longer be a flight from matter but a communion with God in soul and body. The divine grace they will seek will transfigure both the soul and the flesh, regarded as bound together in the New Life and illuminated by the uncreated divine light.

"The Hesychast," wrote St. John Climacus in his *Ladder of Paradise*, "is he who strives to confine the Incorporeal into his bodily house . . . Let the remembrance of Jesus be present with each breath; then you will know the value of solitude." [13] And St. Maximus the Confessor († 662) thus describes the deification which is sought by every Christian, and especially by every Hesychast: "Man becomes God by deification, thereby he experiences a complete abandonment of all that belongs to him by nature . . . because the grace of the Spirit triumphs in him and because God alone, manifestly, acts in him. Thus God, and those who are worthy of God, henceforth have only one and the same activity in all things." [14] The divine vision granted to mystics in deification was identified by St. Gregory of Nyssa (fourth century) and St. Maximus with the vision of Moses on Mount Sinai and with the divine light that was witnessed by the Apostles on Mount Tabor when Christ was transfigured.

Later spiritual writers will place even more emphasis upon the bond between the Prayer of Jesus, the mysticism of deification, and the sacramental life of the Christian community. St. Symeon the New Theologian, the great Byzantine mystic of the eleventh century, found the essential inspiration for his experience of the divine in the Eucharist: his hymns and prayers, both before and after Communion, are some of the most realistic and spiritually moving in the Byzantine *Euchologion*. In the thirteenth and fourteenth centuries the Hesychast revival coincided with a new interest at Byzantium in the sacramental life of the Church. The best-known example of this tendency is Nicholas Cabasilas, whose *Life in Christ*—a comprehensive view of the spiritual life—is in the form of a commentary on the sacraments of Baptism, Chris-

[13] *Ladder of Paradise, Twenty-seventh Step*, tr. by Lazarus Moore (London, 1959), pp. 237, 246.

[14] *Ambigua*, PG 91.1076 B C. On St. Maximus, see P. Sherwood, *The Early Ambigua of St. Maximus the Confessor* (Rome, 1955), and, by the same author, translation and commentary on works of Maximus, in *Ancient Christian Writers*, No. 21.

mation (Confirmation), and the Holy Eucharist. Thus, the Orthodox Hesychasts of this period thought of the Prayer of Jesus not as a subjective and emotional way of communicating with God, but as a method by which they could make more effective, in themselves, the gifts received through the sacraments.

During this period also the practice of saying the Prayer of Jesus according to a particular method began to be widely followed. This consisted of repeating the words of the short prayer "Lord Jesus Christ, Son of God, have mercy on me" in rhythm with one's breathing while at the same time concentrating the mind on the *region of the heart,* regarded as being the focal point for the whole psycho-physiological nature of man.

Though attacked by Barlaam the Calabrian († 1350), a philosopher of both skeptical and Platonizing tendencies, the Hesychast method of prayer was defended in the fourteenth century by the great theologian and monk of Athos, who later became archbishop of Thessalonica, St. Gregory Palamas († 1359). It was the merit of Palamas to have seen clearly the connection between the Orthodox doctrine of God, the deification which the mystics sought to achieve in their mystical experiences, the Hesychast method of prayer, and the sacramental life of the Church. Without attempting to construct a doctrinal *summa,* he assigned to each one of these elements its proper place. God, essentially unsharable and transcendent, is also a living God who communicates Himself voluntarily through His acts: He thus becomes available not merely to knowledge, but sharable or communicable, because of the hypostatic union of divinity and humanity in Jesus Christ. Even then, however, He remains transcendent, since this is His nature: participation in His Being or deification is only possible to the extent that He wills it and in accordance with His

energies or acts. This participation is total in Jesus
Christ, since the Person of the Word incarnate is the
source of all the divine operations. The distinction established here between transcendent essence and "energies" of course involves a philosophical antinomy,
but is God subject to the limitations of our intellect?
This "deification" in Jesus Christ is available to us
through Baptism and the Eucharist: the Incarnate
Word communicates to us the divine life and trans-
forms our whole being from inside. Henceforth, "the
Kingdom of God is within us." This "within us" does
not signify necessarily "in the mind" or "in the soul,"
for human nature is indivisible and shares as a whole
in God. Our body therefore, as well as our mind and
soul, shares in this process through fasting, prayer,
and various acts which make up the duties of the
Christian in his search for the Kingdom of God, and
it can also receive, as of now, the first fruits of glory:
does the Church not venerate the corporal remains of
the saints after their death, and during their life do
the saints not perform miracles which attest the transfiguration already achieved? [15]

Finally, it is the special task of Eastern Orthodox
spirituality to make known to us the presence of God
in history, and to make this known not only in words
but also by providing living examples of God's power.
God is henceforth present in the Church not only in
His written Word, but in the reality of the sacraments
and in the gifts of the Spirit, evident in His saints,
which are available likewise to all Christians who are

[15] We have examined the doctrine of Palamas in some detail
in our Study on Gregory Palamas, and a more rapid sketch of
the Hesychast tradition, both before and after the fourteenth
century, may be found in Saint Grégoire Palamas et la mystique
orthodoxe, Coll. "Maîtres Spirituels," No. 20 (Paris, 1959). The
chief work of Palamas, his Triads for the Defense of the Holy
Hesychasts, has been edited by us with a complete translation
in French, in the series Specilegium Sacrum Lovaniense, Nos.
30-31 (Louvain, 1959), 2 vols.

determined to live in accordance with their baptismal promises. The saints of the Church—from St. Paul who was "raised to the third heaven" to St. Seraphim of Sarov whose face was illumined by a divine light— are all witnesses of this New Life granted to men which transfigures matter itself. Apostles, bishops, martyrs, missionaries, monks, or simple laymen: wherever God is pleased to find them, the saints are the true agents of the Kingdom of God in the world.

In the history of the Orthodox Church Hesychast mysticism has proved to be the most traditional way in which this communion with God, which constitutes the very essence of the Christian life, has expressed itself. Because of its simplicity and uncomplicated nature the Prayer of Jesus became a very popular form of spiritual devotion and was widespread not only among the monks but also among the laity. Its precise definition by great theologians saved it from degenerating into a purely individualistic form of piety. Only in the Church, in the communion of saints, in the sacramental life of the Christian community, can the mystical experience of the individual have, in reality, a truly Christian meaning. Here also is found the ultimate criterion for all spirituality. The Church does not canonize any particular form or method of devotion, but merely sanctions the holiness of those who have been able to express the reality of the Kingdom of God in their lives and in their words.

CHAPTER X

ORTHODOX VIEW OF
THE CHURCH

TODAY more than ever the important topic of discussion among the various separate denominations which together make up the Christian world is the nature of the Church, and we can truthfully say that *inside* each one of the great confessions the ecclesiological problem is far from having been finally settled. Under Pope John XXIII, the Roman Catholic Church is now suddenly becoming aware of the fact that the incomplete and rather hastily arrived-at definitions of the First Vatican Council in 1870 did not provide it with a really balanced and coherent theology of the Church. It intends, therefore, to develop its own doctrine on church unity by clarifying it. Protestants, owing to the remarkable new interest in Biblical theology and the success of the ecumenical movement, have to a large extent abandoned their former aversion to all forms of ecclesiology; without denying any of the principles of the Reformation, they are again discovering the importance of the problem of the Church from the double viewpoint of Tradition and sacramental life. The Orthodox, finally, confronted by entirely new historical situations and obliged to solve problems that were never faced by Byzantium, have been compelled to reformulate their Tradition and readjust the attitudes of the past. It is in response to this new and somewhat "fluid" situation that we shall attempt to outline here some of the essential traits of an Orthodox approach to the ecclesiological problem. The reader will probably have guessed what some of these traits are from our chapters on the history of the Church and Orthodox spirituality. We shall therefore content ourselves here with pointing out the permanent elements in the Orthodox position with regard to the great debate on ecumenism.

Curiously enough, the ecclesiological problem was never formally posed as a real issue in the medieval debate between Constantinople and Rome. It was the question of the *Filioque,* and later that of purgatory and the invocation of the Holy Spirit in the liturgy, or even such questions of an altogether secondary nature as the use of unleavened bread (azymes) in the Western mass, or fasting on Saturdays, which claimed the attention of theologians and controversialists. Some modern theologians like V. Lossky emphasize that there is an intrinsic connection between the Latin doctrine of the Trinity and Roman ecclesiology, but this connection was certainly not clearly perceived or realized in the Middle Ages. In fact, as we have seen, it was the very absence of any common ecclesiological factor which led to the schism. When difficulties arose between East and West, one side appealed to the authority of Tradition and the Councils, while the other appealed to the authority of the Successor of Peter. For a long time—until the capture of Constantinople by the Crusaders in 1204—the Byzantines did not really understand, or did not wish to understand, the new Roman attitude toward the Church, and in their discussions with Latins avoided touching on this point directly. It was only in 1204, when Innocent III appointed a Venetian, Thomas Morosini, to the see of

St. John Chrysostom after the sack of Constantinople, that Byzantine theologians began to discuss seriously the origin of the power which the popes claimed to have.

Their criticism of the Roman position was concerned not so much with the person of the Apostle Peter himself or his position among the Twelve and in the primitive Church, as with the nature of his *succession.* Byzantium did not see why the Church of Rome should be able to claim the *exclusive* right to this succession, when the New Testament furnishes no information about the ministry of Peter in Rome. Could not Antioch, and particularly Jerusalem, where Peter played a key role according to the book of Acts, claim, more logically than Rome, to be the "see of Peter"? The Byzantines recognized, of course, a universal primacy in the Roman Church, but this primacy, according to them, did not have its unique origin in the fact of Peter's death in Rome, but rather in a whole collection of factors of which the chief were that Rome was a church "very great, very ancient, and known to all," as St. Irenaeus put it,[1] and because it had the tombs of the *two* leaders (*coryphaei*) of the Apostles, Peter and Paul, but above all, because it was the capital of the Empire. The famous Canon 28 of the ecumenical council of Chalcedon insists on this latter point.[2] In other words, the Roman primacy was not an exclusive and divine privilege, a power which was possessed by the bishop of Rome by virtue of an express commandment of the Lord, but a *de facto* authority which the Church had formally recognized by the voice of its councils. It went without saying that the pope could not, under such conditions, enjoy

[1] *Against the Heresies,* 3,2.

[2] See our article on "La primauté romaine dans la tradition canonique jusqu'au concile de Chalcedoine," in the periodical *Istina,* No. 4 (1957), pp. 463-82.

any privilege of infallibility. If his presence or that of his legates was considered necessary for a council to be considered "ecumenical," that is to say, truly representative of the episcopate of the whole Empire —the presence of the other great churches was also considered equally necessary—his opinion was never considered to be true *ex sese*. The Eastern churches could live for centuries outside the Roman communion without being unduly perturbed by the fact, and the sixth ecumenical council did not hesitate to condemn the memory of Pope Honorius I for having given support to the Monothelite heresy.

There could be no question therefore, in Byzantine opinion, of holding that the words of Christ, addressed to Peter: "Thou art Peter, and upon this rock I will build my Church" (Matt. xvi.18); "Feed my sheep" (John xxi), etc., related exclusively to the bishops of Rome. This interpretation, generally emphasized in documents issued by the Roman Church from the third century, is not found in any Eastern or Western patristic commentary on the Scriptures, for the Fathers saw in these words, essentially, a recognition by Christ of the fact that Peter had confessed the divine nature of the Son of God on the road to Caesarea Philippi: Peter is declared to be the rock of the Church *to the extent* that he confesses this faith. And all those who imitate Peter and make the same confession likewise inherit the promise. It is on them, on all believers, that the Church is built. This general interpretation of the passage, which we find in Origen and many of the Fathers, received an ecclesiological corrective, however, in the Church's doctrine on the nature of the episcopate, for all bishops are invested with the special charisma to teach. Their special function is to proclaim the true faith. They are therefore *ex officio* the successors of Peter. This conception of the Petrine succession which we find clearly expressed in St. Cyprian of Carthage (third century) and which occurs again and again in the history of theology, will be taken up by Byzantine theologians.

"Well, then," writes Nilus Cabasilas in the fourteenth century, "is the pope not a successor of Peter at all? He is, but only *as a bishop*. . . . For Peter is an Apostle and the head of the Apostles, but the pope is neither an Apostle (for the Apostles did not ordain other Apostles, but pastors and teachers), nor much less the Coryphaeus (leader) of the Apostles. Peter is the teacher of the whole world, whereas the pope is the bishop of Rome. Peter could have ordained a bishop in Antioch, another in Alexandria, and another elsewhere, but the bishop of Rome does not do so . . ." [3] We could multiply texts and quotations proving clearly that the controversy between East and West was due basically to profoundly different attitudes toward the Church. These differences were concerned with the nature of *authority* in the Church, and essentially with the nature of the Church itself.[4]

In the eyes of the East, the Church was above all a communion in which God is present *sacramentally*: the sacrament is, in effect, the way in which the death and resurrection of the Lord are "commemorated" and by which his Second Coming is proclaimed and anticipated. Now the *fullness* of this reality—hence also the fullness of truth and fullness of the magisterium—is present in every local church, in every Christian community gathered around the eucharistic Table and having a bishop at its head, the successor of Peter and the other Apostles. For the bishop is not a successor of any particular Apostle, but of all, and it matters little whether his church has been founded by

[3] PG 149.704 C, D.

[4] For the Orthodox attitude toward the Roman primacy, see *St. Vladimir's Seminary Quarterly*, Vol. IV, Nos. 2-3 (1960), a special issue devoted to *Primacy and Primacies in the Orthodox Church*.

John, Paul, or Peter, or whether it is of more recent
and humbler origin.[5] His function is to teach in accordance with the common teaching of the apostolic
college, of which Peter was the spokesman; he occupies the place of the Lord at the eucharistic Table;
and he is the "image of God" in the church over which
he presides, to use an expression of St. Ignatius of
Antioch (about A.D. 100). These episcopal functions
are essentially the *same*, whether at Rome, Constantinople, or Moscow, and God could not have intended
to grant one Church special privileges in this respect,
since he gave the plenitude of power to *all*.

The local churches, however, are not mere isolated
units living in separation from each other: they are
united by the *identity* of their faith and their witness
to the truth. This identity is manifested particularly
when episcopal consecrations are held, necessarily attended by several bishops. To give greater effectiveness
to the witness of the churches and solve common problems, local councils or synods have been held from time
to time since the third century, and gradually a certain
order of precedence emerged among the various
churches. This order includes a universal primacy—
first that of Rome, then Constantinople—and also
local primacies (metropolitans, today the heads of the
autocephalous churches), but it is capable of further

[5] Several Fathers, particularly St. Irenaeus of Lyons, insist
on the apostolic origin of certain churches in order to establish
the orthodoxy of those churches as compared with the Gnostics.
However, in the East, as Father F. Dvornik has recently shown
in *The Idea of Apostolicity in Byzantium* (Cambridge, Mass.,
Harvard University Press, 1958), apostolic sees never claimed
to have any special authority as a result of the fact of being
"apostolic": there were far too many of them in Asia Minor,
Syria, Palestine, and Greece for such pretensions to be taken
seriously. The Church of Jerusalem, for example, until the
fifth century, was subject to the metropolitan of Caesarea. In
the West, on the other hand, the Church of Rome was the
only church that could claim apostolic origin and no one disputed its prestige based on this fact.

214]   THE ORTHODOX CHURCH

modifications, for it is not of an ontological nature, it
does not restrict the fundamental identity of the local
churches, and it is subject to the formal condition that
the one Orthodox faith must be confessed. A heretical
primate would perforce lose all rights to the primacy.

We thus see where the root of the schism between
East and West lies. In the West, the papacy, as the
result of a long development over the centuries, now
possesses, according to the Vatican definitions of 1870,
both a doctrinal infallibility and an "immediate" jurisdiction over all the faithful. The bishop of Rome therefore is the visible criterion of Truth and the unique
head of the universal Church, without however possessing any sacramental powers different from those of
other bishops. In the Orthodox Church, on the other
hand, no power can exist by divine right outside and
above the local eucharistic community, which corresponds today to what we call the diocese. The relations between bishops and the order of precedence
between them are governed by the canons and are
not something absolute and unchangeable. There does
not exist, therefore, any visible criterion of Truth,
apart from the *consensus* of the Church, the normal
organ of which is the ecumenical council. But this
council, as we have seen above, is not an authority *ex
sese,* outside and above the local churches; it is
merely the expression and witness of their accord. A
council which considers itself formally "ecumenical"
may even be rejected by the Church (examples:
Ephesus in 449, Florence in 1438). The permanence
of Truth in the Church is thus a fact of a supernatural order, similar in every respect to the nature of the
sacrament. It can be detected by religious experience,
but is not amenable to rational explanation or capable
of being subjected to legal norms.

The unity of the Church is, above all, a unity in
faith and not an administrative unity. Administrative

unity can actually only be an expression of a common allegiance to the Truth. If the unity of faith could have been determined by some visible, permanent organ, the doctrinal disputes of the earliest centuries and the councils and controversies of the time of the Fathers would have had no meaning. Today likewise, the reunion with the Church of the churches separated from it presupposes, necessarily and absolutely, their agreement with it in the faith.

Between Rome and the Orthodox Church, therefore, any future dialogue must necessarily hinge on the role still left in Roman ecclesiology for the local church and the episcopate. But if the pope is the final judge in doctrinal matters and exercises an "immediate" jurisdiction over each and every one of the Catholic faithful, can the bishops be anything else than his local vicars? In spite of the enormous obstacle to mutual understanding created by the Vatican Council, there appears to be hope now that a supplementary statement can be made on this point, clarifying the definitions of 1870. The Orthodox, for their part, should reflect more seriously than they have done on the possible forms which the *common* witness could and should take, and especially on the part to be played in this witness by the bishop who is *primus inter pares.* East and West are still united by too long and too common a Biblical and patristic tradition for a discussion not to be possible on this as well as on other points.

On numerous occasions since the sixteenth century the Orthodox have had occasion to define their position with respect to Protestantism. However, they have sometimes done this rather ineptly without fully knowing who their correspondents were and using Roman Catholic arguments against them, as when the Calvinist *Confession* of Loukaris was condemned. Today a new fact of fundamental importance in the

history of Christianity has profoundly altered the outlook of Protestantism, namely the ecumenical movement.[6]

Protestant nineteenth-century missionaries first became fully aware of the tremendous scandal being
caused for non-Christians by the divisions among
Christians. While preaching the same Christ, they
were interpreting his teaching in different ways, were
refusing to communicate from the same Table, were
bitter rivals in missionary countries, and were trans-
planting to Africa and Asia the quarrels and preju-
dicies of sixteenth-century Europe. It did not take
the missionaries very long to become aware of
these facts. This discovery led men of good will, in
Europe and America, to intensify their search for
Christian unity, to found world-wide interconfessional
youth organizations, and finally to organize the first
"ecumenical" conferences. The two trends which made
up the movement—one called *Life and Work,* representing a more practical type of Christianity, the other,
Faith and Order, more concerned with theological implications—were finally merged in the single *ecumenical movement.* Between the two world wars the movement was largely a matter of individual participation.
The theologians and prelates who take part did so on
their own responsibility and did not engage their
churches. But in 1948, at the Amsterdam Conference,
a World Council of *Churches* was formally inaugu-
rated. Henceforth the churches themselves agreed to
take part in the Council and participate in all its activities through their official representatives.

As defined by the Amsterdam Conference, the nature and goal of the Council was to be an "instrument
in the service of the churches, by means of which they
can bear witness together in areas requiring unity of

[6] See R. Rouse and S. Neil, A *History of the Ecumenical
Movement, 1517-1948* (London, S.P.C.K., 1954).

action." It was clearly specified, moreover, that the decisions whether of the General Assembly or of any of the organs of the Council were not to prejudice the individual member churches, who were free to accept or reject them. The promoters of the movement emphasized repeatedly that it was not their intention to create a sort of Super-Church or to impose a centralized organization on the member churches. Under these conditions 153 churches agreed at Amsterdam to take part in the World Council and to bear witness in this way to their common faith in "Jesus Christ, as God and Savior."

The attitude of the Orthodox Church toward the ecumenical movement from the very beginning, and then later toward the World Council of Churches, was laid down in a long series of conferences and contacts between Orthodox and Protestant theologians in the nineteenth century.[7] Orthodox representatives have regularly taken part in the great conferences since 1910, and in 1920 the ecumenical patriarch published an encyclical addressed "to the Churches of Christ throughout the world," urging them to show greater understanding for each other and to co-operate more fully in the practical sphere. Thus, paradoxically, the First See of Orthodoxy assumed the leadership of Orthodox participation in the ecumenical movement by stressing the *Life and Work* aspect of the latter rather than the usefulness of theological discussions with the West. The other Orthodox churches were much more reserved and prudent in their attitude, and remain so to this day. The majority of them, however, were represented at the ecumenical conferences of Stockholm (1925), Lausanne (1927), Oxford (1937), Edinburgh (1937), and Utrecht (1938).

[7] See the remarkable well-documented study of G. Florovsky on this subject, "Orthodox Ecumenism in the 19th Century," in *St. Vladimir's Seminary Quarterly*, Vol. IV, Nos. 3-4.

The Russian Church also was present—though it was not "represented"—in the person of outstanding theologians of the emigration who took a leading part in the discussions.

As a result of the Second World War, three new factors have profoundly modified the status of the problem so far as Orthodox participation in the ecumenical movement is concerned: the establishment of communist regimes in the Orthodox countries of Eastern Europe, with the single exception of Greece; the restoration of the patriarchate of Moscow; and the establishment of the World Council of Churches. Reasons both of a political and a religious nature, the relative importance of which it is difficult to assess, prevented Orthodox delegates, until the New Delhi Assembly of 1961, from taking part in the sessions of the Council in sufficient numbers. While political factors may be largely responsible in the case of Churches behind the Iron Curtain, which include over 90 per cent of all Orthodox, this cannot be the only cause, for Protestant Churches from Czechoslovakia and Hungary have never missed an opportunity to take part in the common work. The rather violent opposition, among certain circles, to participation in the Council by Orthodox Churches in countries which have maintained their political ties with the West, shows that such participation involves crucial problems of a spiritual and theological nature for the Orthodox Church.

Only the Churches of Constantinople, Greece, and Cyprus were represented at Amsterdam in 1948 and agreed to take part in the World Council. Some months later, a conference of the Churches of Russia, Serbia, Rumania, Bulgaria, Poland, Albania, and Czechoslovakia, in the presence of a delegate of the patriarch of Antioch who signed the acts on behalf of the two Oriental patriarchates (Antioch and Alexandria), met in Moscow and declared that the Amsterdam Conference had no other purpose than to "create a new ecumenical Church," that insufficient attention was paid to dogmatic problems in its program, while, on the contrary, political or "imperialist" interests were predominant. The churches meeting at Moscow therefore refused to send representatives.

From 1948, the ecumenical patriarchate of Constantinople was practically the only Orthodox church to take an active part in the Council. A wait-and-see attitude was adopted by the other Oriental patriarchates, which sent no delegates to the sessions until the Central Committee at Rhodes in 1959. A violent controversy raged in Greece between the adversaries and partisans of participation and the Greek hierarchy —in the main hostile to participation—decreed at the beginning of 1959 that only lay theologians who could not engage the Church would be allowed to represent the Greek Church at the ecumenical assemblies in the future. Moreover, they were forbidden to discuss purely dogmatic questions.[8]

Orthodox reservations with regard to the World Council are based primarily on the fear, conscious or otherwise, that the Orthodox Church may find itself bound by an institution which in fact does not represent it. The constitution of the Council and repeated statements by its leaders make it perfectly clear that the member churches remain entirely free, doctrinally and administratively. Nevertheless, the common work of the Council is constantly going forward—is this not precisely the aim of the Council?—in the theological field, as well as in those of the missions, social work, and international affairs. But the Orthodox only take a very small part in this work, since they are represented only by a handful of delegates at the Assemblies and

[8] At Rhodes, in 1959, no bishop under the jurisdiction of the Holy Synod at Athens took part in the official discussions of the Committee.

in the various branches of the organization of the Council. Consequently they naturally feel that they are taking part in an enterprise which they do not control and which is dominated by Protestant thinking. If the Orthodox Church were in a position to make its weight felt in the work of the Council, it is likely that this situation would change considerably. But this is not the only problem.

It is undeniable that Orthodox *ecclesiology* or its attitude toward the Church means that it cannot participate in the work of the Council on the same basis as the other communions that have emerged from the Reformation. Orthodox and Protestants simply do not see the same thing in the World Council of Churches.

Protestants, for whom the Church remains essentially "a communion of forgiven sinners," generally hold that the historical divisions among Christians are divisions in the *Church itself*. The unity of the Church mentioned in the Creed is not realized in any one of the Christian confessions, but all are seeking it. This is precisely what the aim of the World Council should be. Thanks to it, the Church is now drawing nearer to unity and in doing so will gradually become *more fully* the Church. It will "repent" for the sin against unity of which it has been guilty and will thus achieve greater fidelity to God's Word. Many Protestant leaders insist again and again in their discussions of the ecumenical issue that it is necessary for the "churches" to abandon their exclusive dogmatism and emphasis on doctrinal obstacles. This attitude is clearly stated in numerous documents approved by the Protestant majority in the Assemblies of the World Council. "Thus we may speak," declares the Report of Section I of the Assembly of Evanston (1954), "of the oneness of the Church on its earthly pilgrimage as a growth from its unity, as given, to its unity, as fully manifested. In this way we may think of the Church in the same way as we are able to think of the individual believer, who may be said at one and the same time to be both a justified man and a sinner (*simul iustus et peccator*). . . ."

It is obvious that a theology of this kind which regards the Church as both "justified and sinner" cannot be acceptable to the Orthodox Church: for the mystery of the Church consists precisely in the fact that sinners, coming together, form the *infallible Church*. They constitute the Body of Christ, the Temple of the Holy Spirit, and the Column and Foundation of Truth. No analogy can possibly be drawn between the individual member, who is a sinner, and the Church, the Body of Christ. This Protestant thesis appears to the Orthodox to amount to a negation of the full and real presence of Christ in his Church, as a repudiation of the promises which he made to his disciples: "When he will come, the Spirit of Truth, he will guide you into all truth" (John xvi.13). This "all truth" is therefore present in the visible Church, which is one, holy, catholic, and apostolic, and from which other churches are separated. Christian unity is a unity with Christ in the Holy Spirit, and not a unity among men which has been lost at some time in the past. This unity belongs to the One Church, which cannot be divided by human controversies. Men cannot divide God and his Truth, and then later restore them to unity. They may leave them, however, and then return. It is to a return of this kind that the Orthodox Church summons all Christians: a return to the faith of the Fathers and Apostles, which she is conscious of having preserved in its fullness. From this point of view the World Council is therefore primarily a meeting place, a place for witness, for discussion, and eventually for practical collaboration. Orthodox participation does not mean that the Orthodox *Church*, as a divine reality in history, can add anything essential to what it already possesses, but it does mean that the Orthodox as *individuals*—imperfect sinners though they may be—can both help to point out to other Christians the true road to unity and also learn from them how to make better use of the divine gift which they alone possess in its entirety, by being members of the One Church.

This is the task to which the Orthodox delegates are devoting themselves in the ecumenical assemblies —few in number and inadequately prepared as they often are—and it was owing to their efforts that the Toronto Declaration was passed by the Central Committee of the Council (1950), making possible, by its negative language, the continued presence of Orthodox delegates in the Committee: "The World Council cannot and should not be based on any particular conception of the Church. It does not prejudge the ecclesiological problem in advance. . . . Membership in the World Council of Churches does not imply that a Church treats its own conception of the Church as merely relative. . . . Membership does not imply that each Church must regard the other member Churches as Churches in the full sense of the word. . . ."

These conditions, expressed in a language that is absolutely clear, have made possible continued Orthodox participation in the ecumenical *fellowship* without having to renounce, or seem to renounce, their consciousness of being the only true Church and without having to modify their basic attitude toward the other Christian communions. This attitude, however, does not prevent the other member churches from developing an ecumenical theology on their own account. This is precisely what happened, as shown by the Report of the Evanston Assembly, which we have just been quoting. This document was worded in such a way, however, that the Orthodox delegates felt unable to support it and published a separate statement of their own on Section I:

We believe that the return of the communions to the faith of the ancient, united, and indivisible Church of the seven ecumenical councils, namely, to the pure and unchanged and common heritage of the forefathers of all divided Christians shall alone produce the desired reunion of all separated Christians. For, only the unity and fellowship of Christians in a common faith shall have as a necessary result their fellowship in the sacraments and their indissoluble unity in love, as members of one and the same body of the One Church of Christ. . . . We are bound to declare our profound conviction that the Holy Orthodox Church alone has preserved in full and intact 'the faith once delivered unto the saints.' It is not because of our human merit, but because it pleases God to preserve 'his treasure in earthern vessels, that the excellency of the power may be of God' (2 Cor. iv.7).

From the Orthodox point of view, therefore, Christian ecumenism cannot mean a search for unity at any price on the basis of a minimum common denominator: it is the *fullness of truth* that will unite Christians, for Christ is fullness and he can never abandon his Church. The presence of Orthodox representatives in the ecumenical movement is a direct consequence of the universal command of the Lord that we should love our brethren, particularly all those who call themselves Christians, but this love, coming from God as it does, cannot be a love without truth. The Son of God made himself *visible* in the course of history, he became man and founded on earth a *visible* communion, which was to possess sacramentally the fullness of his redemptive grace. This fullness is present in each community which professes the true faith. In the eyes of the Orthodox, "certain fundamental elements which make up the reality of the fullness of the Church are lacking in the separated communions" (Declaration of the Orthodox Delegation at Evanston): these elements must therefore be restored. The Protestant conception of the unity and fullness of the Church as either something of an invisible nature or belonging to an eschatological future seems, to Orthodox Christians, to amount to a denial of the reality of salvation, as a repudiation of that which God himself has given us.

The Orthodox representatives have always been free to express these views clearly in the Assemblies of the World Council. But they have been present there in too few numbers, up until now, to be able to carry on an effective discussion with the Protestant majority. To be more fruitful and to be able to exercise some influence on the course of the discussions, they ought to participate more effectively and be present in greater numbers. If this is not done in the near future, it is certain that the Protestant majority in the Council, by a process of internal logic, will lead the organization more and more in a direction incompatible with Orthodox principles[9] and make their presence impossible. The issuance of separate, negative statements, and spasmodic collaboration in specialized areas, particularly those relating to material aid, do not constitute an adequate witness for the Orthodox Church. The full participation of the Moscow patriarchate and of the other Eastern European Orthodox Churches, which became a reality since New Delhi (1961), will certainly ensure a much more efficient Orthodox witness in the Council. One must simply pray and hope that political pressures and conflicts will not prevent

[9] See on this subject A. Schmemann, "Orthodox Agony in the World Council," in *Christianity Today*, Vol. II (January 8, 1958).

them from expressing the essential meaning of the Orthodox message.

Since we do not have the space to be able to deal with all aspects of Orthodox ecclesiology *systematically* and in detail, we have confined ourselves to a discussion of the Orthodox position with respect to Western Christianity and have emphasized recent developments. The reader can now see how this position differs from the others and what its peculiar features are. As opposed to Protestantism and Roman Catholicism, the Orthodox Church claims to be the true Church of Christ from which Western Christians have separated. Its claims are as exclusive and categorical as those of Rome, but they are put forth in the name of a different conception of the Church. The historic development of the papacy culminating in the proclamation of the Vatican dogma has conferred on Roman Catholicism a monolithic structure and given it a permanent criterion of Truth, which is nevertheless compatible with a great deal of doctrinal and liturgical divergence. Rome is more anxious that all Christians accept the existence of a final criterion than a particular doctrinal system. But the Orthodox Church does not claim to possess any infallible and permanent criterion of Truth or any monolithic structure: it sees unity in a communion of faith, of which the Church itself—or rather the Holy Spirit always dwelling in the Church—is the unique judge. The Spirit of Truth dwells in the communion of the faithful who are united by the bond of charity, and while he normally speaks through those who have the charisma to teach, namely, the bishops, he belongs properly to the Church as a Body. This Body is totally present everywhere that the Eucharist is celebrated, in every local church, and no authority, apart from that of the Spirit, can possibly impose itself on the people of God united in Jesus Christ. The Christian is by definition free, free

with a *true* liberty which permits him to accept the
Truth which God reveals to him. He is therefore also
responsible for this Truth: he finds it and preserves it
in the Church, in the communion of the Spirit, in a
reasonable obedience to the authorities in the Church
(magisterium), and in the unity of love with his
brethren.[10]

This freedom the Orthodox enjoys in his relations
with God makes it possible for him to carry on a dialogue with all Christians, Protestants or Catholics, and
to appeal to his separated brethren to accept, not some
external "criterion"—Rome or *sola scriptura*—but the
living Truth as experienced in a liturgical communion
and in the Church as the Temple of the Holy Spirit.
On the other hand, the great responsibility which he
feels has been placed on his own shoulders makes him
acutely aware of the importance of all doctrinal questions. Not only will he never consent to cast doubt
on any of the dogmas of the Church, but he even believes that any change in the rites or government of
the Church is a matter that personally concerns him,
even when the change is of a purely routine or trivial
nature.

The "liberty of the children of God" is indeed a
heavy burden to bear at the present time, because it
involves such a heavy *responsibility*. And yet this liberty is one of the keys to Christian ecclesiology. The
Orthodox Church clings to this above all else, and in
doing so feels that it is defending the very mystery of
God's presence in the Christian communion.

[10] This responsibility of all Christians for the truth is brought
out by the Encyclical of the Oriental patriarchs in 1848, as we
have seen. The idea has been developed particularly by Russian theologians in the nineteenth century. The most famous of
these, without question, was A. S. Khomiakov (see A. Gratieux,
A. S. Khomiakov [Paris, Éditions du Cerf, 1950], 2 vols.; cf. also
J. S. Romanides, "Orthodox Ecclesiology According to Alexis
Khomiakov," in *The Greek Orthodox Theological Review*, Vol.
II, no. 1 [1956]). The same idea is echoed, on a different
level, in Dostoevsky's famous *Legend of the Grand Inquisitor*.

CONCLUSION

OUR PAGES on the origin of the Church in the brief account of Orthodox history and particularly the chapter on Orthodox doctrine and spirituality will help the reader to see that the essential element in the Orthodox message today is its emphasis upon a genuine "Catholic" tradition, catholicity being understood here in a broad sense with respect to truth, continuity, and fullness, rather than in a mere geographical sense.

It is a historical fact which no one can deny that the Christian East has remained aloof from the great changes which have occurred in the West as a result of papal centralization and the great Scholastic movement during the Middle Ages, the Reformation, and the Counter-Reformation. From the ninth to the fifteenth century Byzantium went on developing and living according to the great tradition of the Fathers, their theology, spirituality, and above all their sacramental conception of the Church. It deliberately refused to identify itself with any particular synthesis of philosophical thought and Revelation such as the Scholastic system, and preferred to remain faithful to patristic thought. Its theology, and particularly its doctrine on the sacraments and the Church, were never formulated in accordance with the dictates and terminology of a given philosophical system, and the constitution of the Orthodox Church was never thought of solely in terms of the laws by which a law-dominated institution was governed. Its God remained a living, acting God, the God of the Bible, the God of Abraham, Isaac, and Jacob; He was never transformed into the God of philosophers. As a matter of fact, the Church never provided itself with a complete system of canon law: the canons of those councils which it acknowledged as authentic were regarded merely as an expression of the Church's nature under certain concrete circumstances, a kind of "jurisprudence of the Holy Spirit," as it were, reflecting the eternal *order* of the Body of Christ. They were never transformed into a kind of juridical supergovernment and were never looked upon as a means by which to exercise an effective control over all members of the Church, centrally or from above. By defining the position of the Orthodox Church rather negatively and opposing it to Western Christianity in this way, it is not our intention to imply that the latter has *completely* transformed revealed doctrine into a philosophical theory or the constitution of the Church into a mere juridical system. We merely wish to point out that in its desire to bear witness to the Truth and do so effectively, the West has gone much further in these two directions than the East, and in so doing it has formulated a certain number of dogmas making any return to the past difficult. Therefore the ecumenical task of Orthodoxy, in its discussions with both Protestants and Catholics, should be to question the appropriateness of certain formulas handed down from the Latin Middle Ages and the period of the Counter-Reformation, without, however, giving the impression of wishing to deny the traditional doctrines which they are intended to express; and to urge Roman Catholics on the one hand fraternally to return to the common sources, and Protestants on the other to be more receptive to the idea of Tradition.

In order to play this role effectively, however, the Orthodox must do a bit of rethinking and reflecting themselves. If the truth which they are conscious of possessing is really Catholic truth, it must of course be valid for all men, all times, and all countries. It must be capable of supplying an answer to the very real problems raised by Western Christians during the centuries which have elapsed since the separation. It must face the challenge of the modern world. In order to make their message meaningful, the Orthodox must learn to live these problems *from inside,* not externally. It is not enough merely to conform outwardly to Western customs or make a few liturgical adjustments; they must learn to discipline themselves spiritually; there must be an act of love as well as of humility. It is all too obvious that while the Church as a supernatural body always possesses the fullness of divine life and truth, individuals, groups, nations, and local churches fail to conform to this life and this truth in all respects. In this regard, what may be called historical Orthodoxy, that is, the various nations which formerly made up or still make up the Orthodox world, have much to ask forgiveness for. Granted their history has been a particularly tragic one. The Arab, Turkish, and Mongol invasions and the recent martyrdom occasioned by the Russian Revolution have all been so many terrible disasters interrupting the course of development in the East. External factors of this kind largely explain, perhaps, the present weakness of Eastern Christianity. But there are also other weaknesses for which the Orthodox have only themselves to blame, in particular, the bane of excessive nationalism which has resulted in the harmful isolation of Orthodox churches from each other.

The future of the Orthodox Church and its spiritual influence is now clearly at stake, both in the communist-dominated countries of the East and in the West, where Providence has led millions of the Orthodox and compelled them to bear witness to their faith.

In the communist-dominated countries, especially in Russia, there have been many martyrs on behalf of the faith during the terrible revolutionary period and more recently in the post-revolutionary years. The Russian Church has learned on the whole, rather quickly, to distinguish between the absolute values of religion and the relative values of politics, and its continued survival, a veritable miracle, may be attributed to this fact. However, if the Christians of Russia accept as normal and satisfactory the present condition of relative tranquility and prosperity, they may be succumbing to a new and even subtler form of temptation. The Russian Church is forbidden to have anything to do with certain vital areas: it may not educate the young, it may not publish any religious works, it may not engage in missionary or charitable work, and finally it is not free to pass judgment on the policies of the government. So far, the Church has succeeded in showing that it is not the mere "vestige of capitalism" which the Soviet authorities claim that it is; however, its future depends very much on the possibility of being able to make an effective appeal to youth and thus on being able to get its message across to the coming generation.

The Orthodox presence in the West is a rather new phenomenon. Following the two world wars large numbers of emigrants from Eastern Europe sought new homes in Western Europe, and particularly in America. The social and religious consequences of this migration are not yet clearly discernible, but we may venture to say that it will certainly be regarded as of great importance in the history of Christianity. The Orthodox Church has now ceased to be an exclusively Eastern Church. This fact can readily be observed in the United States, for example, where several millions of the faithful have largely adopted the language, culture, and ways of thought of their new country, while at the same time remaining faithful to the Church of their forefathers. To some extent, they have even succeeded in breathing into the latter a new missionary spirit and in imbuing it with a new zeal for organization such as it has never known before. By surmounting national differences inherited from the past, by training a clergy that can cope with the new conditions in which the Church finds itself, and by their skill in reconciling a faithfulness to tradition with the needs of the modern world, the Western Orthodox can give an entirely new meaning to their witness to the faith. This is the task to which their Church calls them, a Church which claims to be the true Church of Christ, and it is by this standard that they will be judged by history, by their brothers, by other Christians, and finally by God himself.

SELECTED BIBLIOGRAPHY

1. The Orthodox Faith

CLÉMENT, O., *L'Église orthodoxe, Collection* "Que sais-je?" Paris, 1961.

BULGAKOV, S., *The Orthodox Church.* London, 1935; 2nd ed., New York, 1960.

EVDOKIMOV, P., *L'Orthodoxie.* Neuchâtel-Paris, Delachaux et Niestlé, 1960.

GAVIN, F., *Some Aspects of Contemporary Greek Orthodox Thought.* London, 1936.

LOSSKY, V., *The Mystical Theology of the Eastern Church.* Napierville, Ill., Allenson, 1957.

Die Orthodoxe Kirche in griechischer Sicht. Stuttgart, Evangelisches Verlagswerk, 1959. A symposium in German, edited by P. Bratsiotis, Professor at the University of Athens.

2. Orthodox Ecclesiology

Primacy and Primacies in the Orthodox Church (articles by V. Kesich, J. Meyendorff, A. Schmemann, and S. Verkhovsky), special issue of *St. Vladimir's Seminary Quarterly*, Vol. IV, 1960.

La Primauté de Pierre dans l'Église orthodoxe. Neuchâtel-Paris, Delachaux et Niestlé, 1960, Bibliothèque orthodoxe, No. 1. A symposium in French of articles by

N. Afanassief, N. Koulomzine, J. Meyendorff, and
A. Schmemann, which will shortly appear in English.

3. Orthodox Liturgy and Spirituality

CABASILAS, N., *A Commentary on the Divine Liturgy*, tr.
by J. M. Hussey and McNulty. London, S.P.C.K.,
1960.

FEDOTOV, G. P., *The Russian Religious Mind*. New York,
1960 (Harper Torchbook).

FEDOTOV, G. P., *A Treasury of Russian Spirituality*. New
York, 1961 (Harper Torchbook).

MEYENDORFF, J., *St. Grégoire Palamas et la mystique orthodoxe*. Paris, Éditions du Seuil, 1959.

*Orthodox Spirituality: An Outline of the Orthodox Asceti-
cal and Mystical Tradition,* by a Monk of the Eastern
Church. London, S.P.C.K., 1945.

4. History and the Contemporary Situation

ANDERSON, P., *People, Church and State in Modern Russia*. New York, Macmillan, 1944.

CURTISS, J. S., *The Russian Church and the Soviet State,
1917-1950*. Boston, Little, Brown, 1953.

DVORNIK, F., *The Idea of Apostolicity in Byzantium and
the Legend of the Apostle Andrew*. Cambridge,
Mass., Harvard University Press, 1958.

DVORNIK, F., *The Photian Schism: History and Legend*.
Cambridge, 1948.

EVERY, G., *The Byzantine Patriarchate*. London, 1947.

FLOROVSKY, G., "The Orthodox Churches and the Ecumenical Movement Prior to 1910," in R. Rouse and
S. Neill, *A History of the Ecumenical Movement,
1517-1948*. Philadelphia, The Westminster Press,
1954. Pp. 171-217.

FRENCH, R. M., *The Eastern Orthodox Church*. London,
Hutchinson University Library, 1961, 3rd impression.

HAMMOND, P., *The Waters of Marah: The Present State of the Greek Church*. London, Rockliff, 1956.

RUNCIMAN, S., *The Eastern Schism: A Study of the Papacy and the Eastern Churches During the XIth and XIIth Centuries*. New York, Oxford University Press, 1955.

SPINKA, M., *The Church in Soviet Russia*. New York, Oxford University Press, 1956.

ZERNOV, N., "The Eastern Churches and the Ecumenical Movement in the Twentieth Century," in Rouse and Neill, *A History of the Ecumenical Movement, 1517-1948*. Philadelphia, The Westminster Press, 1954. Pp. 645-77.

ZERNOV, N., *The Russians and Their Church*. London, S.P.C.K., 1945.

INDEX